Happy Kanako's Killer Life

3

story & art by:
TOSHIYA WAKABAYASHI

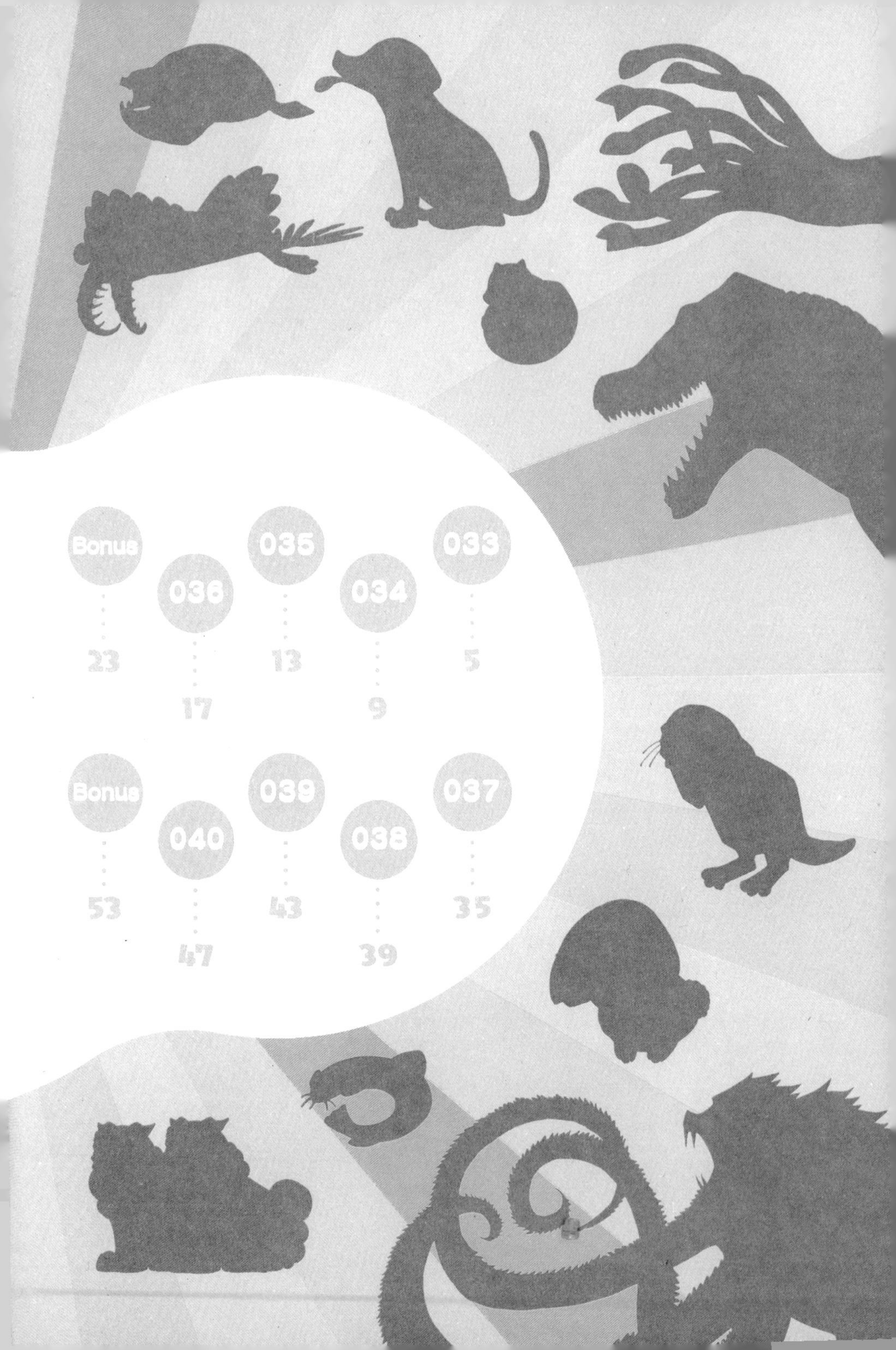

CONTENTS

Happy Kanako's
Killer Life

He's such a pala- mute!!

033

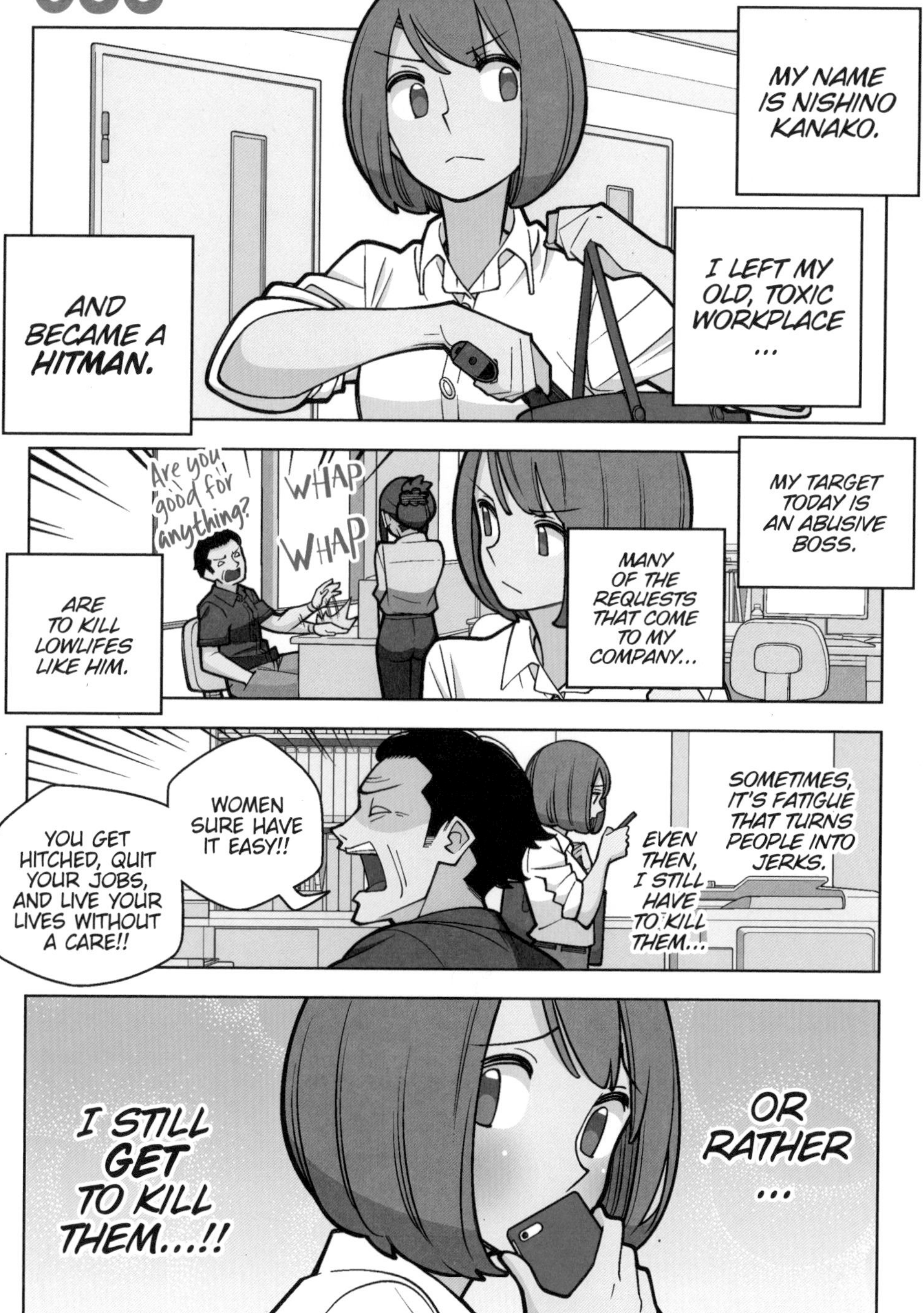
MY NAME IS NISHINO KANAKO.
I LEFT MY OLD, TOXIC WORKPLACE ...
AND BECAME A HITMAN.
MY TARGET TODAY IS AN ABUSIVE BOSS.
MANY OF THE REQUESTS THAT COME TO MY COMPANY...
WHAP
WHAP
Are you good for anything?
ARE TO KILL LOWLIFES LIKE HIM.
SOMETIMES, IT'S FATIGUE THAT TURNS PEOPLE INTO JERKS.
EVEN THEN, I STILL HAVE TO KILL THEM...
WOMEN SURE HAVE IT EASY!!
YOU GET HITCHED, QUIT YOUR JOBS, AND LIVE YOUR LIVES WITHOUT A CARE!!
OR RATHER ...
I STILL GET TO KILL THEM...!!

It's a job to kill for. ☆

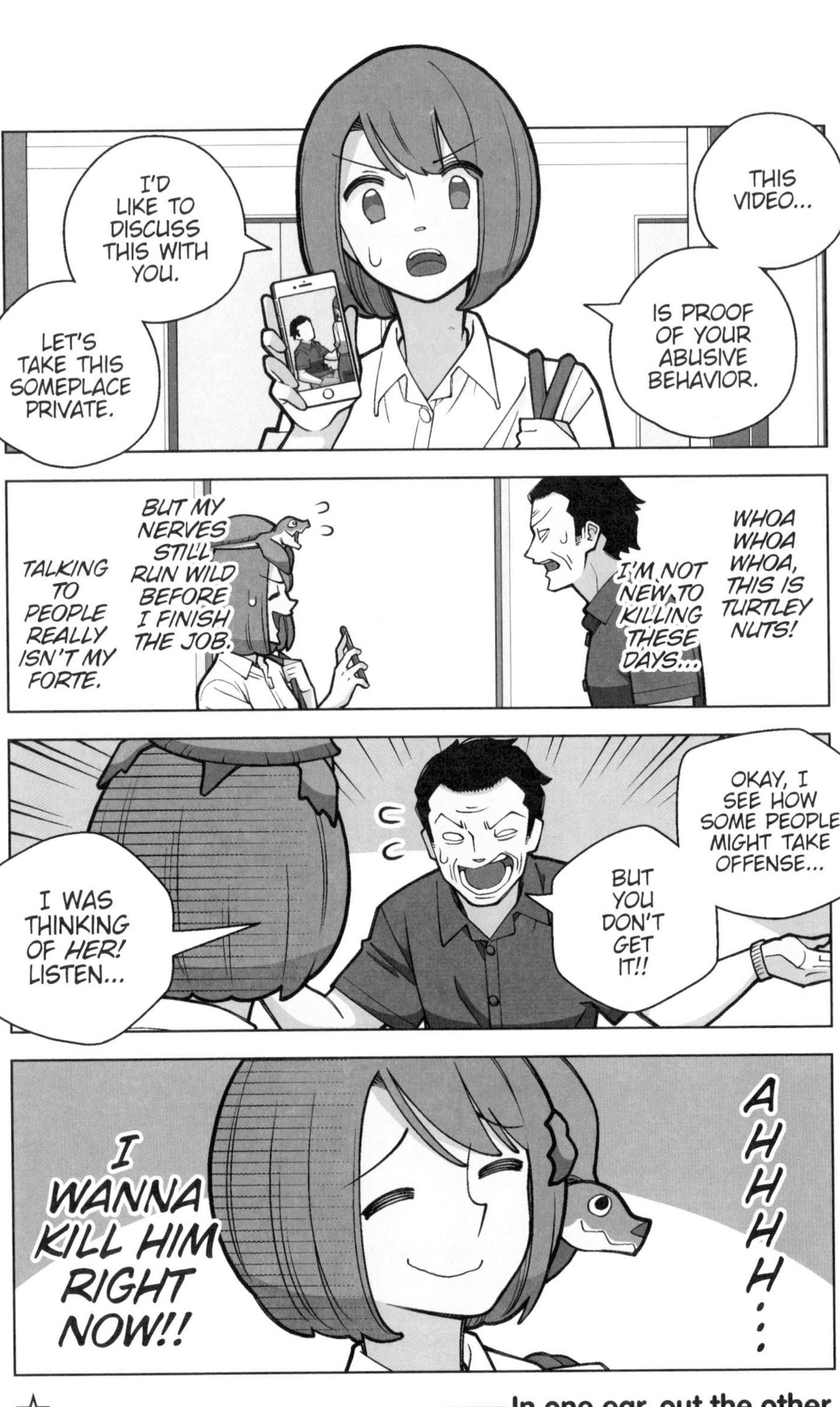
THIS VIDEO...
IS PROOF OF YOUR ABUSIVE BEHAVIOR.
I'D LIKE TO DISCUSS THIS WITH YOU.
LET'S TAKE THIS SOMEPLACE PRIVATE.
WHOA WHOA WHOA, THIS IS TURTLEY NUTS!
I'M NOT NEW TO KILLING THESE DAYS...
BUT MY NERVES STILL RUN WILD BEFORE I FINISH THE JOB.
TALKING TO PEOPLE REALLY ISN'T MY FORTE.
OKAY, I SEE HOW SOME PEOPLE MIGHT TAKE OFFENSE...
BUT YOU DON'T GET IT!!
I WAS THINKING OF *HER*! LISTEN...
AHHHH...
I WANNA KILL HIM RIGHT NOW!!

☆ —— **In one ear, out the other.**

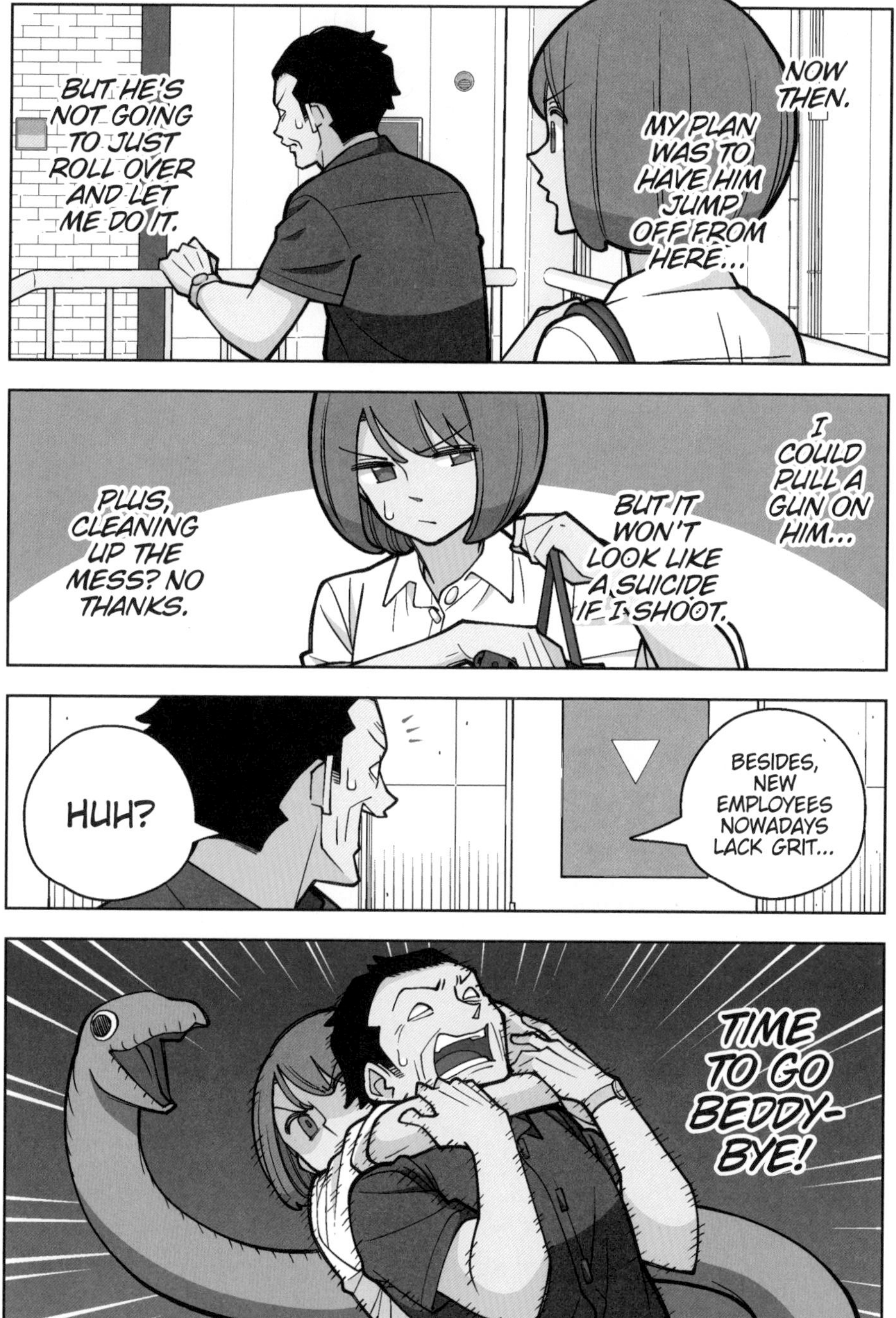
NOW THEN.
MY PLAN WAS TO HAVE HIM JUMP OFF FROM HERE...
BUT HE'S NOT GOING TO JUST ROLL OVER AND LET ME DO IT.
I COULD PULL A GUN ON HIM...
BUT IT WON'T LOOK LIKE A SUICIDE IF I SHOOT.
PLUS, CLEANING UP THE MESS? NO THANKS.
BESIDES, NEW EMPLOYEES NOWADAYS LACK GRIT...
HUH?
TIME TO GO BEDDY-BYE!

No slithering out of this one, you sneaky snake! ———— ☆

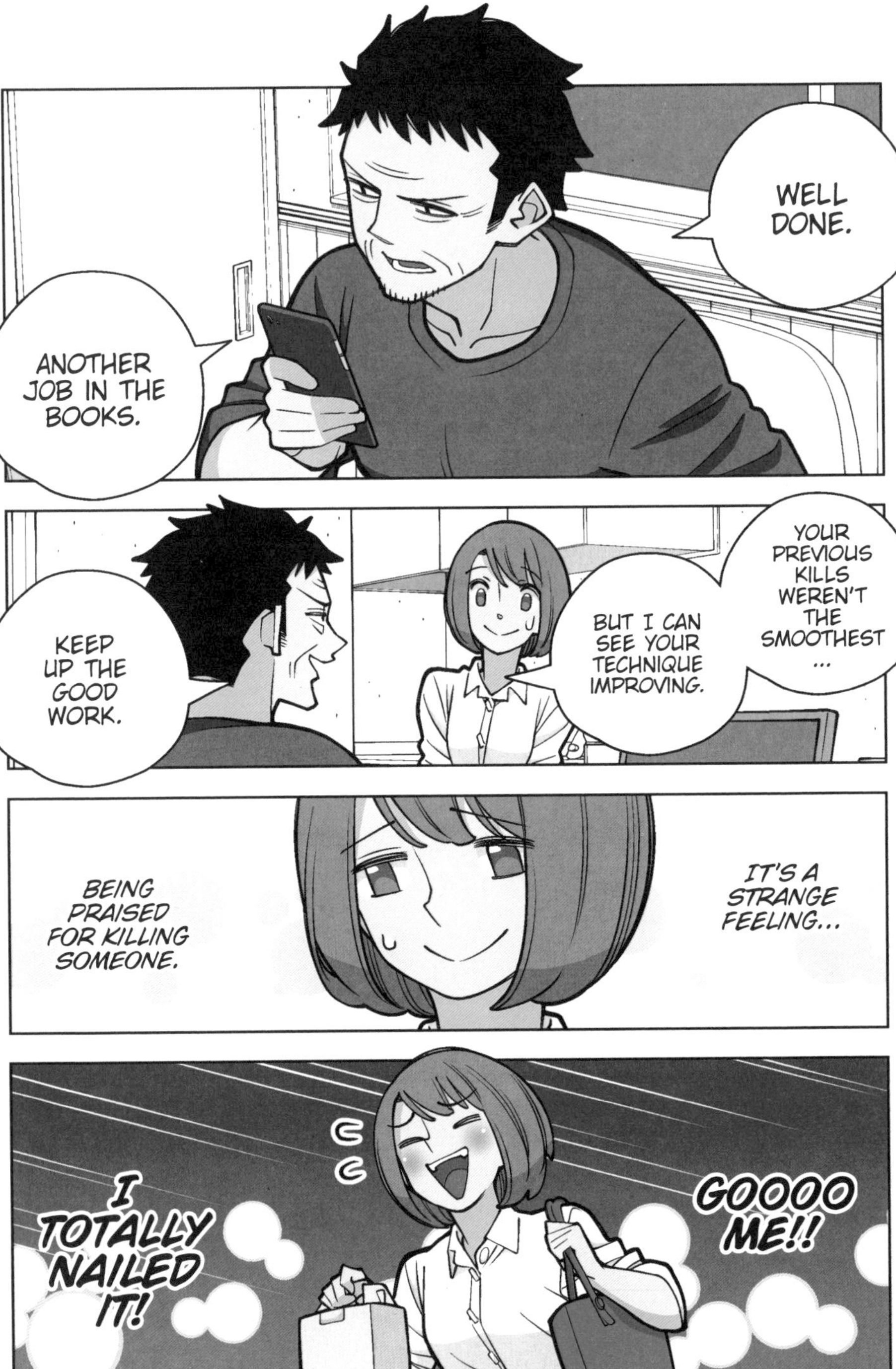
WELL DONE.
ANOTHER JOB IN THE BOOKS.
YOUR PREVIOUS KILLS WEREN'T THE SMOOTHEST...
BUT I CAN SEE YOUR TECHNIQUE IMPROVING.
KEEP UP THE GOOD WORK.
IT'S A STRANGE FEELING...
BEING PRAISED FOR KILLING SOMEONE.
GOOOO ME!!
I TOTALLY NAILED IT!

☆——— **Gonnna treat myself to four pieces of cake tonight!**

034

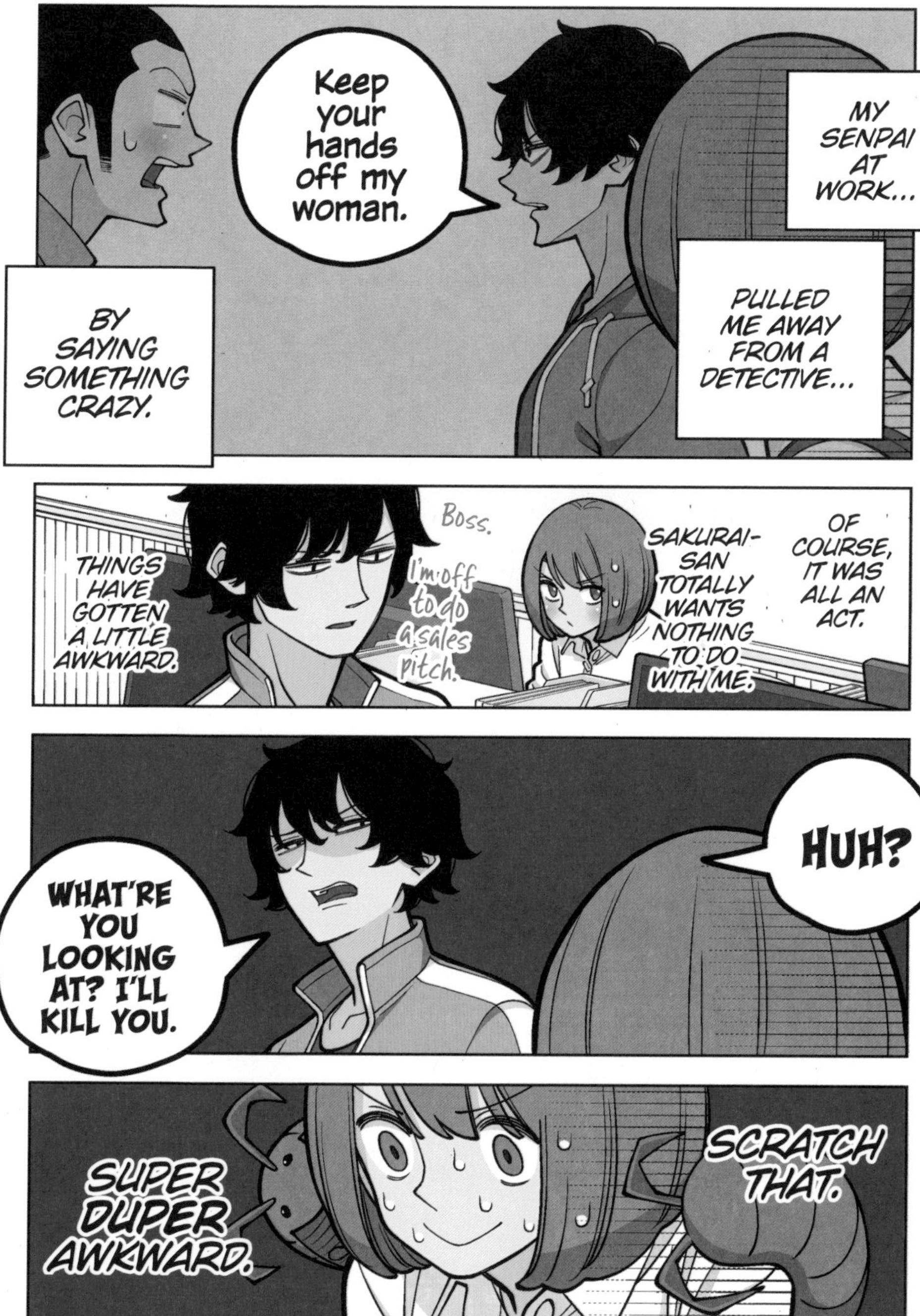
MY SENPAI AT WORK...
PULLED ME AWAY FROM A DETECTIVE...
Keep your hands off my woman.
BY SAYING SOMETHING CRAZY.
OF COURSE, IT WAS ALL AN ACT.
SAKURAI-SAN TOTALLY WANTS NOTHING TO DO WITH ME.
Boss.
I'm off to do a sales pitch.
THINGS HAVE GOTTEN A LITTLE AWKWARD.
HUH?
WHAT'RE YOU LOOKING AT? I'LL KILL YOU.
SCRATCH THAT.
SUPER DUPER AWKWARD.

Holy moly roly poly! ☆

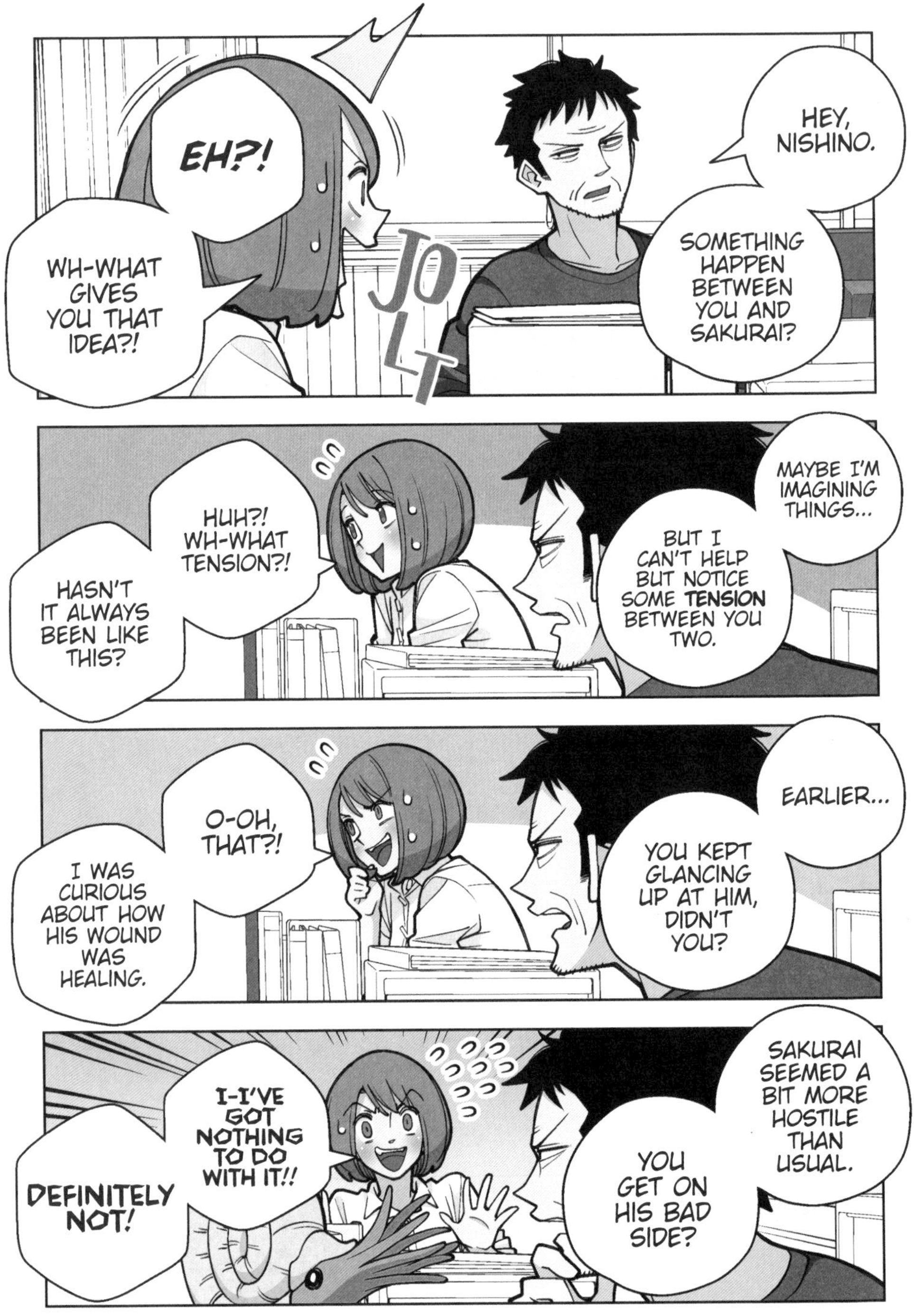
HEY, NISHINO.
SOMETHING HAPPEN BETWEEN YOU AND SAKURAI?
JOLT
EH?!
WH-WHAT GIVES YOU THAT IDEA?!
MAYBE I'M IMAGINING THINGS...
BUT I CAN'T HELP BUT NOTICE SOME **TENSION** BETWEEN YOU TWO.
HUH?! WH-WHAT TENSION?!
HASN'T IT ALWAYS BEEN LIKE THIS?
EARLIER...
YOU KEPT GLANCING UP AT HIM, DIDN'T YOU?
O-OH, THAT?!
I WAS CURIOUS ABOUT HOW HIS WOUND WAS HEALING.
SAKURAI SEEMED A BIT MORE HOSTILE THAN USUAL.
YOU GET ON HIS BAD SIDE?
I-I'VE GOT NOTHING TO DO WITH IT!!
DEFINITELY NOT!

☆ —— **Definitely naut(ilus)!**

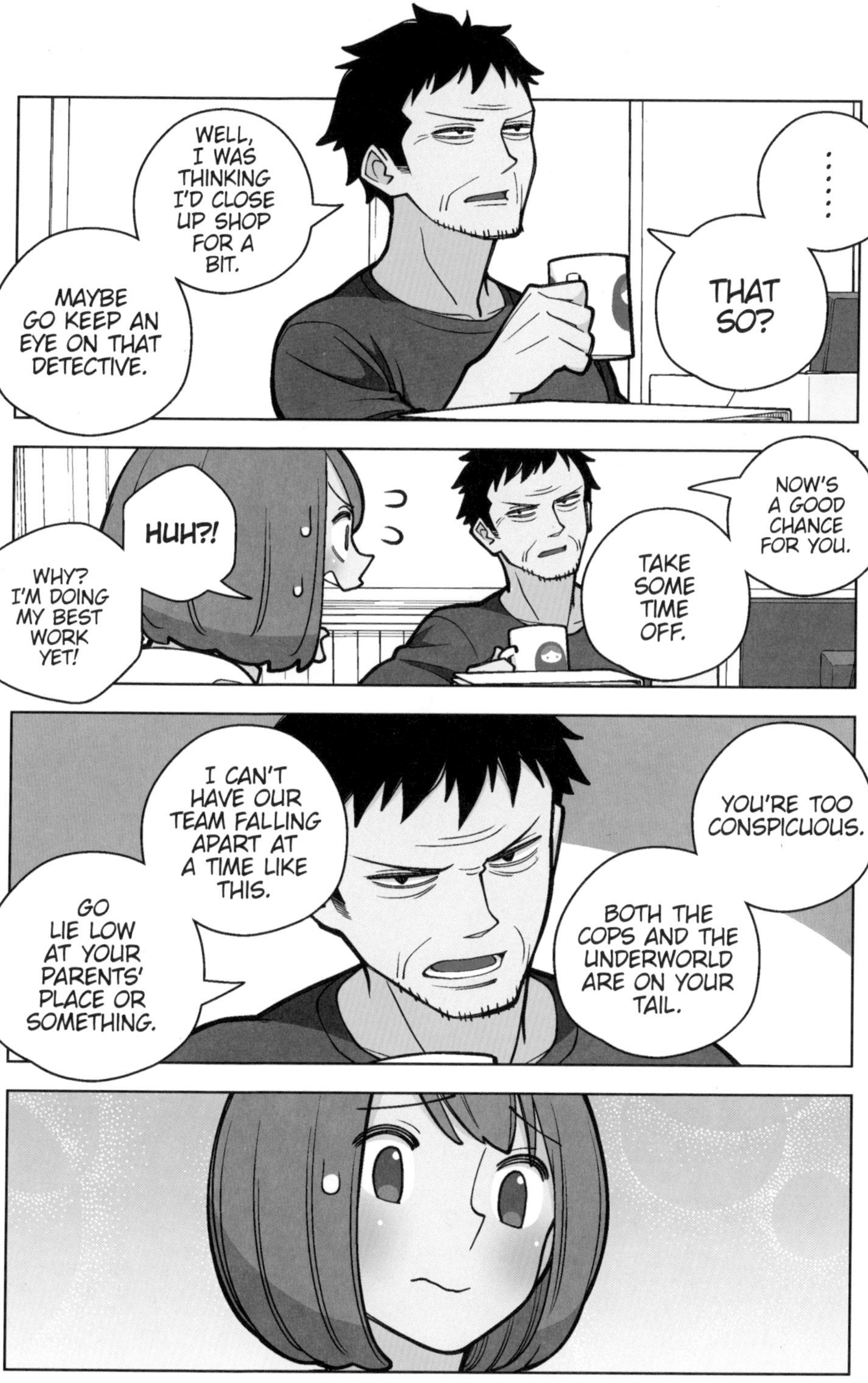
……
THAT SO?
WELL, I WAS THINKING I'D CLOSE UP SHOP FOR A BIT.
MAYBE GO KEEP AN EYE ON THAT DETECTIVE.
NOW'S A GOOD CHANCE FOR YOU.
TAKE SOME TIME OFF.
HUH?!
WHY? I'M DOING MY BEST WORK YET!
YOU'RE TOO CONSPICUOUS.
BOTH THE COPS AND THE UNDERWORLD ARE ON YOUR TAIL.
I CAN'T HAVE OUR TEAM FALLING APART AT A TIME LIKE THIS.
GO LIE LOW AT YOUR PARENTS' PLACE OR SOMETHING.

I got in trouble for being too good at my job.——☆

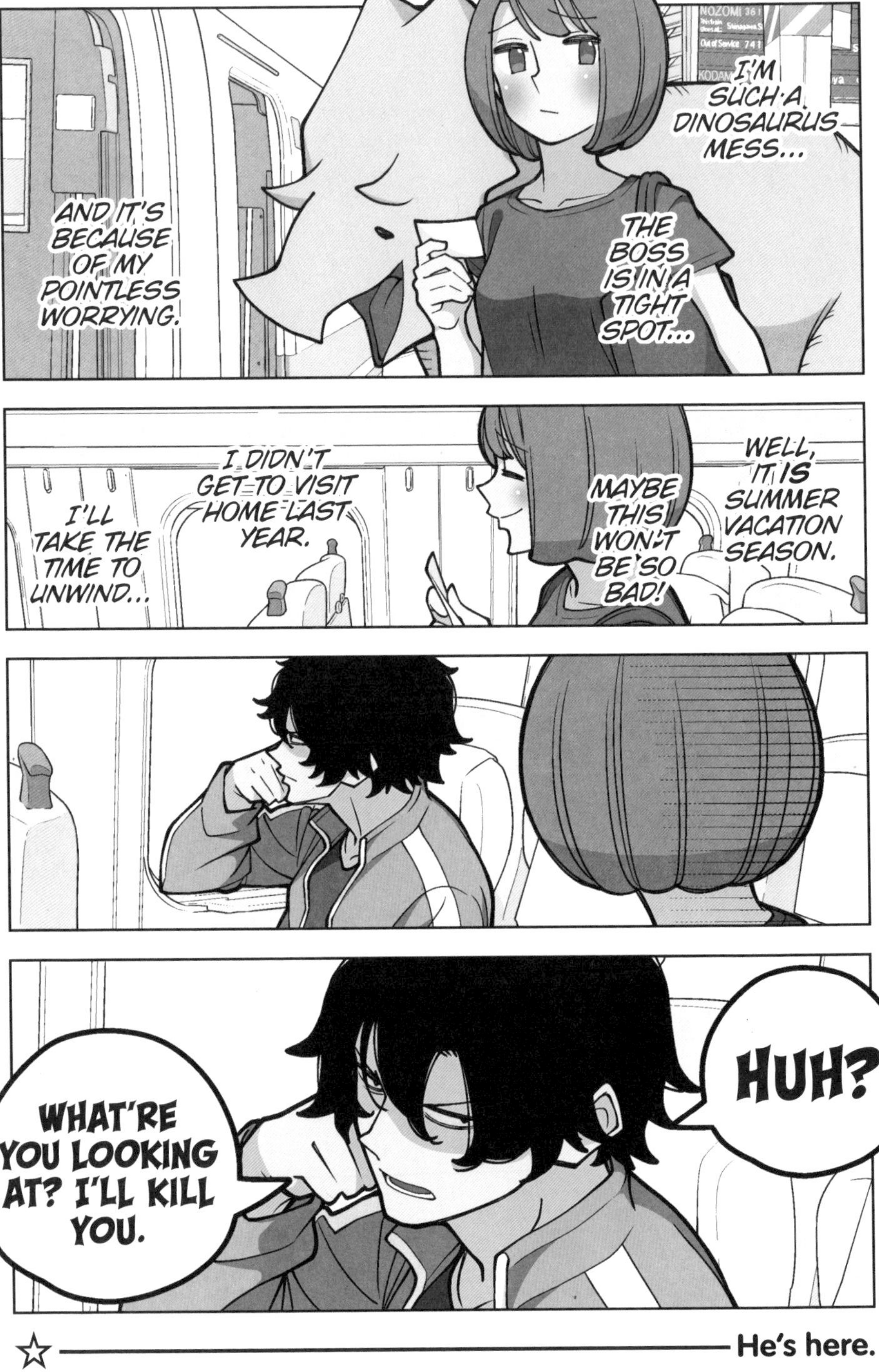
NOZOMI 361
Out of Service 741
I'M SUCH A DINOSAURUS MESS...
THE BOSS IS IN A TIGHT SPOT...
AND IT'S BECAUSE OF MY POINTLESS WORRYING.
WELL, IT IS SUMMER VACATION SEASON.
MAYBE THIS WON'T BE SO BAD!
I DIDN'T GET TO VISIT HOME LAST YEAR.
I'LL TAKE THE TIME TO UNWIND...
HUH?
WHAT'RE YOU LOOKING AT? I'LL KILL YOU.

☆ He's here.

035

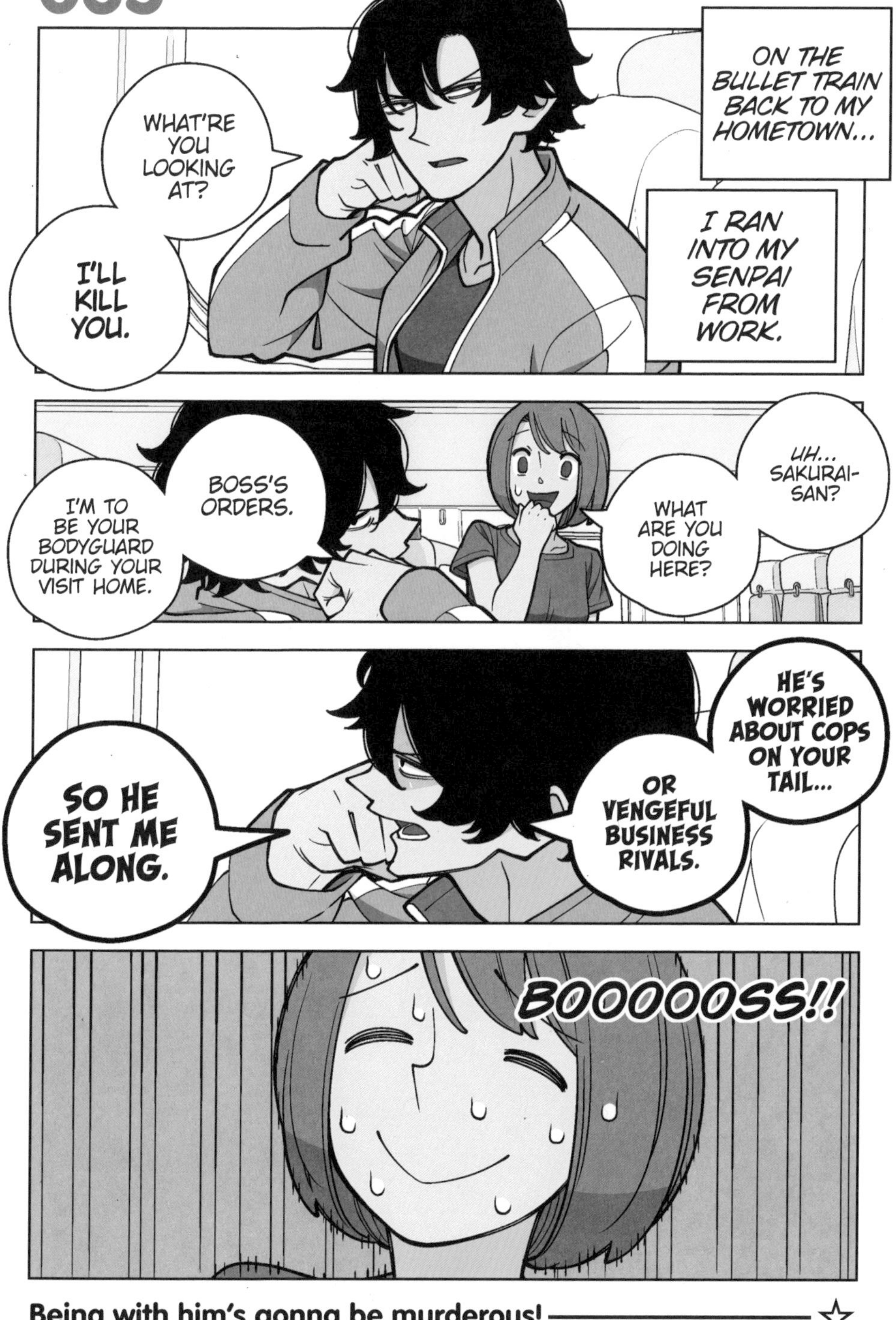

ON THE BULLET TRAIN BACK TO MY HOMETOWN...
I RAN INTO MY SENPAI FROM WORK.
WHAT'RE YOU LOOKING AT?
I'LL KILL YOU.
UH... SAKURAI-SAN?
WHAT ARE YOU DOING HERE?
BOSS'S ORDERS.
I'M TO BE YOUR BODYGUARD DURING YOUR VISIT HOME.
HE'S WORRIED ABOUT COPS ON YOUR TAIL...
OR VENGEFUL BUSINESS RIVALS.
SO HE SENT ME ALONG.
BOOOOOSS!!

Being with him's gonna be murderous! ☆

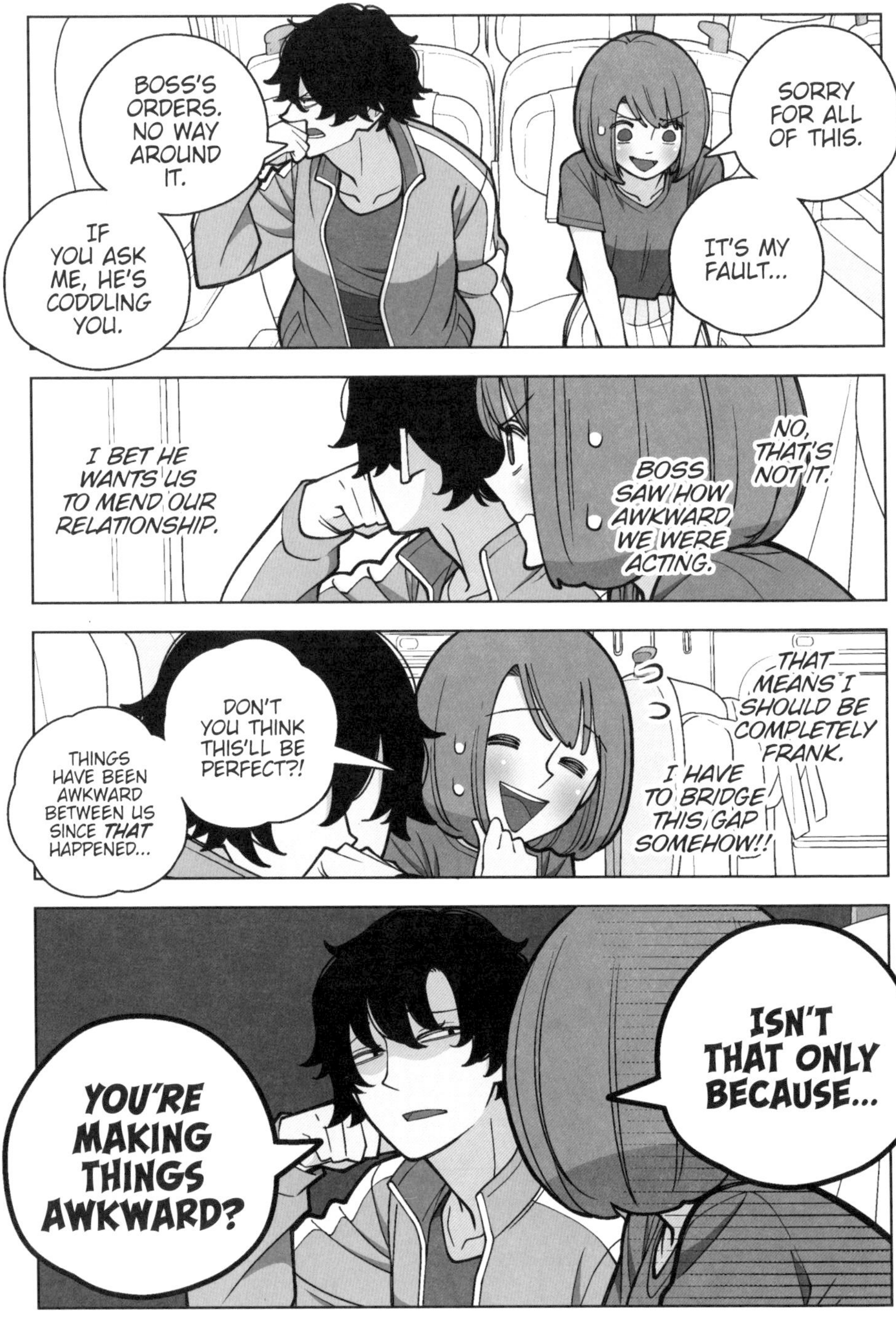
SORRY FOR ALL OF THIS.
IT'S MY FAULT...
BOSS'S ORDERS. NO WAY AROUND IT.
IF YOU ASK ME, HE'S CODDLING YOU.
NO, THAT'S NOT IT.
BOSS SAW HOW AWKWARD WE WERE ACTING.
I BET HE WANTS US TO MEND OUR RELATIONSHIP.
THAT MEANS I SHOULD BE COMPLETELY FRANK.
I HAVE TO BRIDGE THIS GAP SOMEHOW!!
DON'T YOU THINK THIS'LL BE PERFECT?!
THINGS HAVE BEEN AWKWARD BETWEEN US SINCE *THAT* HAPPENED...
ISN'T THAT ONLY BECAUSE...
YOU'RE MAKING THINGS AWKWARD?

☆ — **No *waaaaaaayyy!***

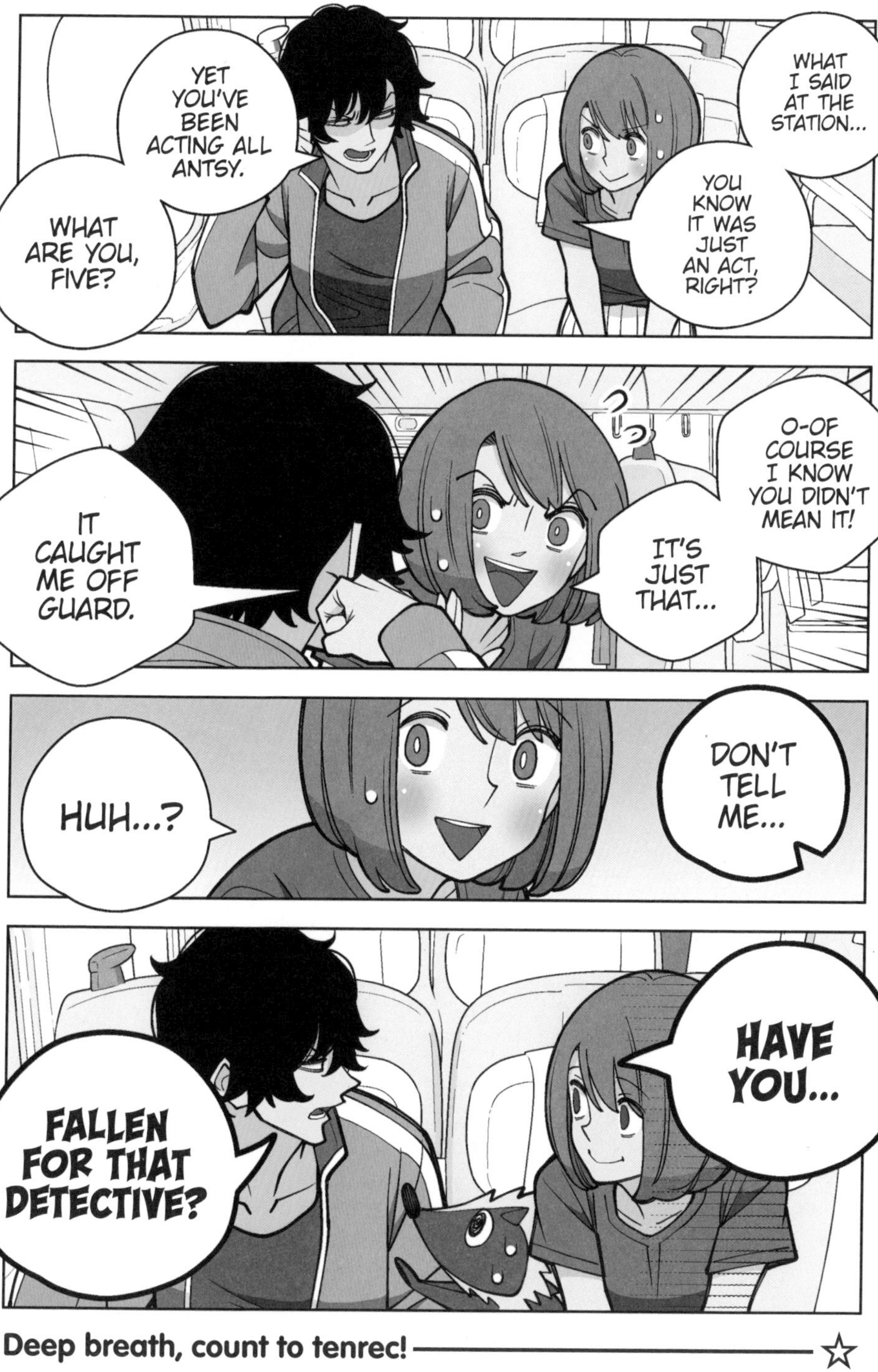
WHAT I SAID AT THE STATION...
YOU KNOW IT WAS JUST AN ACT, RIGHT?
YET YOU'VE BEEN ACTING ALL ANTSY.
WHAT ARE YOU, FIVE?
O-OF COURSE I KNOW YOU DIDN'T MEAN IT!
IT'S JUST THAT...
IT CAUGHT ME OFF GUARD.
DON'T TELL ME...
HUH...?
HAVE YOU...
FALLEN FOR THAT DETECTIVE?

Deep breath, count to tenrec! ☆

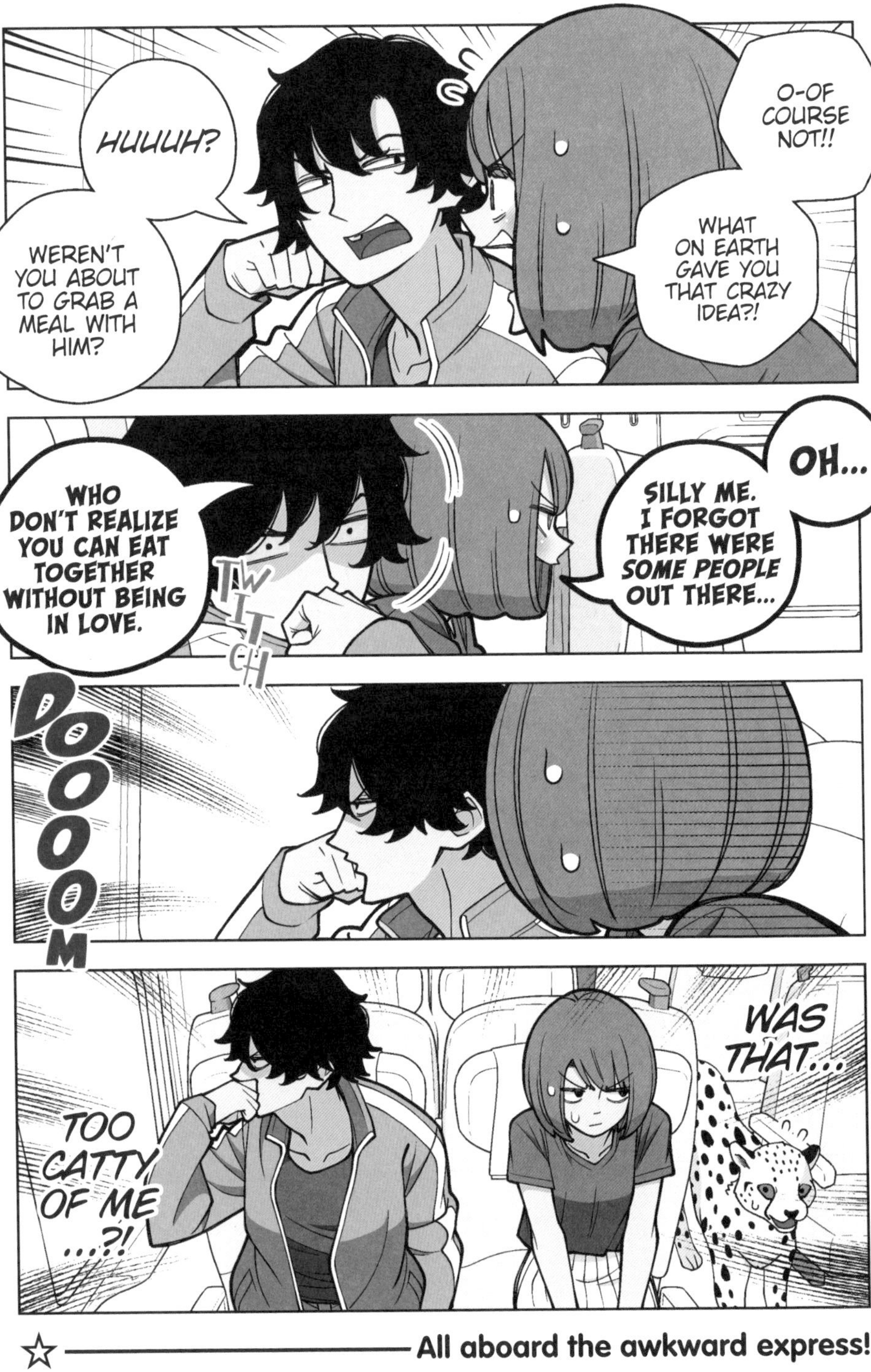
O-OF COURSE NOT!!
HUUUH?
WHAT ON EARTH GAVE YOU THAT CRAZY IDEA?!
WEREN'T YOU ABOUT TO GRAB A MEAL WITH HIM?
OH...
SILLY ME. I FORGOT THERE WERE SOME PEOPLE OUT THERE...
WHO DON'T REALIZE YOU CAN EAT TOGETHER WITHOUT BEING IN LOVE.
TWITCH
DOOOOOOM
WAS THAT...
TOO CATTY OF ME ...?!

☆ — All aboard the awkward express!

036

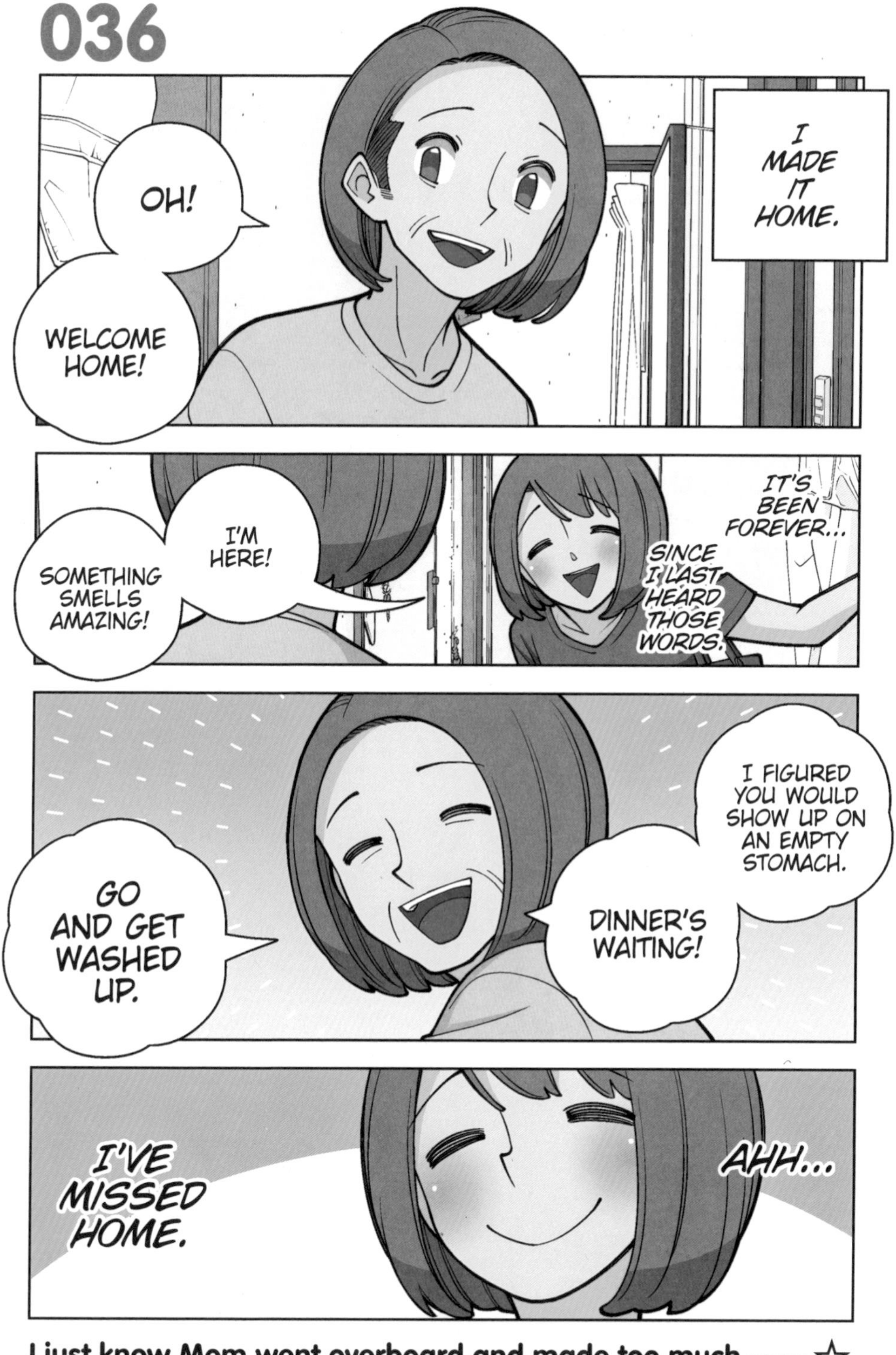
I MADE IT HOME.
OH!
WELCOME HOME!
IT'S BEEN FOREVER...
SINCE I LAST HEARD THOSE WORDS.
I'M HERE!
SOMETHING SMELLS AMAZING!
I FIGURED YOU WOULD SHOW UP ON AN EMPTY STOMACH.
DINNER'S WAITING!
GO AND GET WASHED UP.
AHH...
I'VE MISSED HOME.

I just know Mom went overboard and made too much.—— ☆

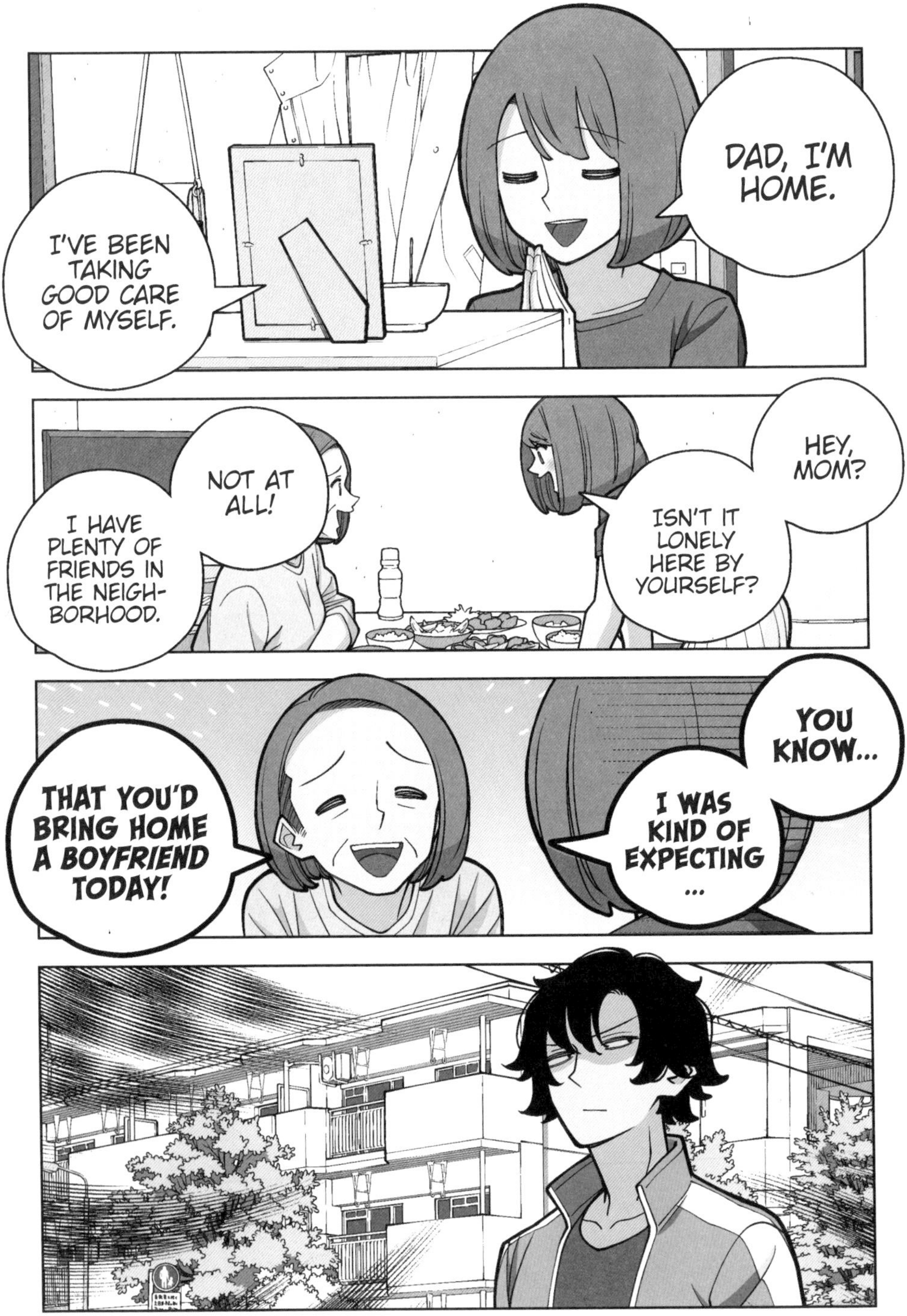
DAD, I'M HOME.
I'VE BEEN TAKING GOOD CARE OF MYSELF.
HEY, MOM?
ISN'T IT LONELY HERE BY YOURSELF?
NOT AT ALL!
I HAVE PLENTY OF FRIENDS IN THE NEIGH-BORHOOD.
YOU KNOW...
I WAS KIND OF EXPECTING...
THAT YOU'D BRING HOME A *BOYFRIEND* TODAY!

☆ —— My senpai from work is outside.

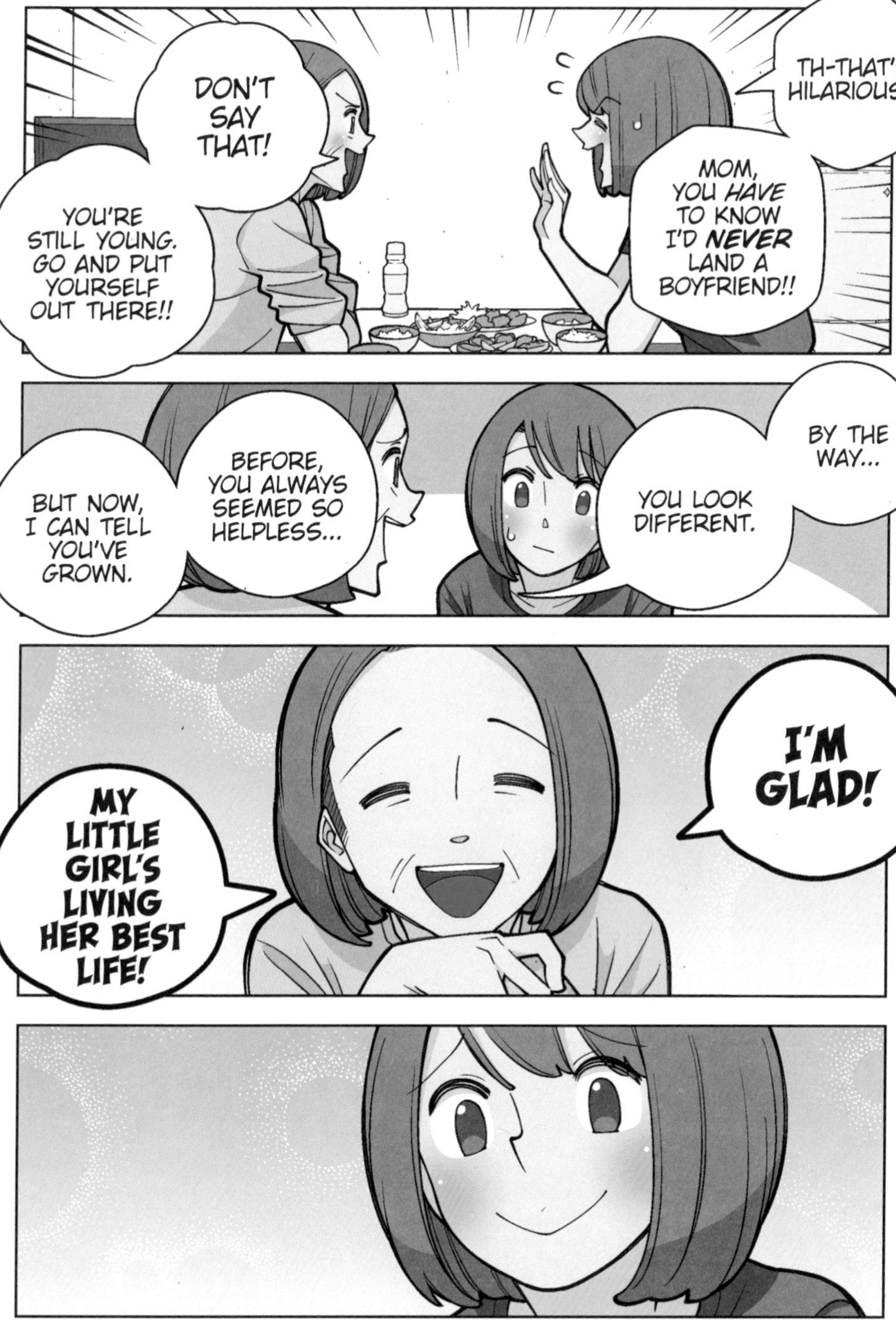
TH-THAT'S HILARIOUS!!
MOM, YOU *HAVE* TO KNOW I'D **NEVER** LAND A BOYFRIEND!!
DON'T SAY THAT!
YOU'RE STILL YOUNG. GO AND PUT YOURSELF OUT THERE!!
BY THE WAY...
YOU LOOK DIFFERENT.
BEFORE, YOU ALWAYS SEEMED SO HELPLESS...
BUT NOW, I CAN TELL YOU'VE GROWN.
I'M GLAD!
MY LITTLE GIRL'S LIVING HER BEST LIFE!

Please don't ask for details. ☆

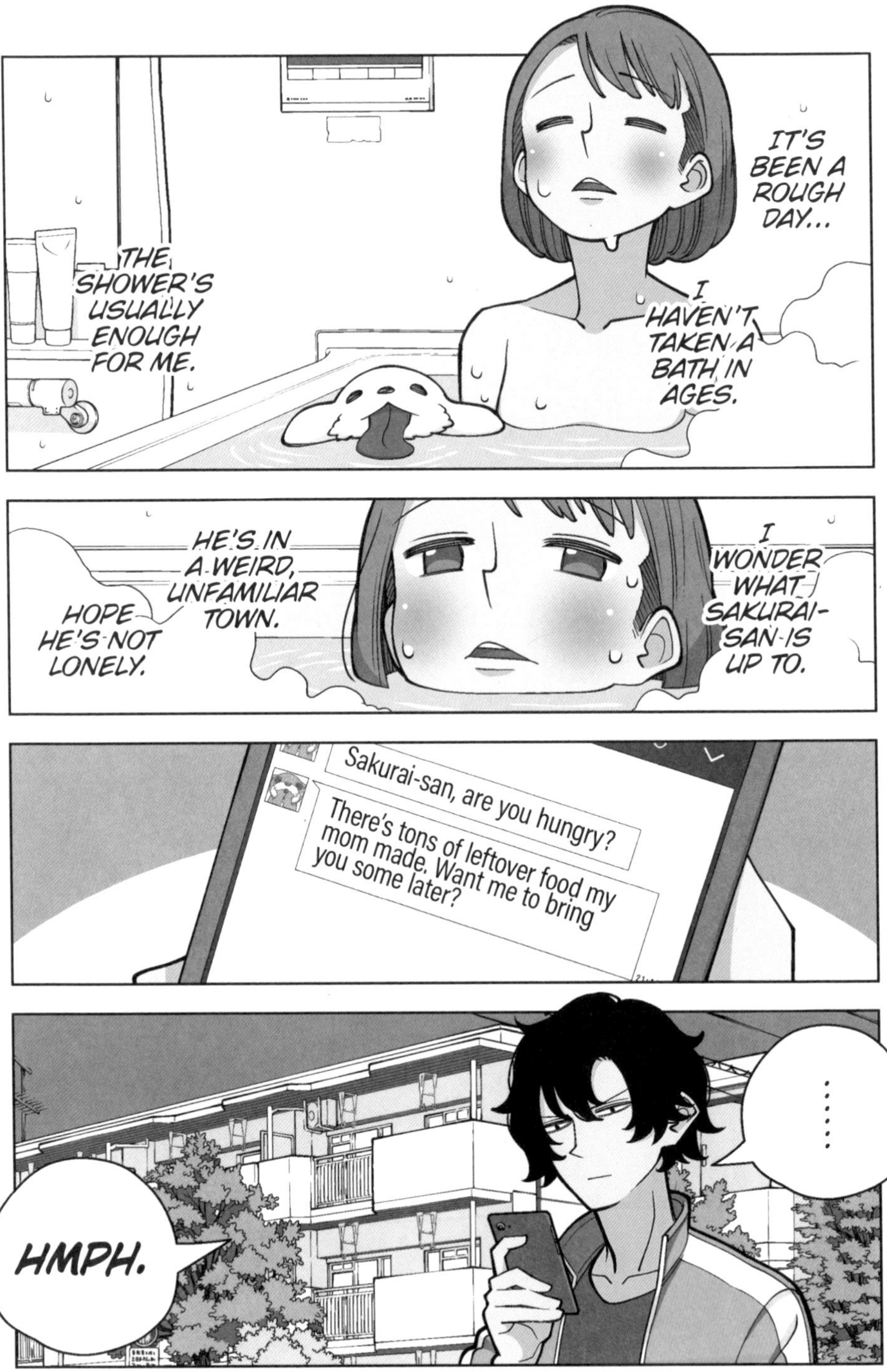
IT'S BEEN A ROUGH DAY...
I HAVEN'T TAKEN A BATH IN AGES.
THE SHOWER'S USUALLY ENOUGH FOR ME.
I WONDER WHAT SAKURAI-SAN IS UP TO.
HE'S IN A WEIRD, UNFAMILIAR TOWN.
HOPE HE'S NOT LONELY.
Sakurai-san, are you hungry?
There's tons of leftover food my mom made. Want me to bring you some later?
......
HMPH.

☆ Reconciliation.

Happy Kanako's
Killer Life

Holy
Moly
Roly
Poly!!

Happy Kanako's
Killer Life

Right on the nose!!

Bonus

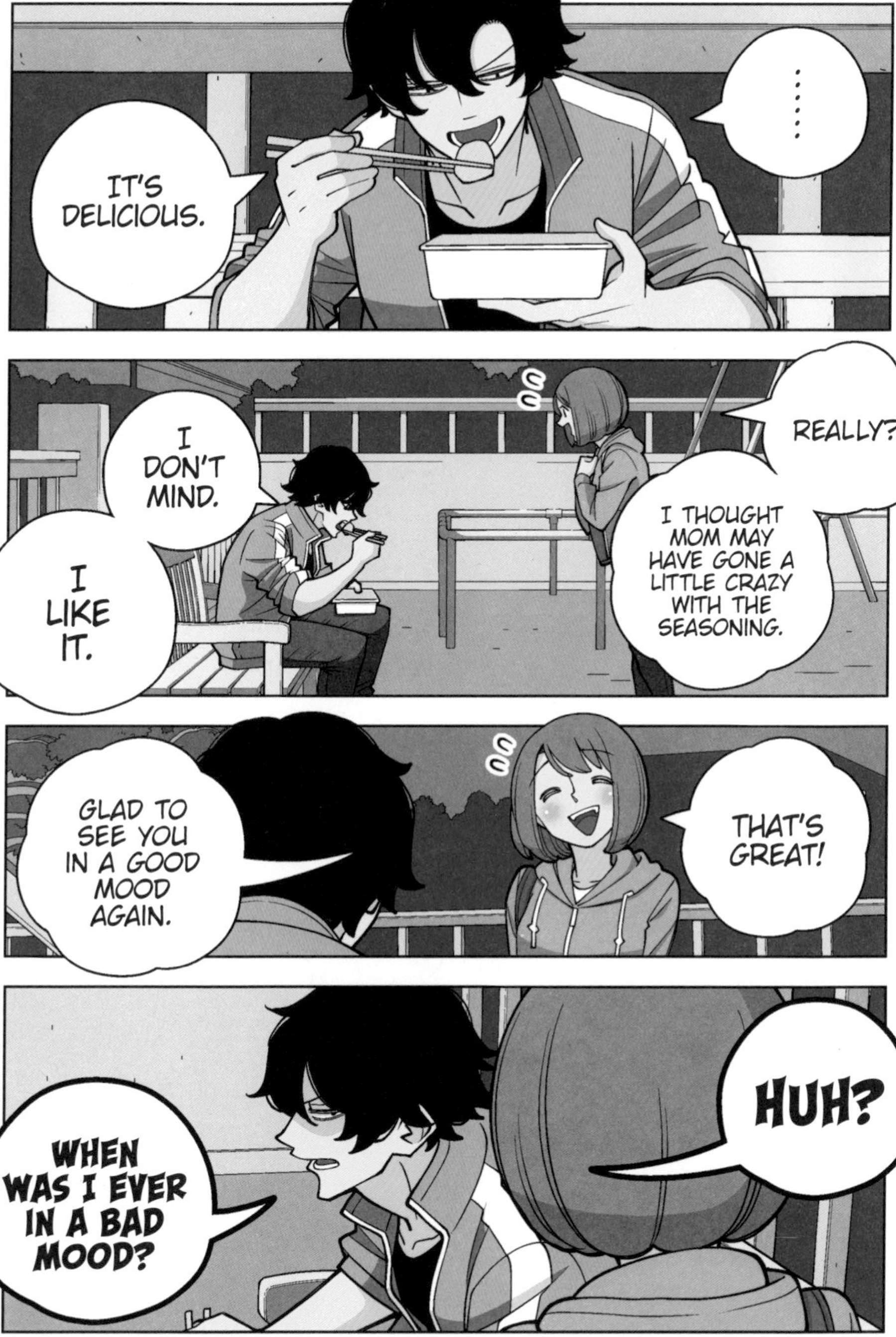
......
IT'S DELICIOUS.
REALLY?
I THOUGHT MOM MAY HAVE GONE A LITTLE CRAZY WITH THE SEASONING.
I DON'T MIND.
I LIKE IT.
THAT'S GREAT!
GLAD TO SEE YOU IN A GOOD MOOD AGAIN.
HUH?
WHEN WAS I EVER IN A BAD MOOD?

Always quick to counter. ☆

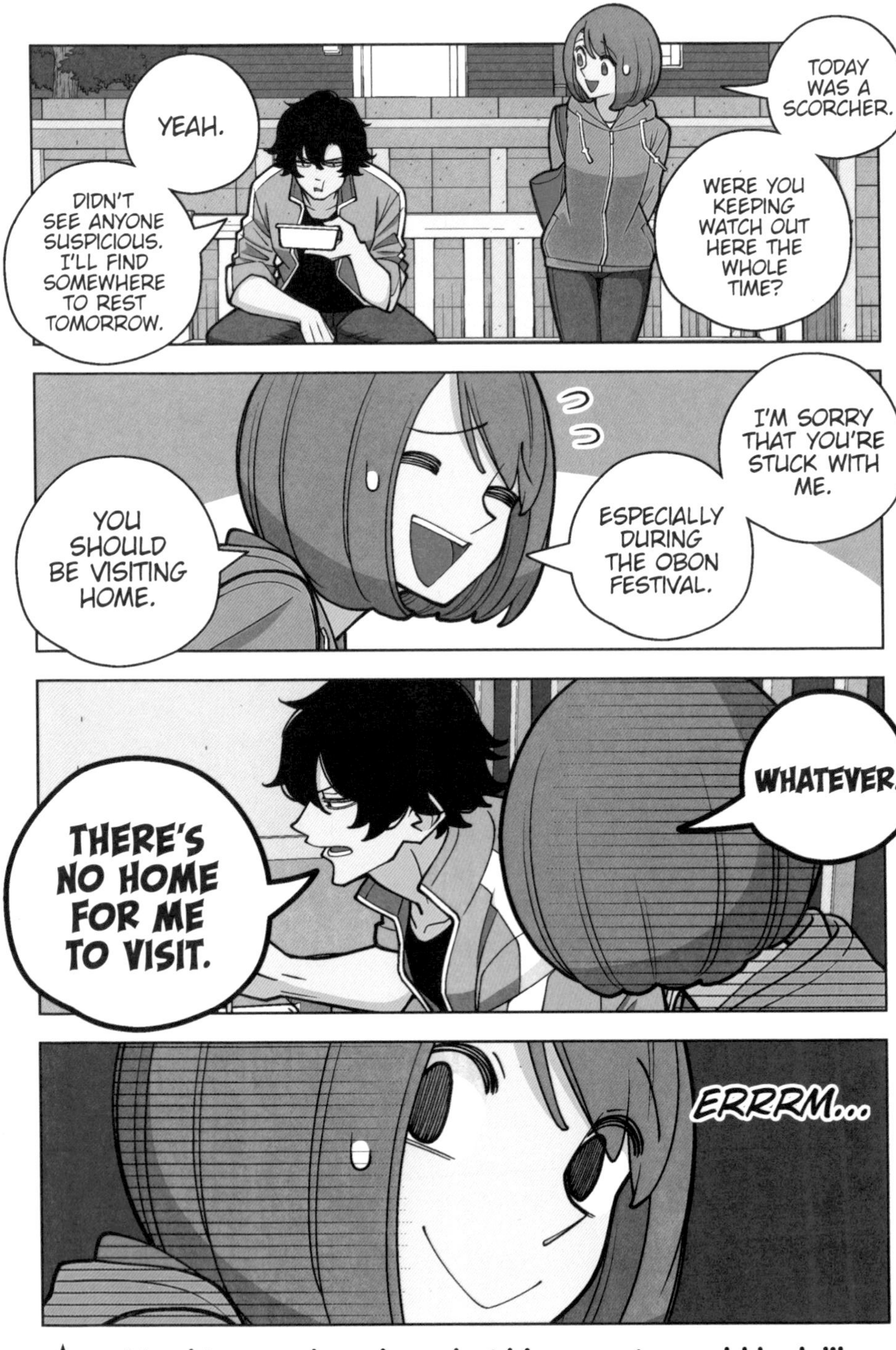
TODAY WAS A SCORCHER.
WERE YOU KEEPING WATCH OUT HERE THE WHOLE TIME?
YEAH.
DIDN'T SEE ANYONE SUSPICIOUS. I'LL FIND SOMEWHERE TO REST TOMORROW.
I'M SORRY THAT YOU'RE STUCK WITH ME.
ESPECIALLY DURING THE OBON FESTIVAL.
YOU SHOULD BE VISITING HOME.
WHATEVER.
THERE'S NO HOME FOR ME TO VISIT.
ERRRM...

☆—Hard to even imagine what his parents would look like...

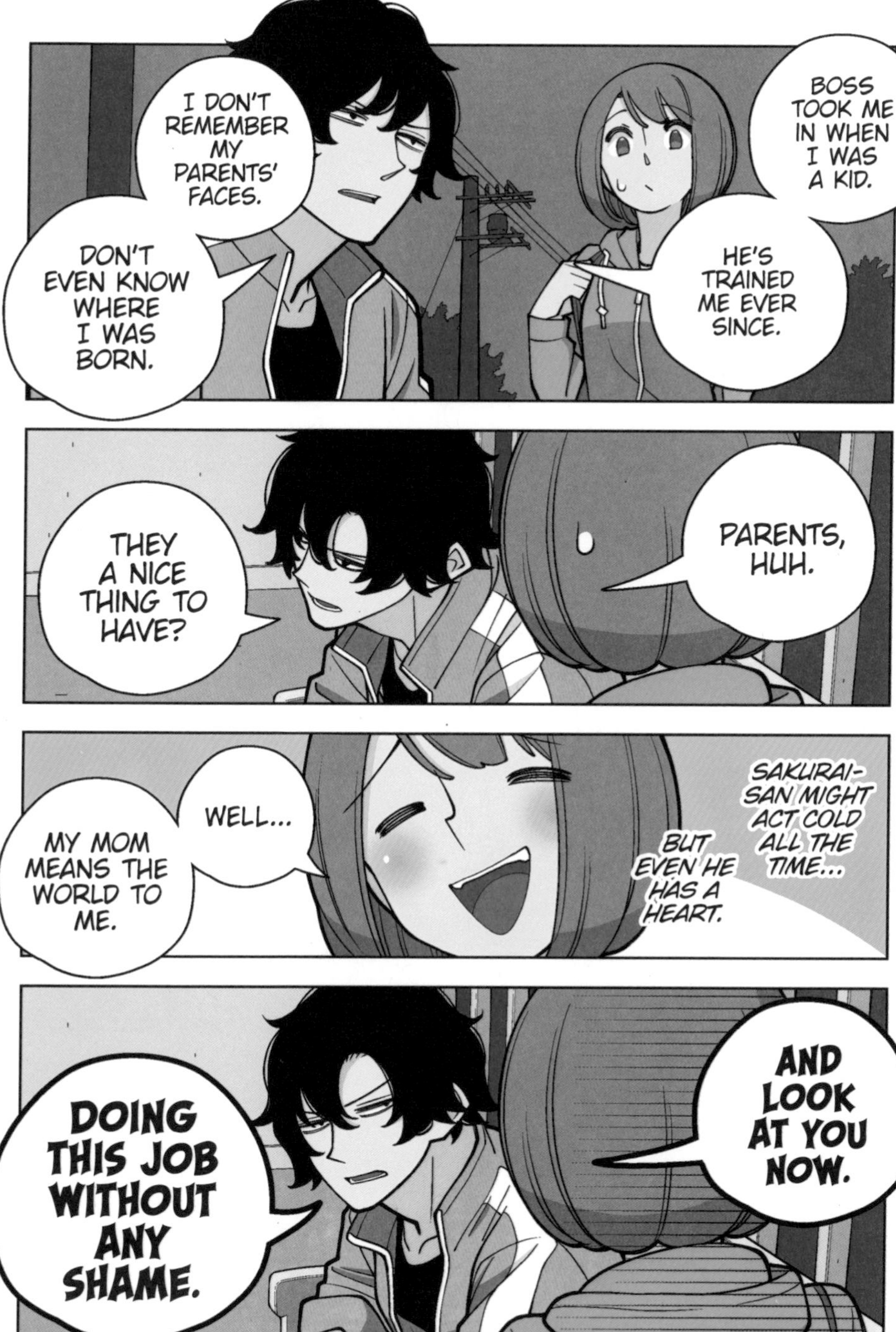
BOSS TOOK ME IN WHEN I WAS A KID.
HE'S TRAINED ME EVER SINCE.
I DON'T REMEMBER MY PARENTS' FACES.
DON'T EVEN KNOW WHERE I WAS BORN.
PARENTS, HUH.
THEY A NICE THING TO HAVE?
SAKURAI-SAN MIGHT ACT COLD ALL THE TIME...
BUT EVEN HE HAS A HEART.
WELL...
MY MOM MEANS THE WORLD TO ME.
AND LOOK AT YOU NOW.
DOING THIS JOB WITHOUT ANY SHAME.

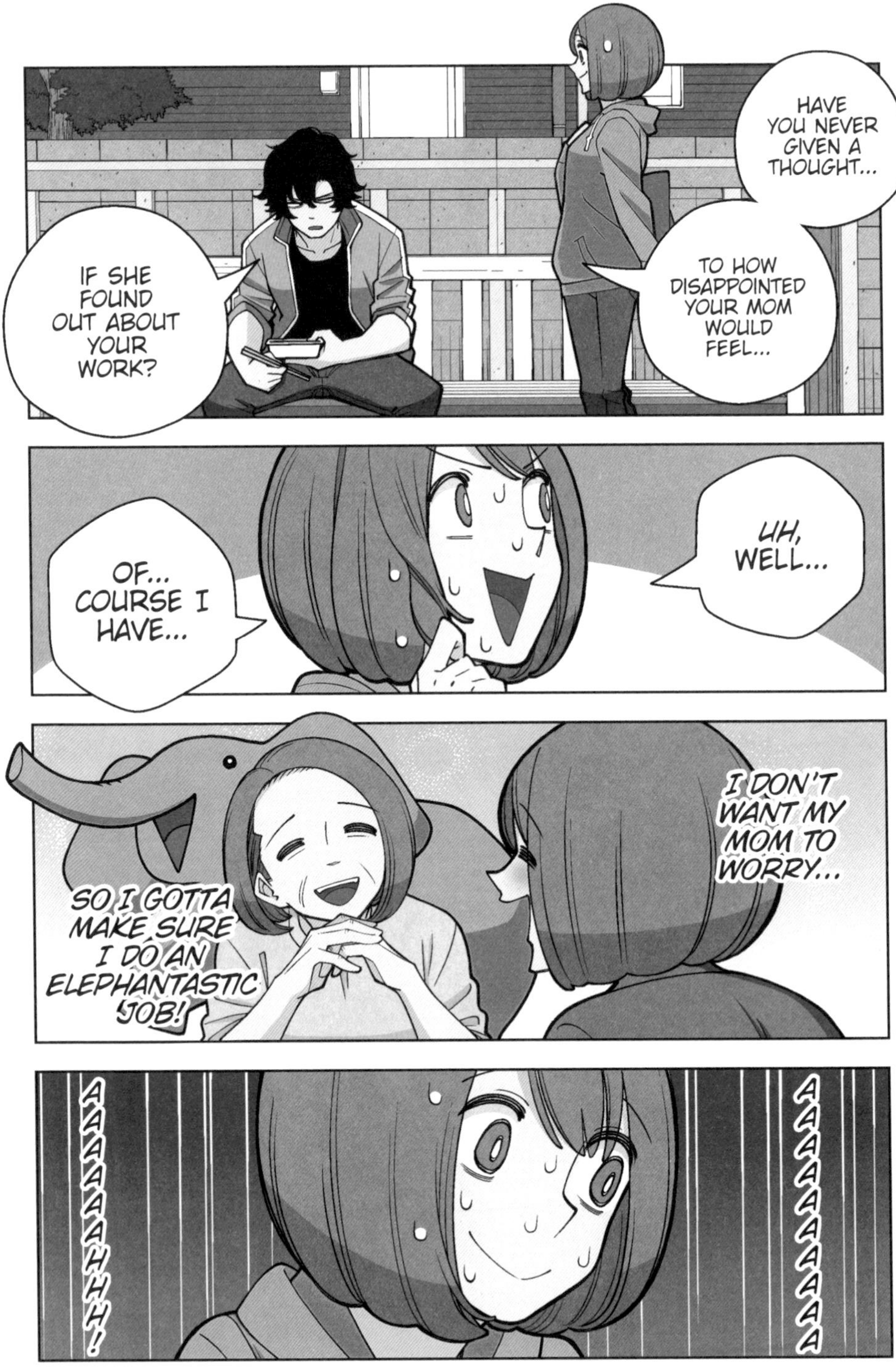
HAVE YOU NEVER GIVEN A THOUGHT...
TO HOW DISAPPOINTED YOUR MOM WOULD FEEL...
IF SHE FOUND OUT ABOUT YOUR WORK?
UH, WELL...
OF... COURSE I HAVE...
I DON'T WANT MY MOM TO WORRY...
SO I GOTTA MAKE SURE I DO AN ELEPHANTASTIC JOB!
AAAAAAAAAA
AAAAAAHHHH!

☆ —— A good girl at heart.

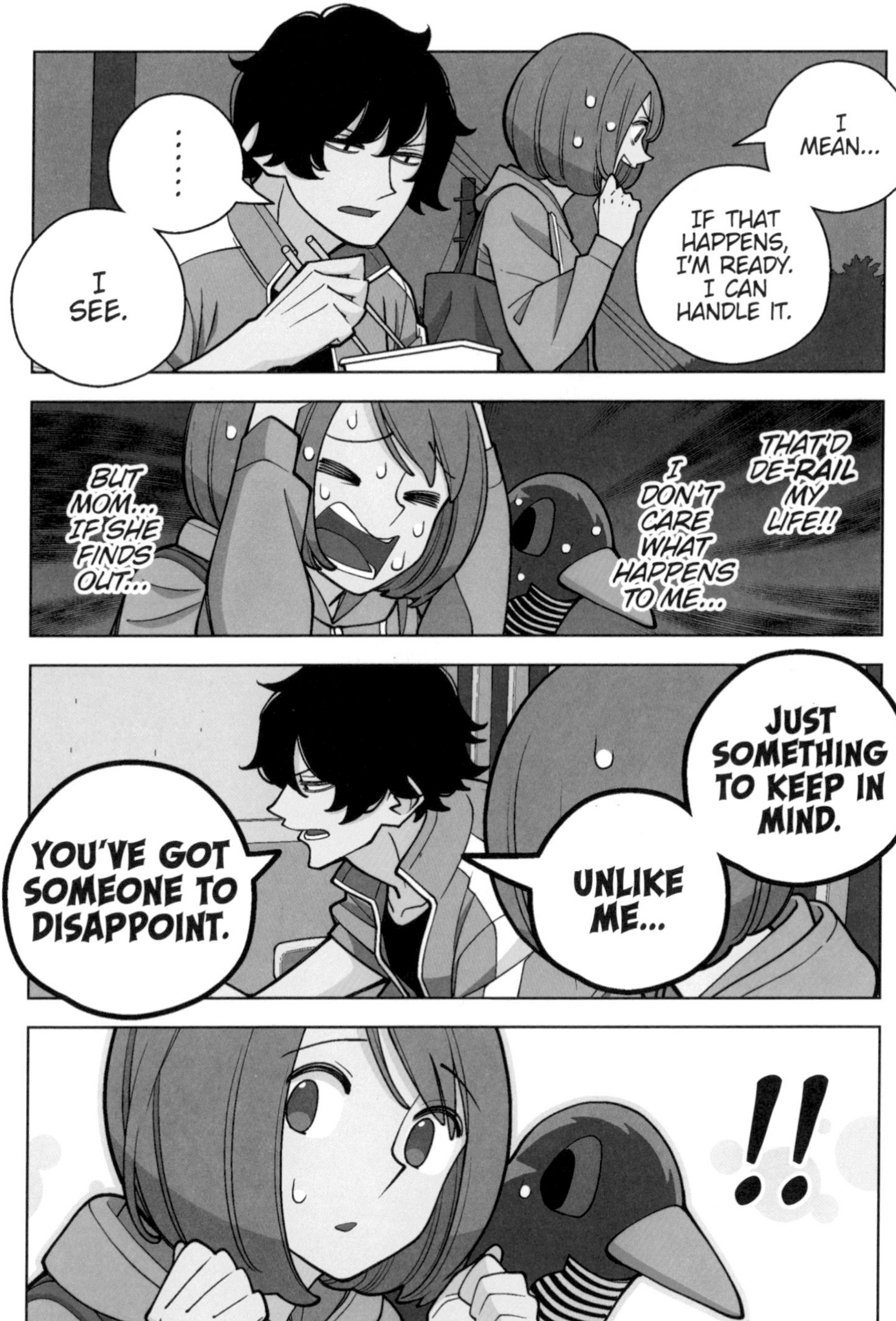
I MEAN...
IF THAT HAPPENS, I'M READY. I CAN HANDLE IT.
......
I SEE.
BUT MOM... IF SHE FINDS OUT...
I DON'T CARE WHAT HAPPENS TO ME...
THAT'D DE-RAIL MY LIFE!!
YOU'VE GOT SOMEONE TO DISAPPOINT.
UNLIKE ME...
JUST SOMETHING TO KEEP IN MIND.
!!

Don't say something so gloomy. ☆

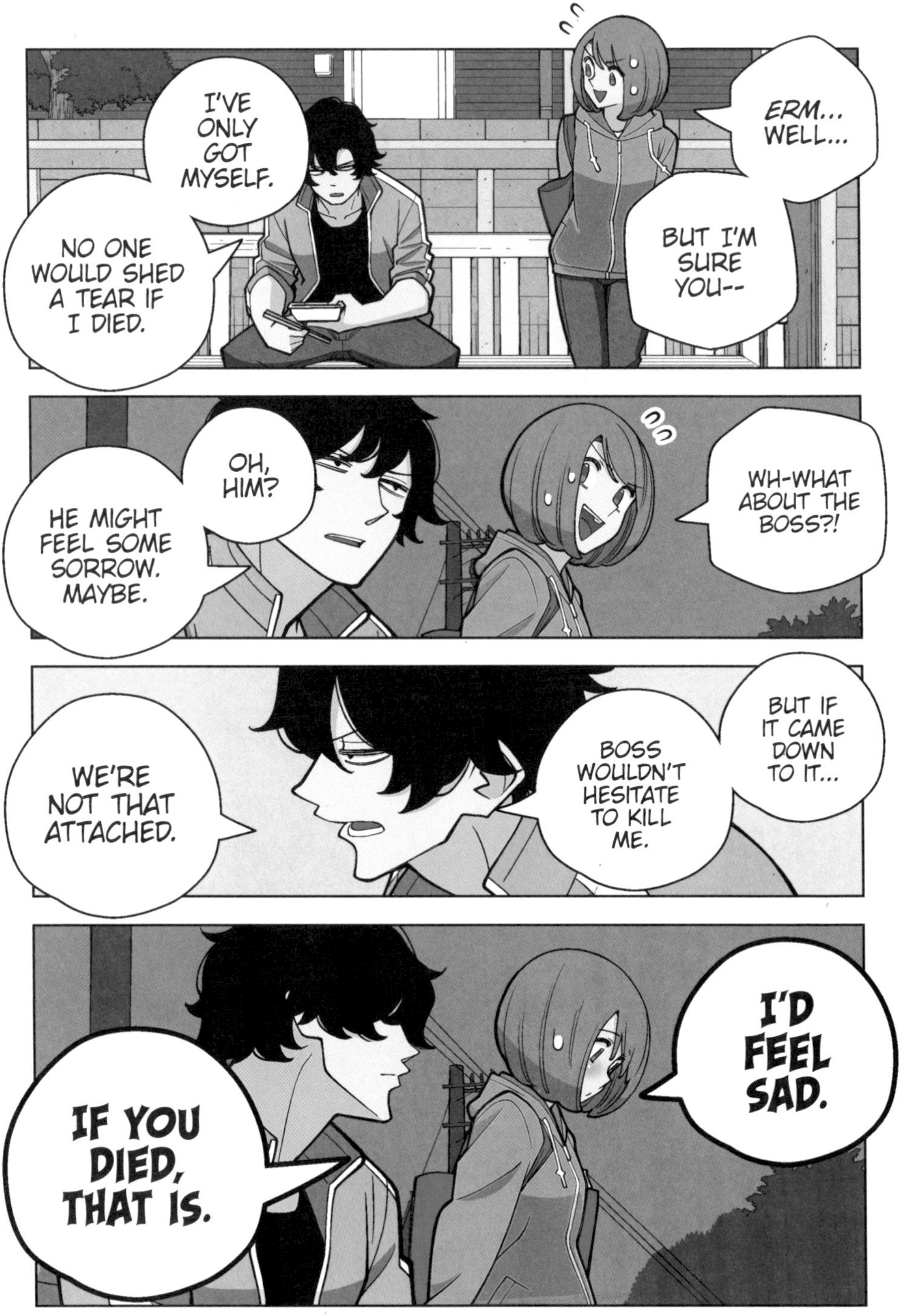
ERM... WELL...
BUT I'M SURE YOU--
I'VE ONLY GOT MYSELF.
NO ONE WOULD SHED A TEAR IF I DIED.
WH-WHAT ABOUT THE BOSS?!
OH, HIM?
HE MIGHT FEEL SOME SORROW. MAYBE.
BUT IF IT CAME DOWN TO IT...
BOSS WOULDN'T HESITATE TO KILL ME.
WE'RE NOT THAT ATTACHED.
I'D FEEL SAD.
IF YOU DIED, THAT IS.

☆ —— Chances are pretty good I'd cry, even.

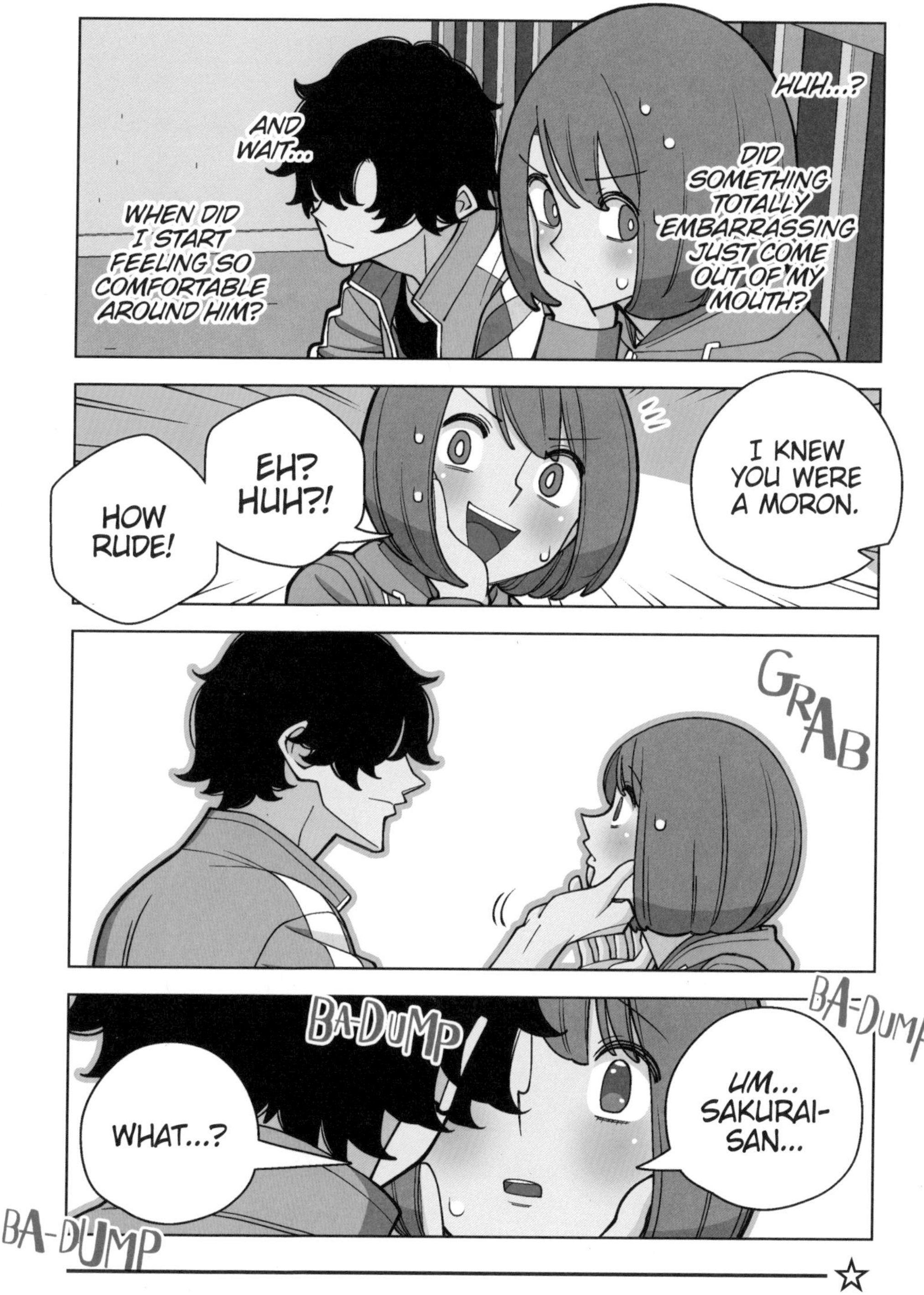
HUH...?
DID SOMETHING TOTALLY EMBARRASSING JUST COME OUT OF MY MOUTH?
AND WAIT...
WHEN DID I START FEELING SO COMFORTABLE AROUND HIM?
I KNEW YOU WERE A MORON.
EH? HUH?!
HOW RUDE!
GRAB
BA-DUM
UM... SAKURAI-SAN...
BA-DUMP
WHAT...?
BA-DUMP

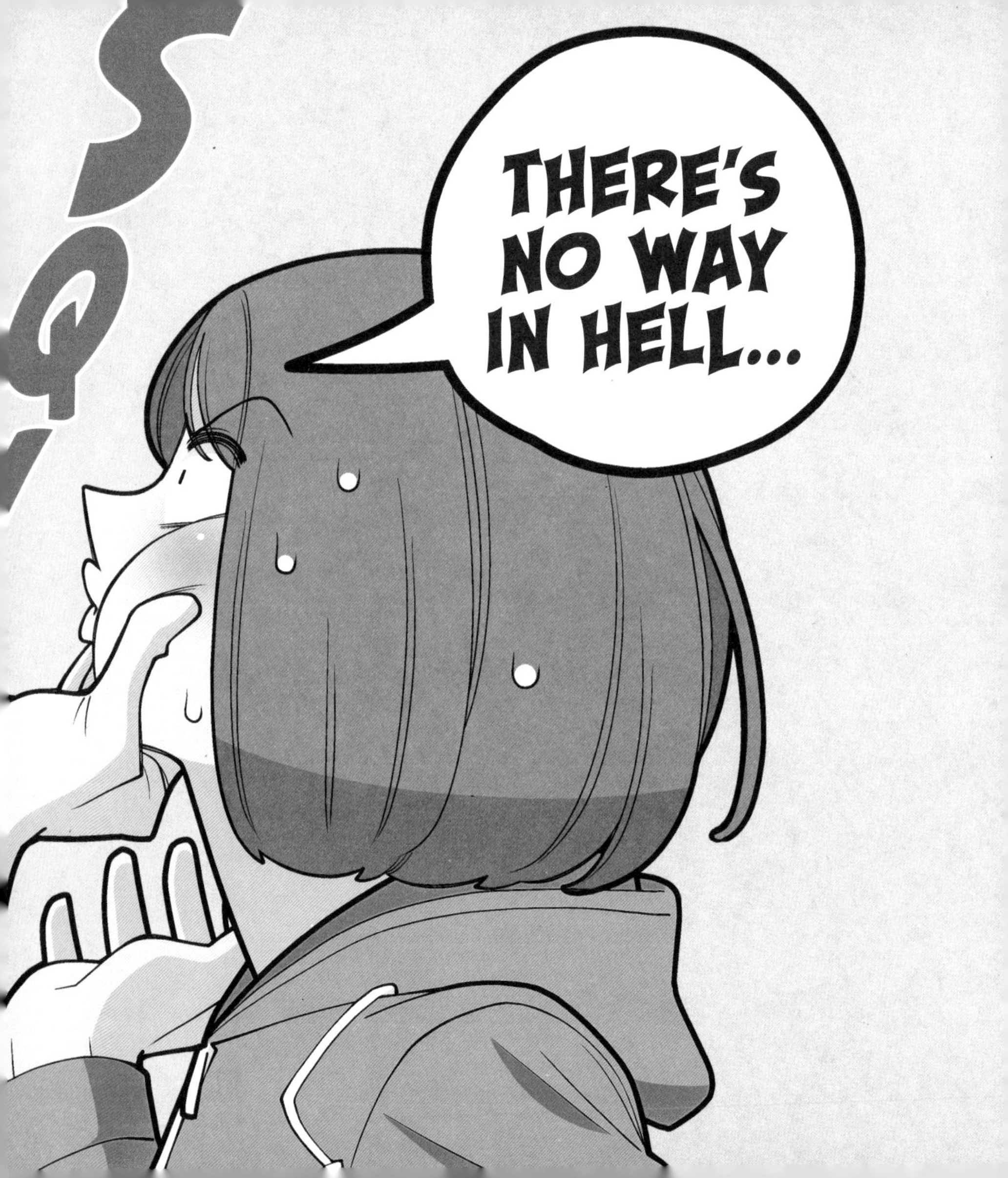
THERE'S NO WAY IN HELL...

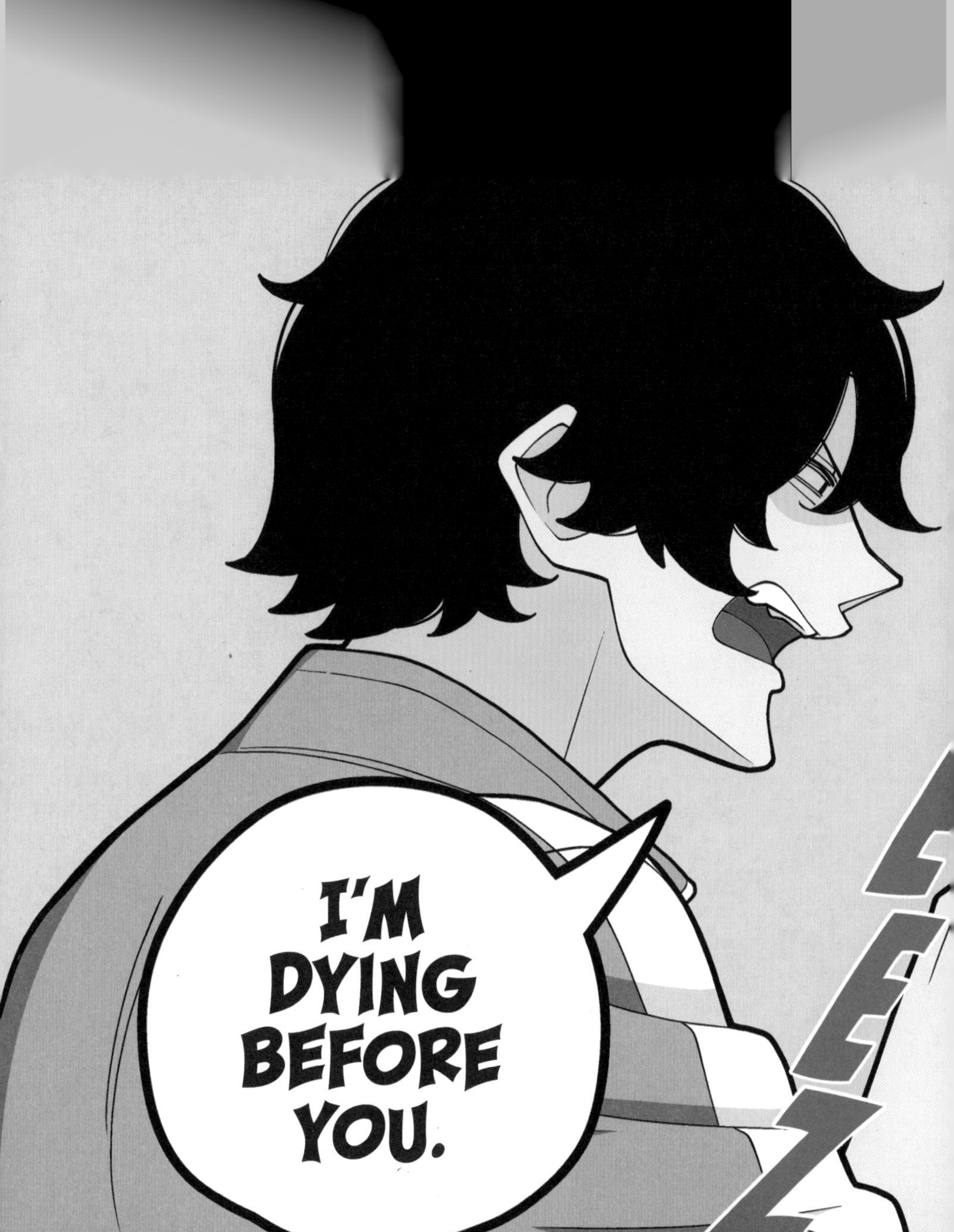
I'M DYING BEFORE YOU.

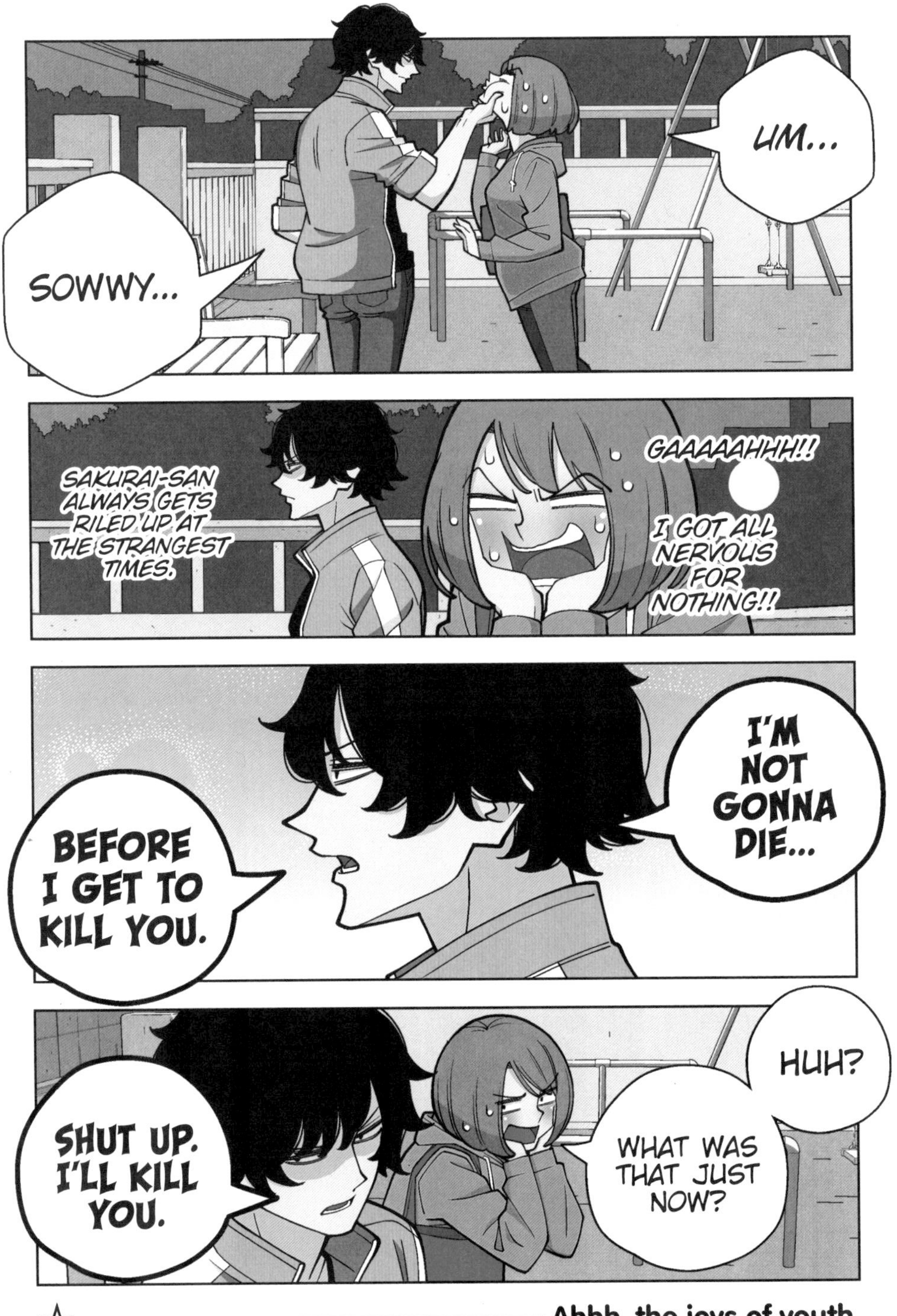

UM...
SOWWY...
GAAAAAHHH!!
I GOT ALL NERVOUS FOR NOTHING!!
SAKURAI-SAN ALWAYS GETS RILED UP AT THE STRANGEST TIMES.
I'M NOT GONNA DIE...
BEFORE I GET TO KILL YOU.
HUH?
WHAT WAS THAT JUST NOW?
SHUT UP. I'LL KILL YOU.

☆ —— Ahhh, the joys of youth.

Happy Kanako's
Killer Life

Let's
party
hard!

Happy Kanako's
Killer Life

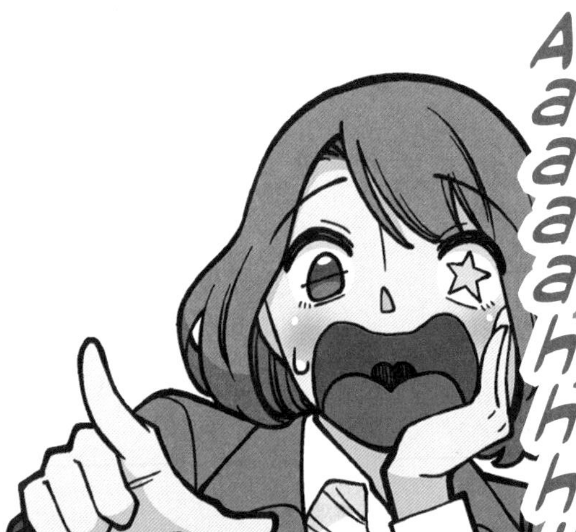
Aaaaaahhhh!!

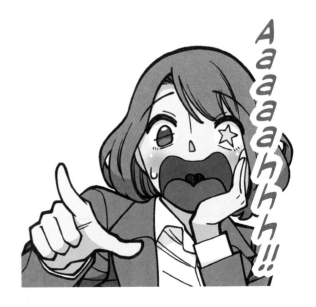

037

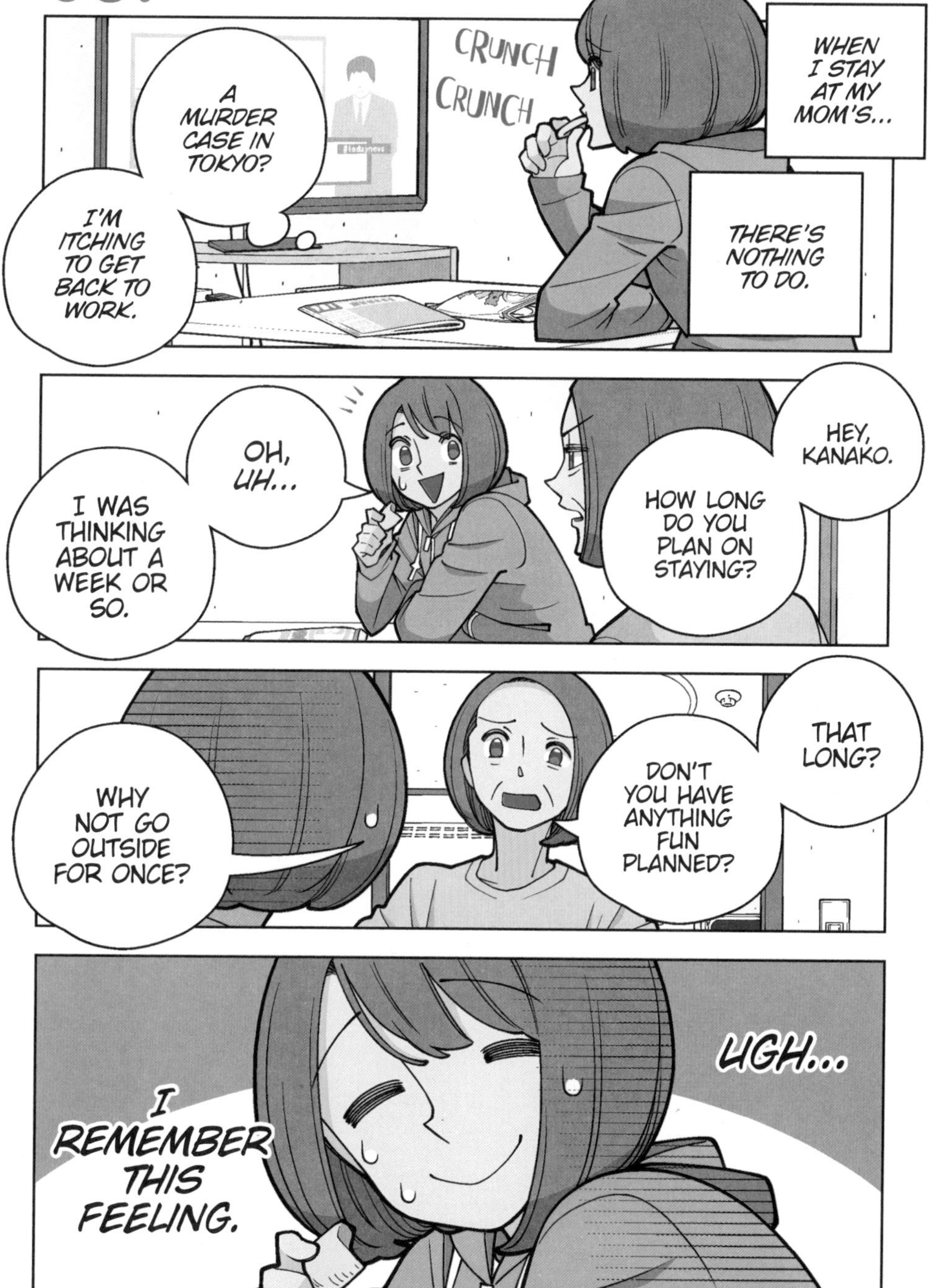
WHEN I STAY AT MY MOM'S...
THERE'S NOTHING TO DO.
CRUNCH
CRUNCH
A MURDER CASE IN TOKYO?
I'M ITCHING TO GET BACK TO WORK.
HEY, KANAKO.
HOW LONG DO YOU PLAN ON STAYING?
OH, UH...
I WAS THINKING ABOUT A WEEK OR SO.
THAT LONG?
DON'T YOU HAVE ANYTHING FUN PLANNED?
WHY NOT GO OUTSIDE FOR ONCE?
UGH...
I REMEMBER THIS FEELING.

Miss Never-Left-the-House-on-Sundays. ——— ☆

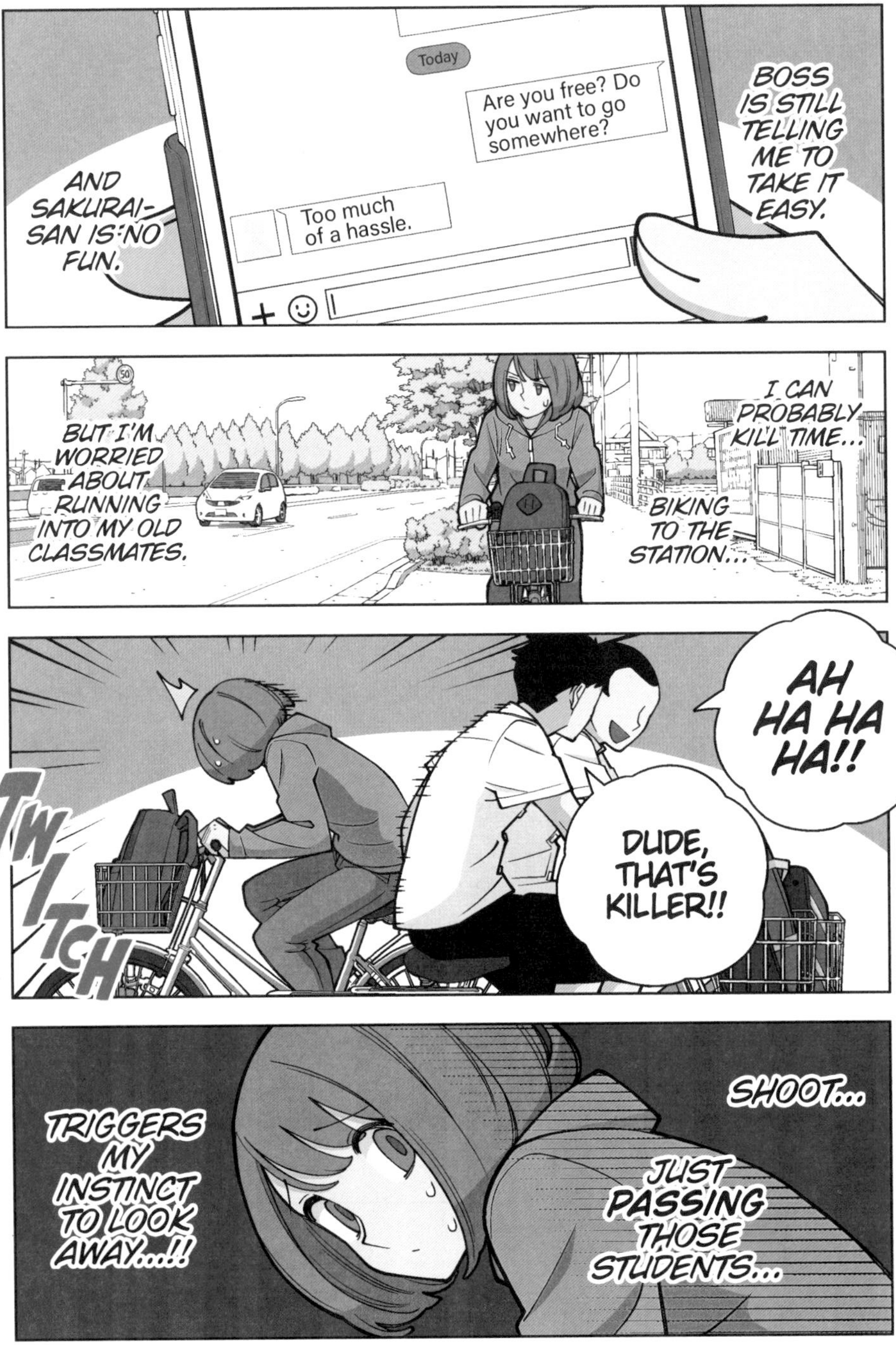
BOSS IS STILL TELLING ME TO TAKE IT EASY.
Today
Are you free? Do you want to go somewhere?
Too much of a hassle.
AND SAKURAI-SAN IS NO FUN.
I CAN PROBABLY KILL TIME...
BIKING TO THE STATION...
BUT I'M WORRIED ABOUT RUNNING INTO MY OLD CLASSMATES.
AH HA HA HA!!
DUDE, THAT'S KILLER!!
TWITCH
SHOOT...
JUST PASSING THOSE STUDENTS...
TRIGGERS MY INSTINCT TO LOOK AWAY...!!

☆ —— A life of constant dread.

GOSH DARN DOG-GONE IT...

THE MORE THE OLD ME RESURFACES.

THE LONGER I'M HERE...

THE LIBRARY BECAME MY SAFE HAVEN.

AND IN HIGH SCHOOL, IT FELT SUFFOCATING TO BE AT HOME.

IN JUNIOR HIGH, I SKIPPED SCHOOL ALL THE TIME.

AND IT'LL BE COOL WITH THE AC ON!!

THE LIBRARY IS PERFECT FOR TIMES LIKE THESE.

IT SHOULD BE OPEN DURING OBON!

THE LIBRARY! THAT'S IT!!

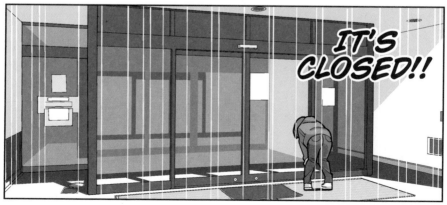

IT'S CLOSED!!

Closed on Mondays! ————————————— ☆

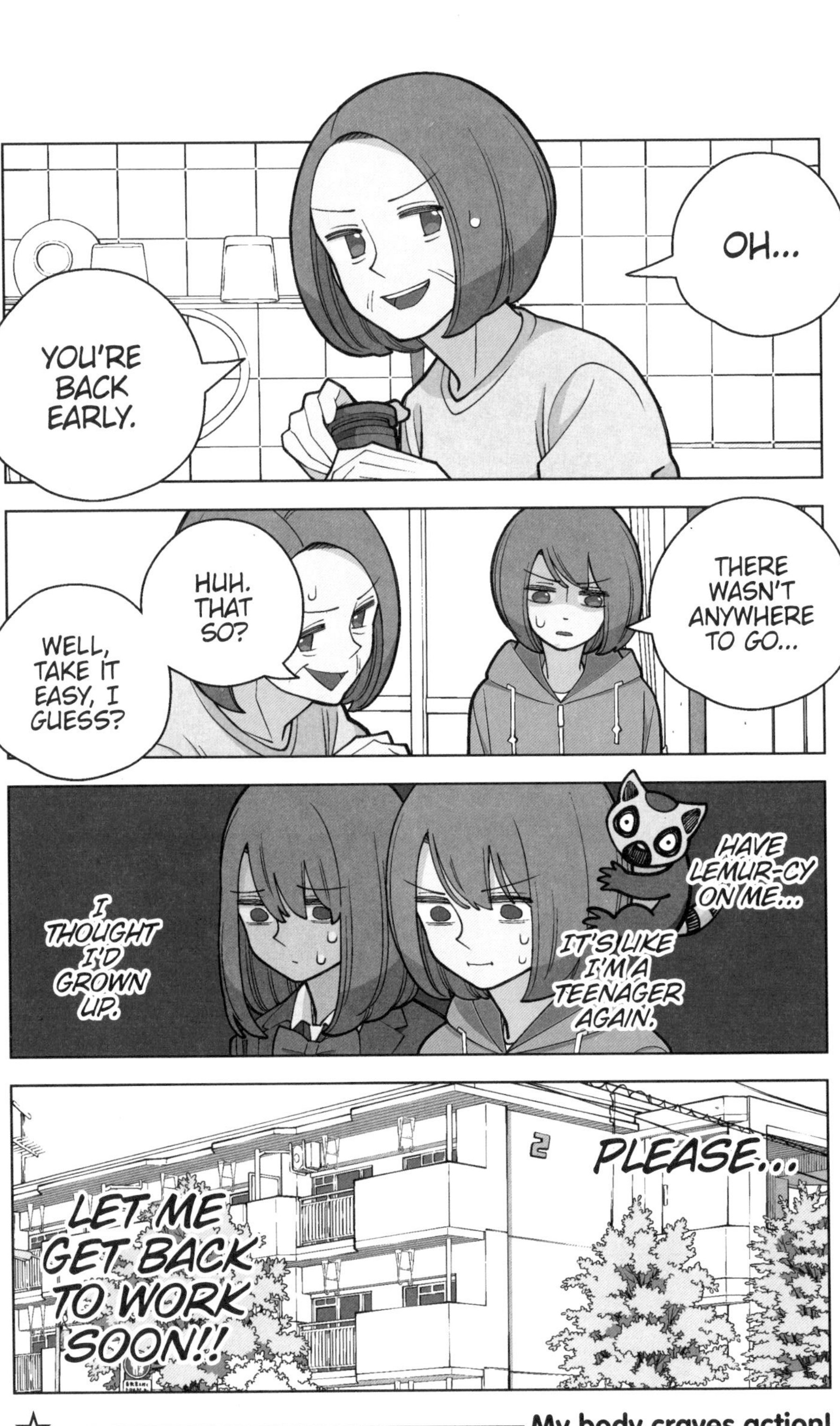
OH...
YOU'RE BACK EARLY.
THERE WASN'T ANYWHERE TO GO...
HUH. THAT SO?
WELL, TAKE IT EASY, I GUESS?
HAVE LEMUR-CY ON ME...
IT'S LIKE I'M A TEENAGER AGAIN.
I THOUGHT I'D GROWN UP.
PLEASE...
LET ME GET BACK TO WORK SOON!!

☆ — **My body craves action!**

038

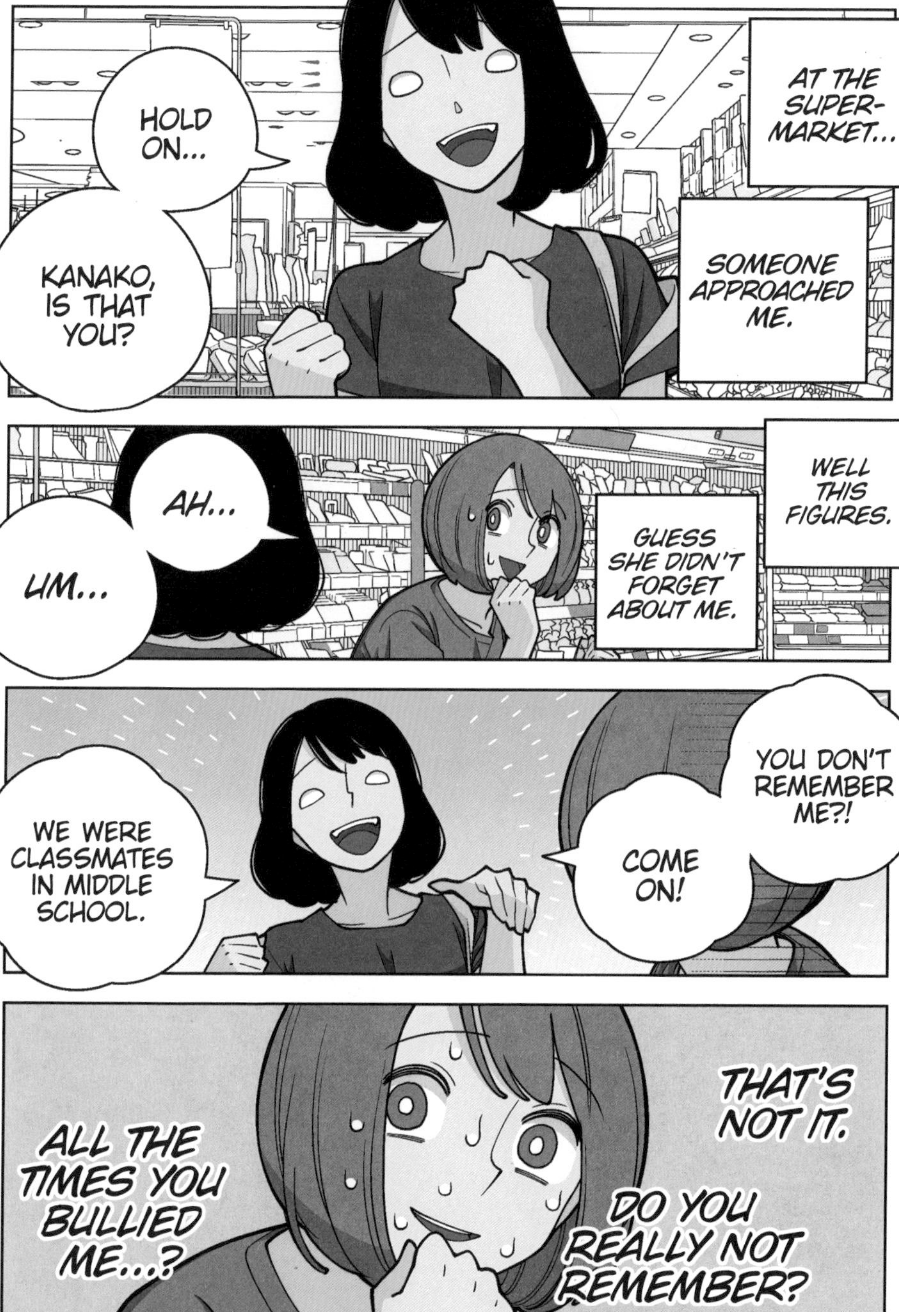
AT THE SUPER-MARKET...
SOMEONE APPROACHED ME.
HOLD ON...
KANAKO, IS THAT YOU?
WELL THIS FIGURES.
GUESS SHE DIDN'T FORGET ABOUT ME.
AH...
UM...
YOU DON'T REMEMBER ME?!
COME ON!
WE WERE CLASSMATES IN MIDDLE SCHOOL.
THAT'S NOT IT.
DO YOU REALLY NOT REMEMBER?
ALL THE TIMES YOU BULLIED ME...?

What I wouldn't give to forget. ☆

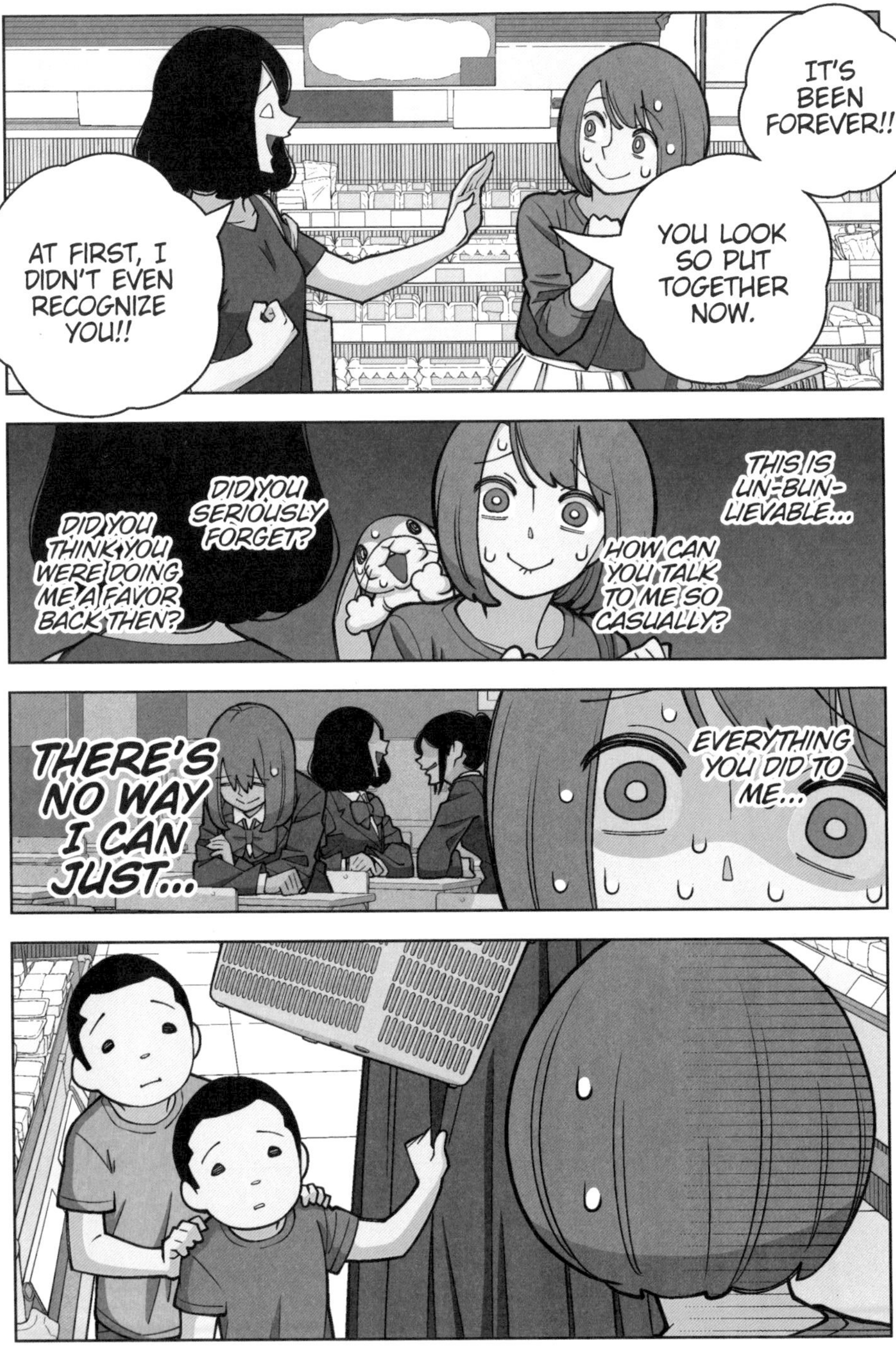
IT'S BEEN FOREVER!!
YOU LOOK SO PUT TOGETHER NOW.
AT FIRST, I DIDN'T EVEN RECOGNIZE YOU!!
THIS IS UN-BUN-LIEVABLE...
HOW CAN YOU TALK TO ME SO CASUALLY?
DID YOU SERIOUSLY FORGET?
DID YOU THINK YOU WERE DOING ME A FAVOR BACK THEN?
EVERYTHING YOU DID TO ME...
THERE'S NO WAY I CAN JUST...

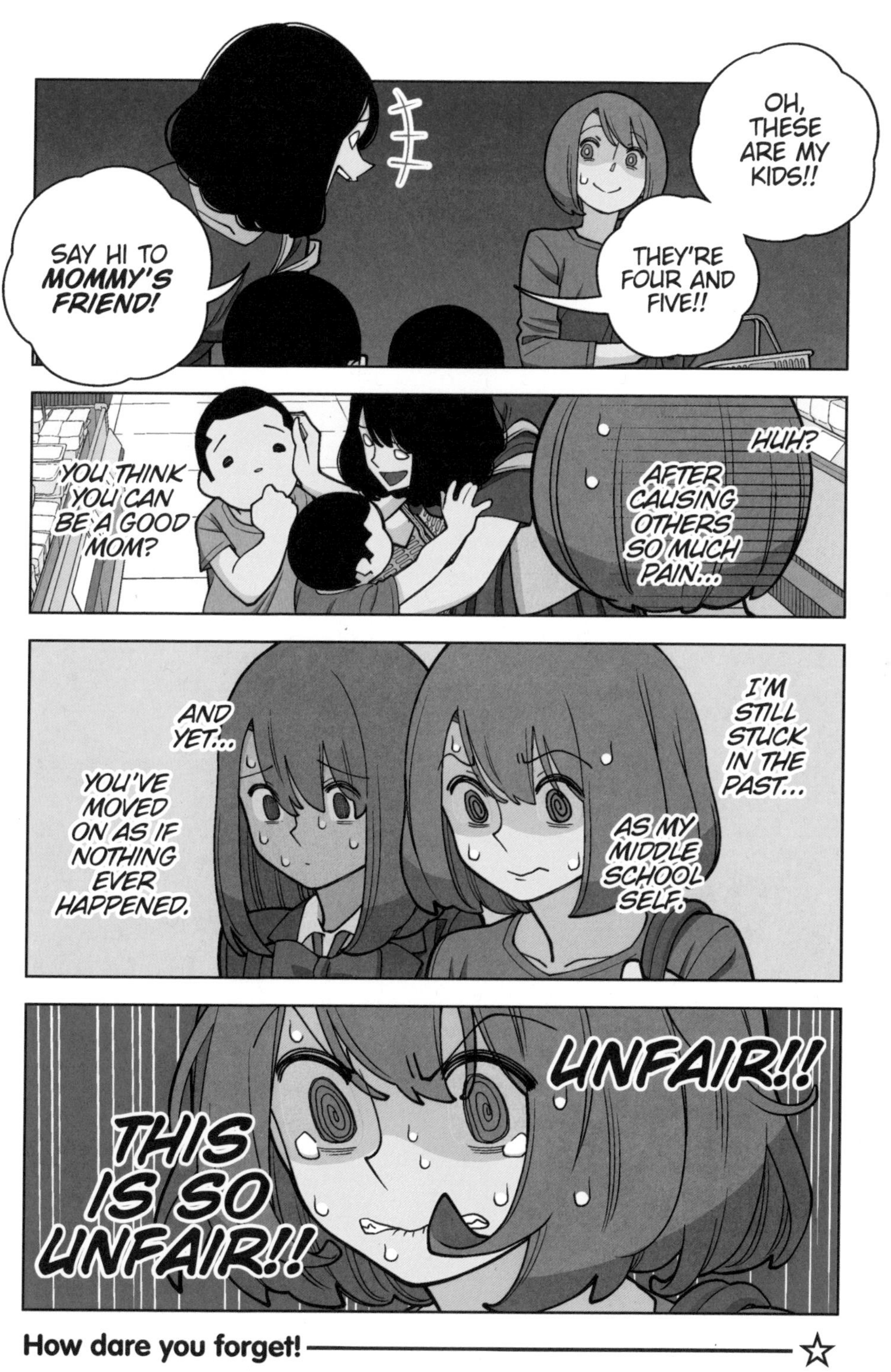
OH, THESE ARE MY KIDS!!
THEY'RE FOUR AND FIVE!!
SAY HI TO MOMMY'S FRIEND!
HUH?
AFTER CAUSING OTHERS SO MUCH PAIN...
YOU THINK YOU CAN BE A GOOD MOM?
I'M STILL STUCK IN THE PAST...
AS MY MIDDLE SCHOOL SELF.
AND YET...
YOU'VE MOVED ON AS IF NOTHING EVER HAPPENED.
UNFAIR!!
THIS IS SO UNFAIR!!

How dare you forget! ——— ☆

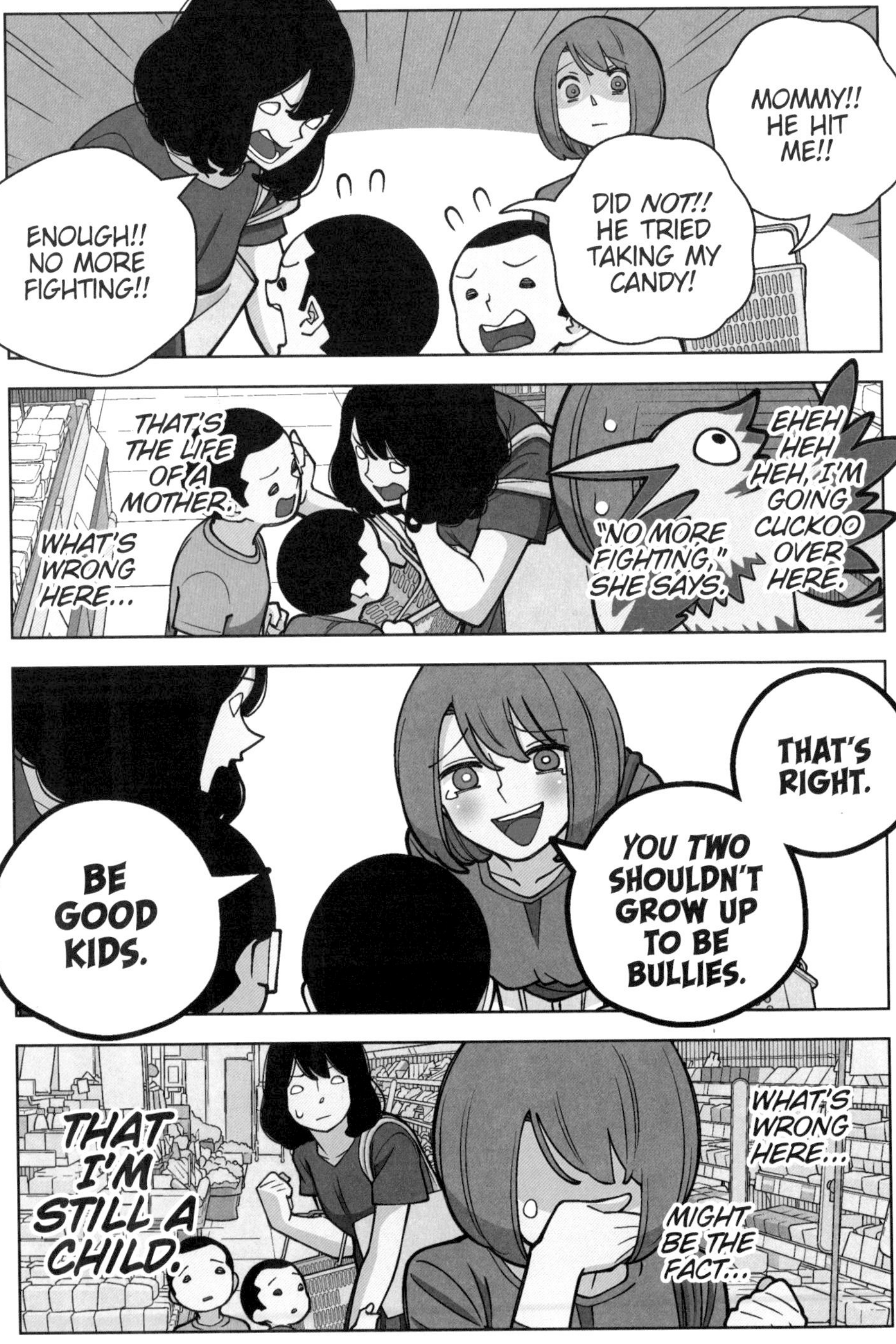
MOMMY!! HE HIT ME!!
DID NOT!! HE TRIED TAKING MY CANDY!
ENOUGH!! NO MORE FIGHTING!!
EHEH HEH HEH, I'M GOING CUCKOO OVER HERE.
"NO MORE FIGHTING," SHE SAYS.
THAT'S THE LIFE OF A MOTHER.
WHAT'S WRONG HERE...
THAT'S RIGHT.
YOU TWO SHOULDN'T GROW UP TO BE BULLIES.
BE GOOD KIDS.
WHAT'S WRONG HERE...
MIGHT BE THE FACT...
THAT I'M STILL A CHILD.

☆ —— **Dishing out revenge.**

039

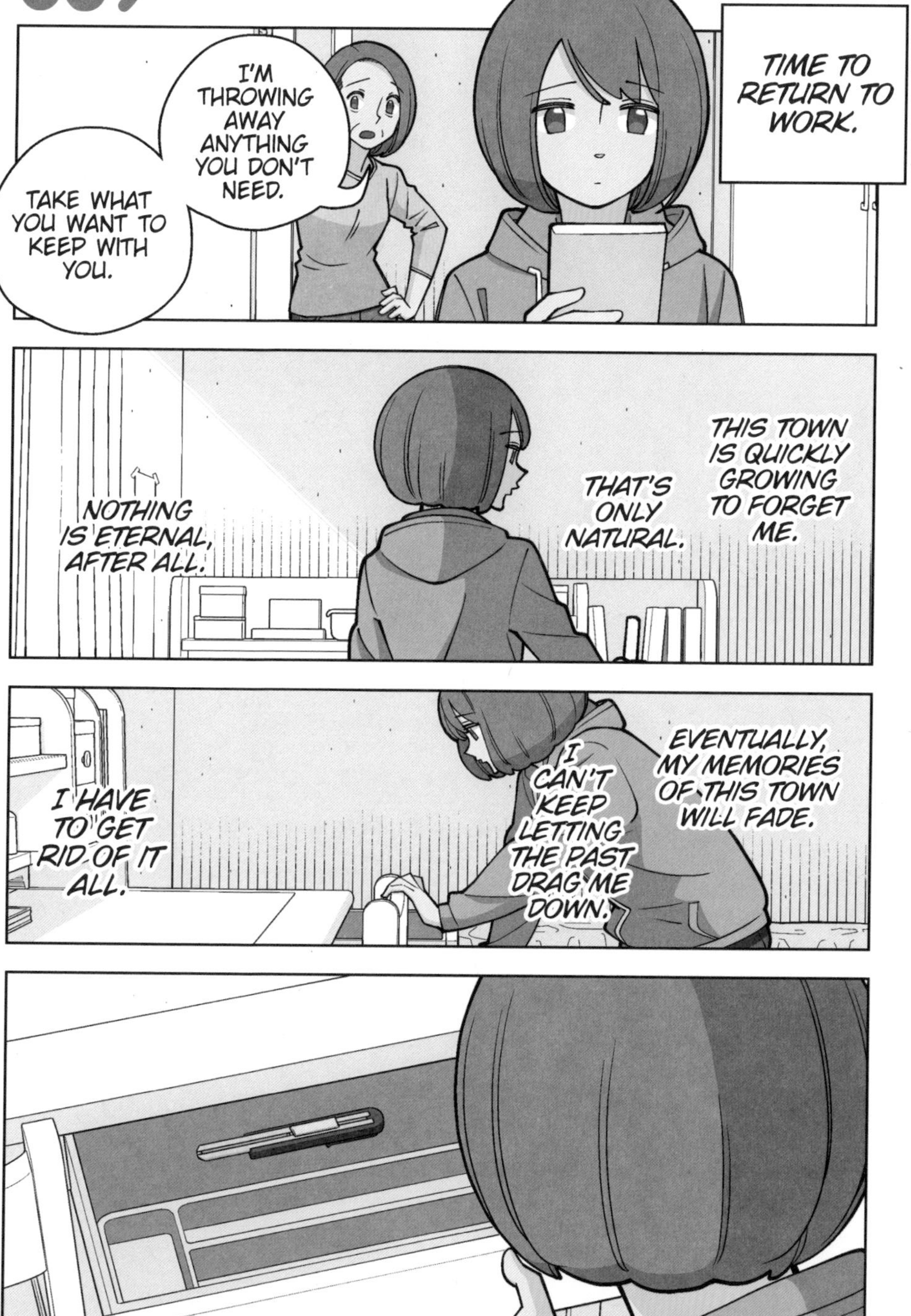

TIME TO RETURN TO WORK.
I'M THROWING AWAY ANYTHING YOU DON'T NEED.
TAKE WHAT YOU WANT TO KEEP WITH YOU.
THIS TOWN IS QUICKLY GROWING TO FORGET ME.
THAT'S ONLY NATURAL.
NOTHING IS ETERNAL, AFTER ALL.
EVENTUALLY, MY MEMORIES OF THIS TOWN WILL FADE.
I CAN'T KEEP LETTING THE PAST DRAG ME DOWN.
I HAVE TO GET RID OF IT ALL.

Box Cutter . ☆

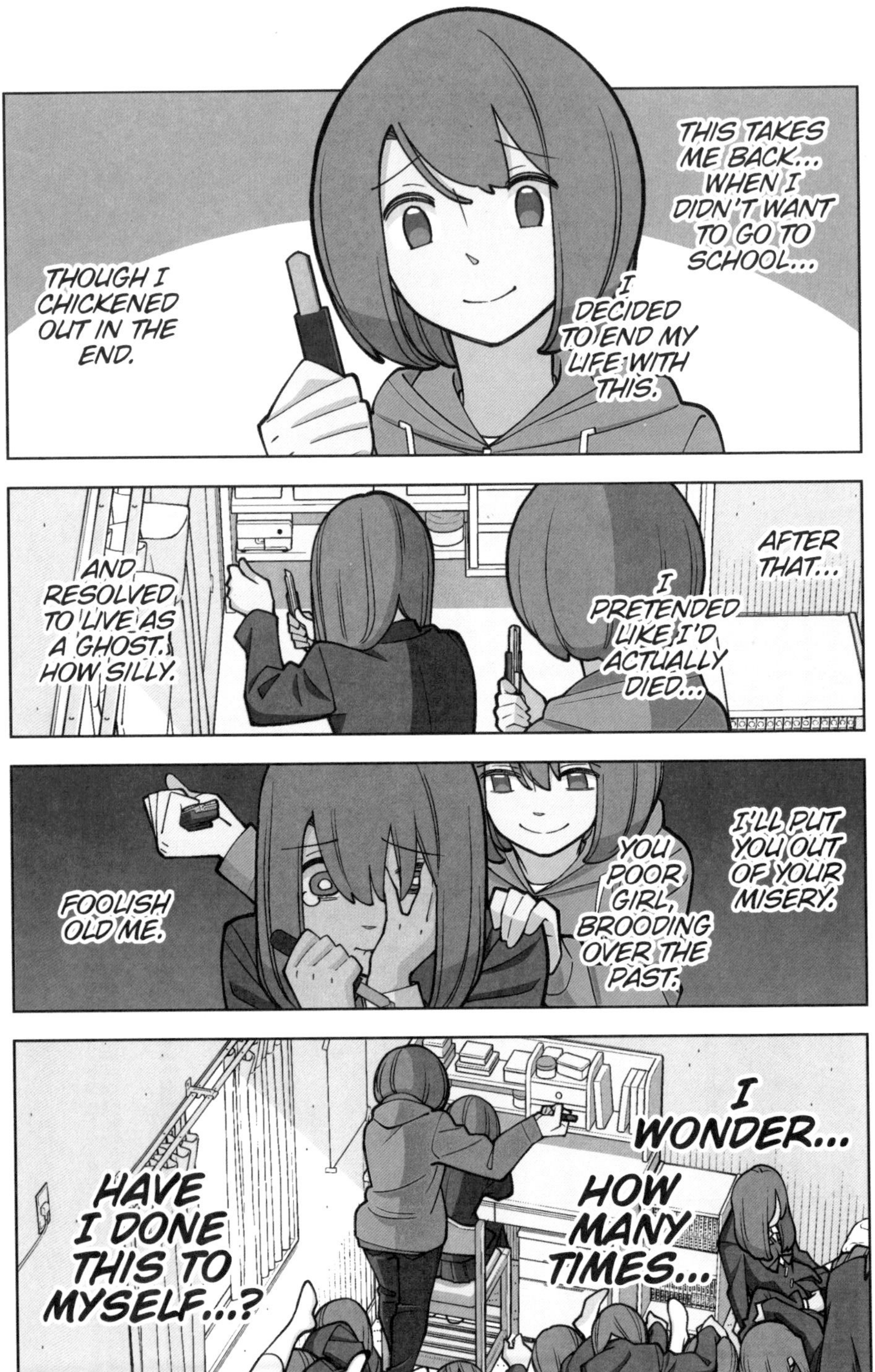
THIS TAKES ME BACK... WHEN I DIDN'T WANT TO GO TO SCHOOL...
I DECIDED TO END MY LIFE WITH THIS.
THOUGH I CHICKENED OUT IN THE END.
AFTER THAT...
I PRETENDED LIKE I'D ACTUALLY DIED...
AND RESOLVED TO LIVE AS A GHOST. HOW SILLY.
I'LL PUT YOU OUT OF YOUR MISERY.
YOU POOR GIRL, BROODING OVER THE PAST.
FOOLISH OLD ME.
I WONDER...
HOW MANY TIMES...
HAVE I DONE THIS TO MYSELF...?

☆ —— A room full of corpses.

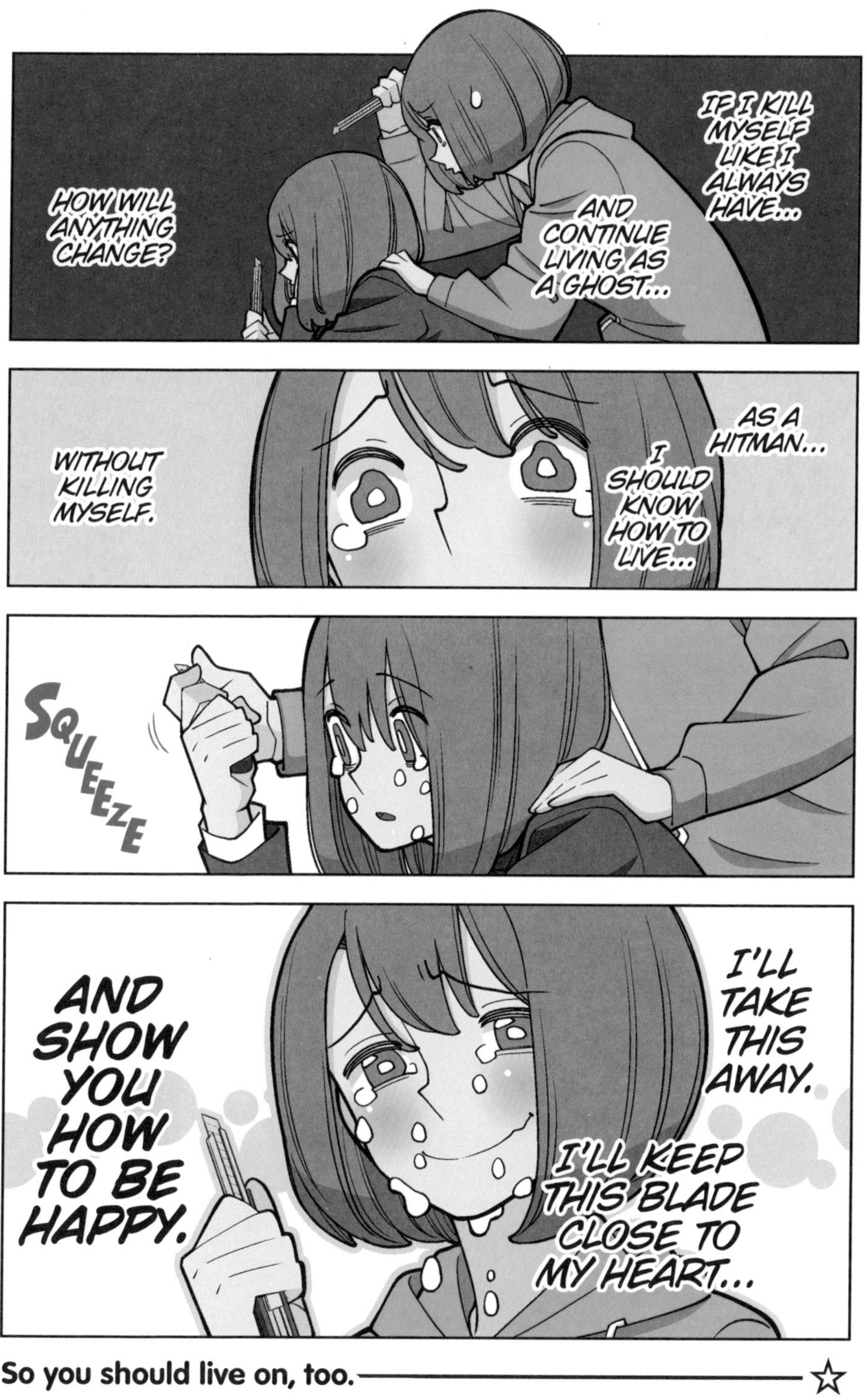
IF I KILL MYSELF LIKE I ALWAYS HAVE...
AND CONTINUE LIVING AS A GHOST...
HOW WILL ANYTHING CHANGE?
AS A HITMAN...
I SHOULD KNOW HOW TO LIVE...
WITHOUT KILLING MYSELF.
SQUEEZE
I'LL TAKE THIS AWAY.
I'LL KEEP THIS BLADE CLOSE TO MY HEART...
AND SHOW YOU HOW TO BE HAPPY.

So you should live on, too. ☆

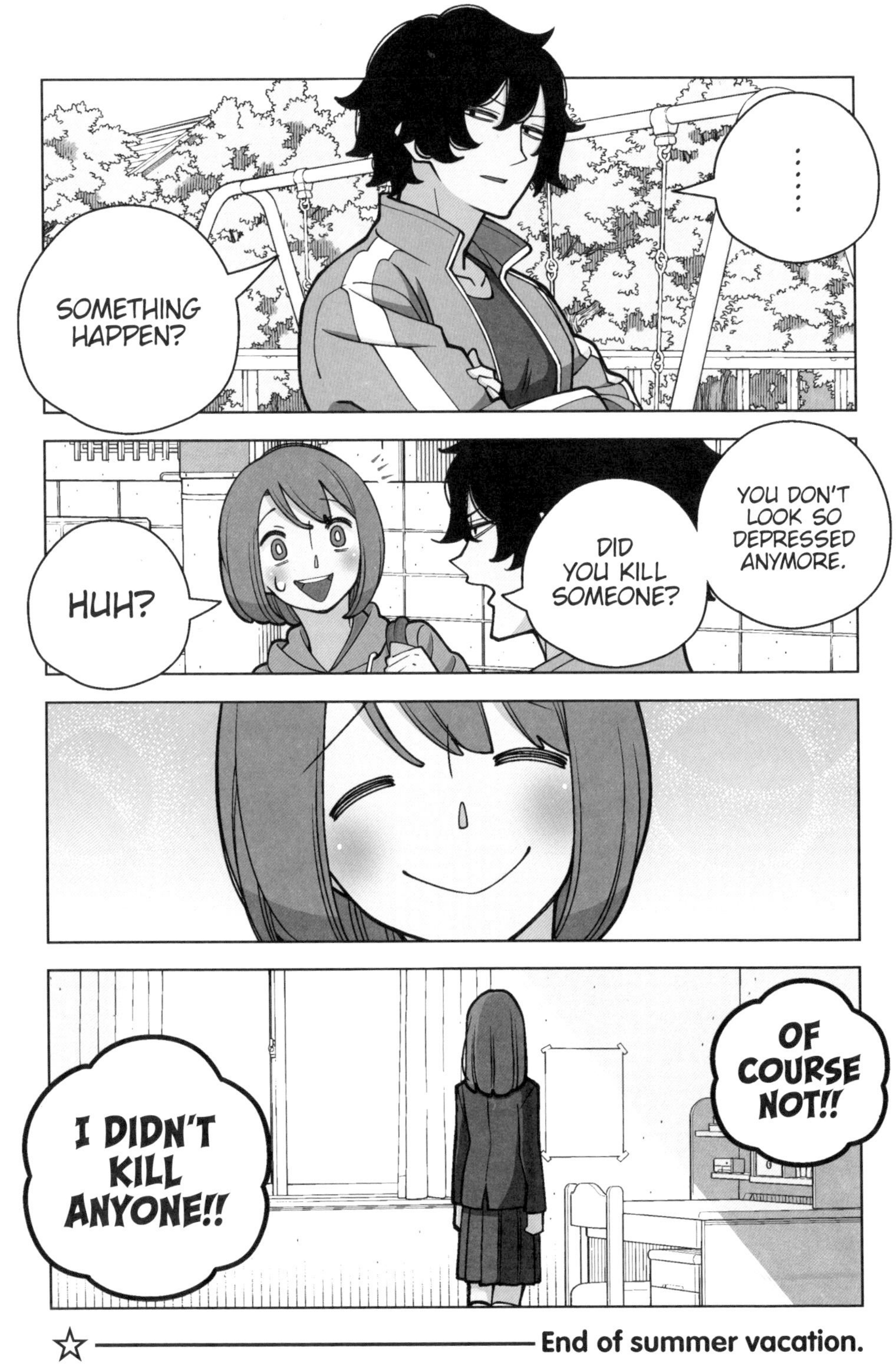
……
SOMETHING HAPPEN?
YOU DON'T LOOK SO DEPRESSED ANYMORE.
DID YOU KILL SOMEONE?
HUH?
OF COURSE NOT!!
I DIDN'T KILL ANYONE!!

☆ —— **End of summer vacation.**

040

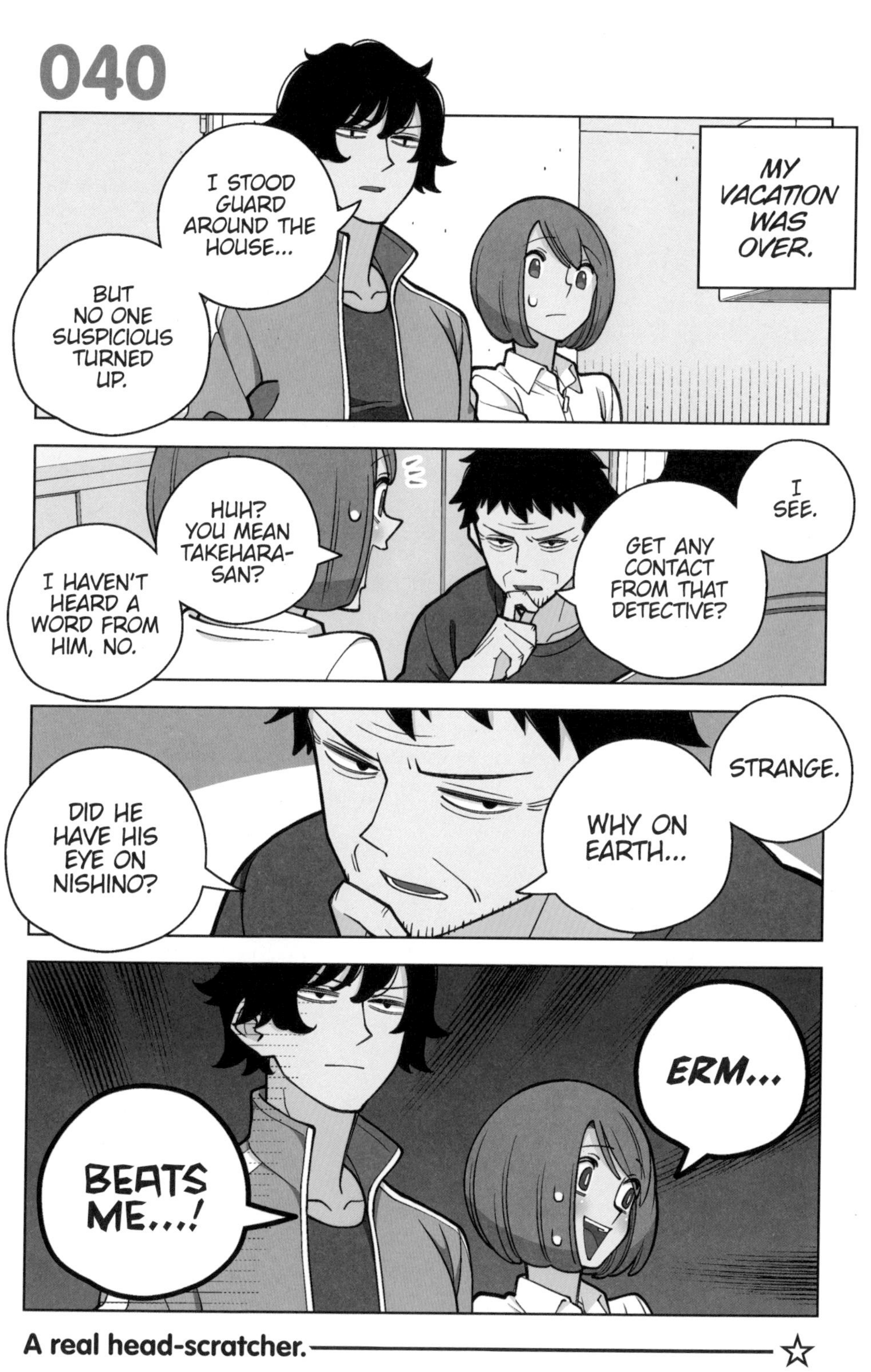
MY VACATION WAS OVER.
I STOOD GUARD AROUND THE HOUSE...
BUT NO ONE SUSPICIOUS TURNED UP.
I SEE.
GET ANY CONTACT FROM THAT DETECTIVE?
HUH? YOU MEAN TAKEHARA-SAN?
I HAVEN'T HEARD A WORD FROM HIM, NO.
STRANGE.
WHY ON EARTH...
DID HE HAVE HIS EYE ON NISHINO?
ERM...
BEATS ME...!

A real head-scratcher. ☆

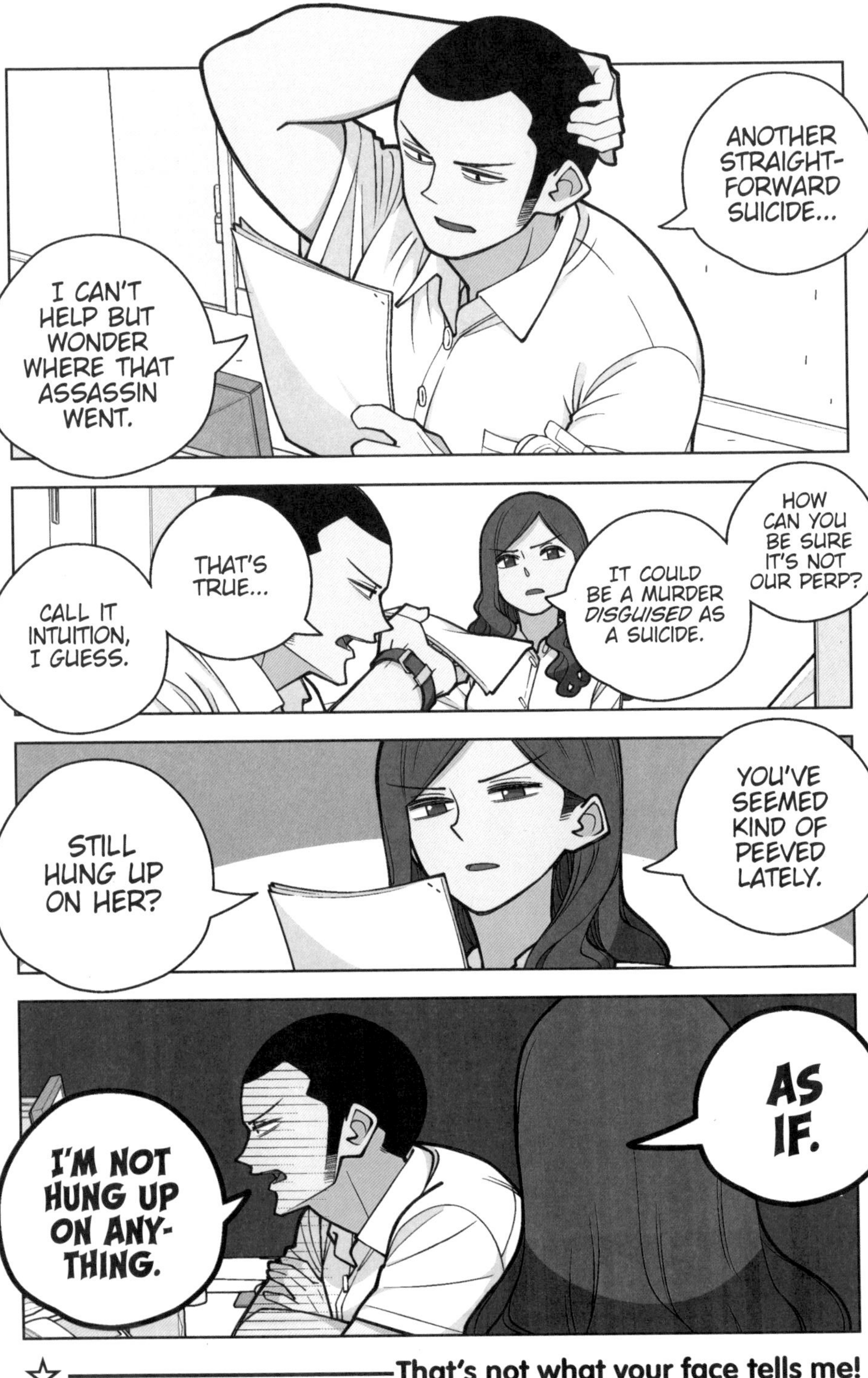
ANOTHER STRAIGHT-FORWARD SUICIDE...
I CAN'T HELP BUT WONDER WHERE THAT ASSASSIN WENT.
HOW CAN YOU BE SURE IT'S NOT OUR PERP?
IT COULD BE A MURDER *DISGUISED* AS A SUICIDE.
THAT'S TRUE...
CALL IT INTUITION, I GUESS.
YOU'VE SEEMED KIND OF PEEVED LATELY.
STILL HUNG UP ON HER?
AS IF.
I'M NOT HUNG UP ON ANYTHING.

☆ ——That's not what your face tells me!

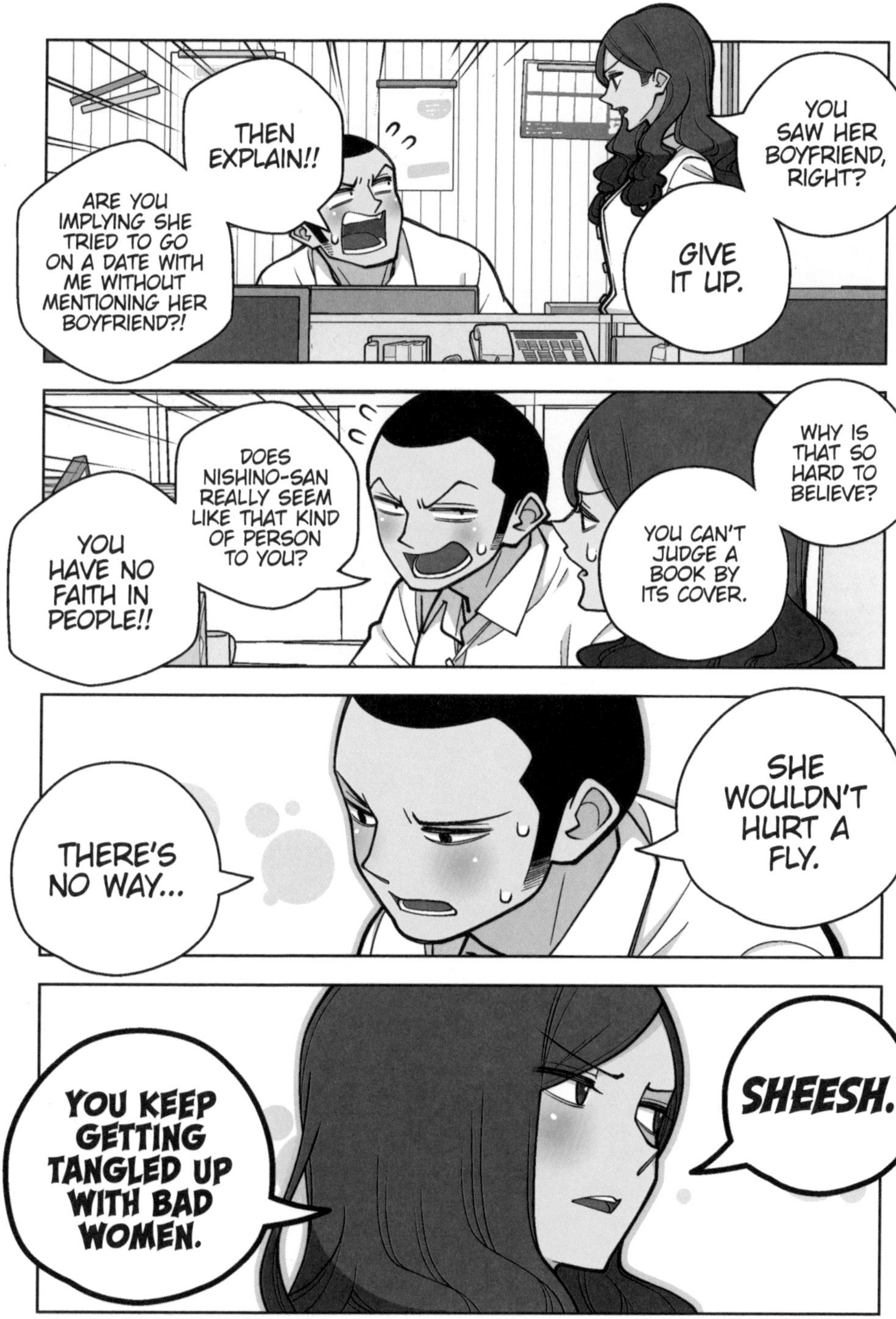
YOU SAW HER BOYFRIEND, RIGHT?
GIVE IT UP.
THEN EXPLAIN!!
ARE YOU IMPLYING SHE TRIED TO GO ON A DATE WITH ME WITHOUT MENTIONING HER BOYFRIEND?!
WHY IS THAT SO HARD TO BELIEVE?
YOU CAN'T JUDGE A BOOK BY ITS COVER.
DOES NISHINO-SAN REALLY SEEM LIKE THAT KIND OF PERSON TO YOU?
YOU HAVE NO FAITH IN PEOPLE!!
SHE WOULDN'T HURT A FLY.
THERE'S NO WAY...
SHEESH.
YOU KEEP GETTING TANGLED UP WITH BAD WOMEN.

Right on the money. ☆

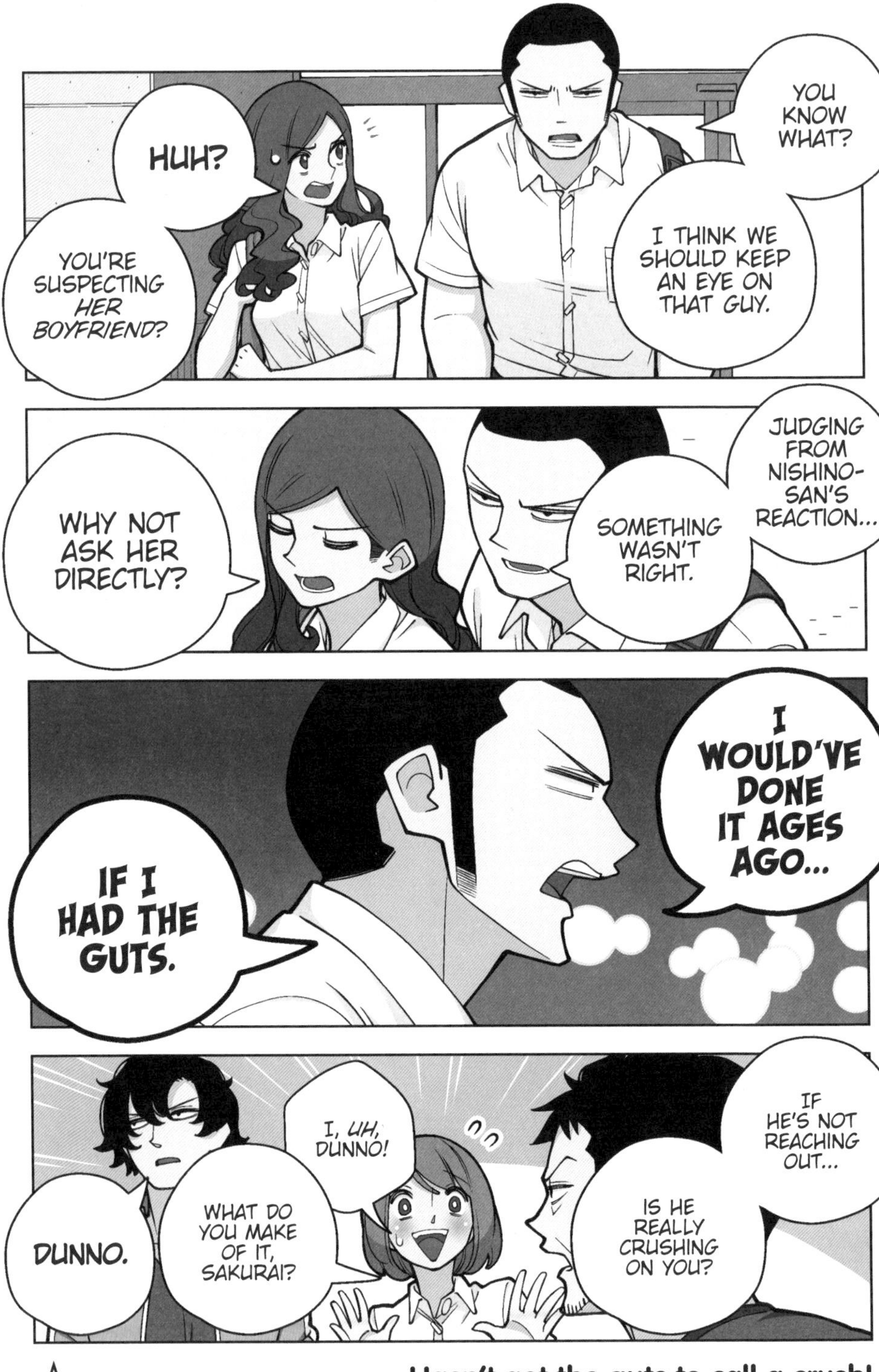
YOU KNOW WHAT?
I THINK WE SHOULD KEEP AN EYE ON THAT GUY.
HUH?
YOU'RE SUSPECTING *HER* BOYFRIEND?
JUDGING FROM NISHINO-SAN'S REACTION...
SOMETHING WASN'T RIGHT.
WHY NOT ASK HER DIRECTLY?
I WOULD'VE DONE IT AGES AGO...
IF I HAD THE GUTS.
IF HE'S NOT REACHING OUT...
IS HE REALLY CRUSHING ON YOU?
I, *UH*, DUNNO!
WHAT DO YOU MAKE OF IT, SAKURAI?
DUNNO.

☆ —— **Hasn't got the guts to call a crush!**

Happy Kanako's
Killer Life

Happy Kanako's
Killer Life

I feel so much better now, but...

Bonus

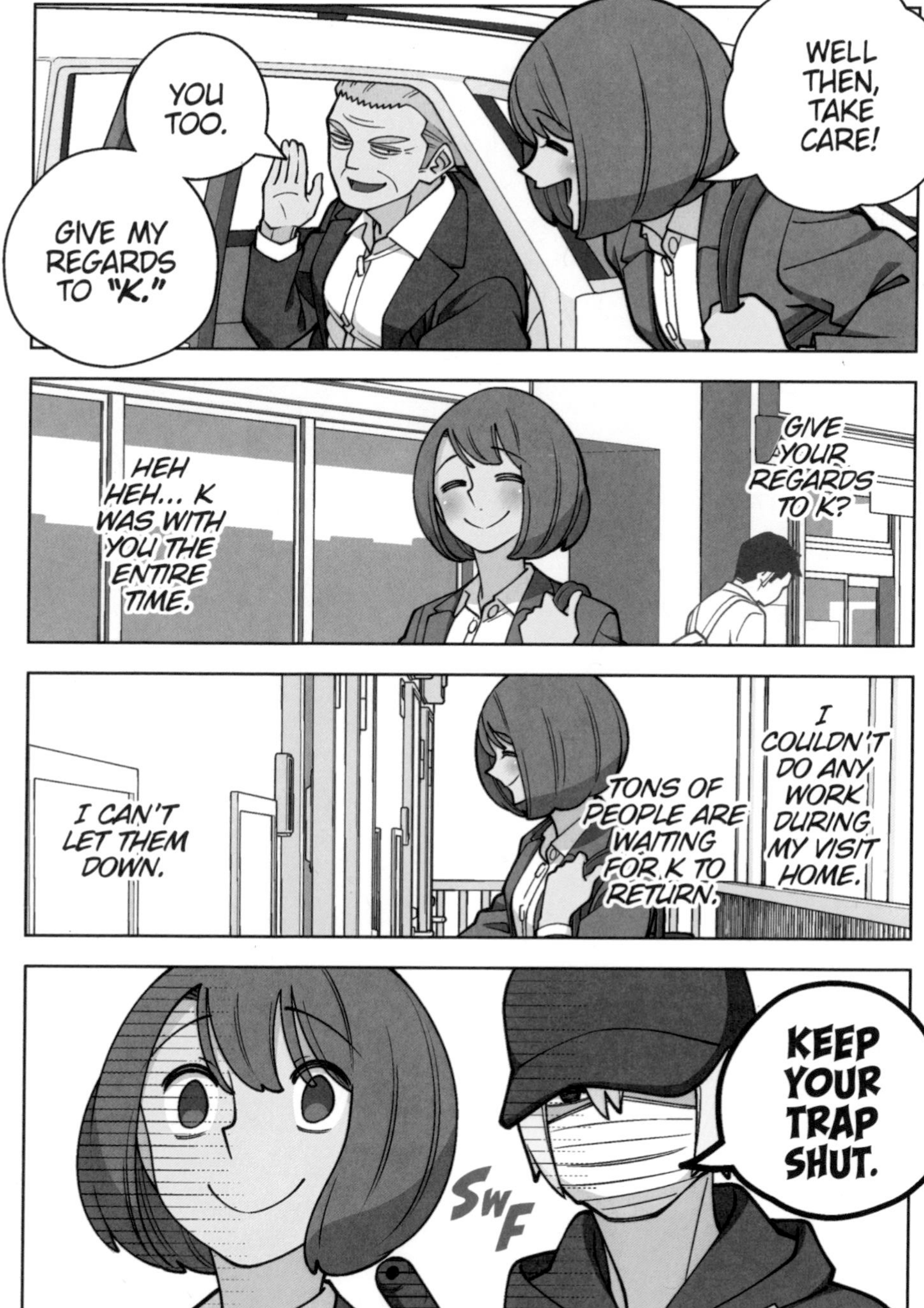
WELL THEN, TAKE CARE!
YOU TOO.
GIVE MY REGARDS TO "K."
GIVE YOUR REGARDS TO K?
HEH HEH... K WAS WITH YOU THE ENTIRE TIME.
I COULDN'T DO ANY WORK DURING MY VISIT HOME.
TONS OF PEOPLE ARE WAITING FOR K TO RETURN.
I CAN'T LET THEM DOWN.
KEEP YOUR TRAP SHUT.
SWF

Someone got tired of waiting! ☆

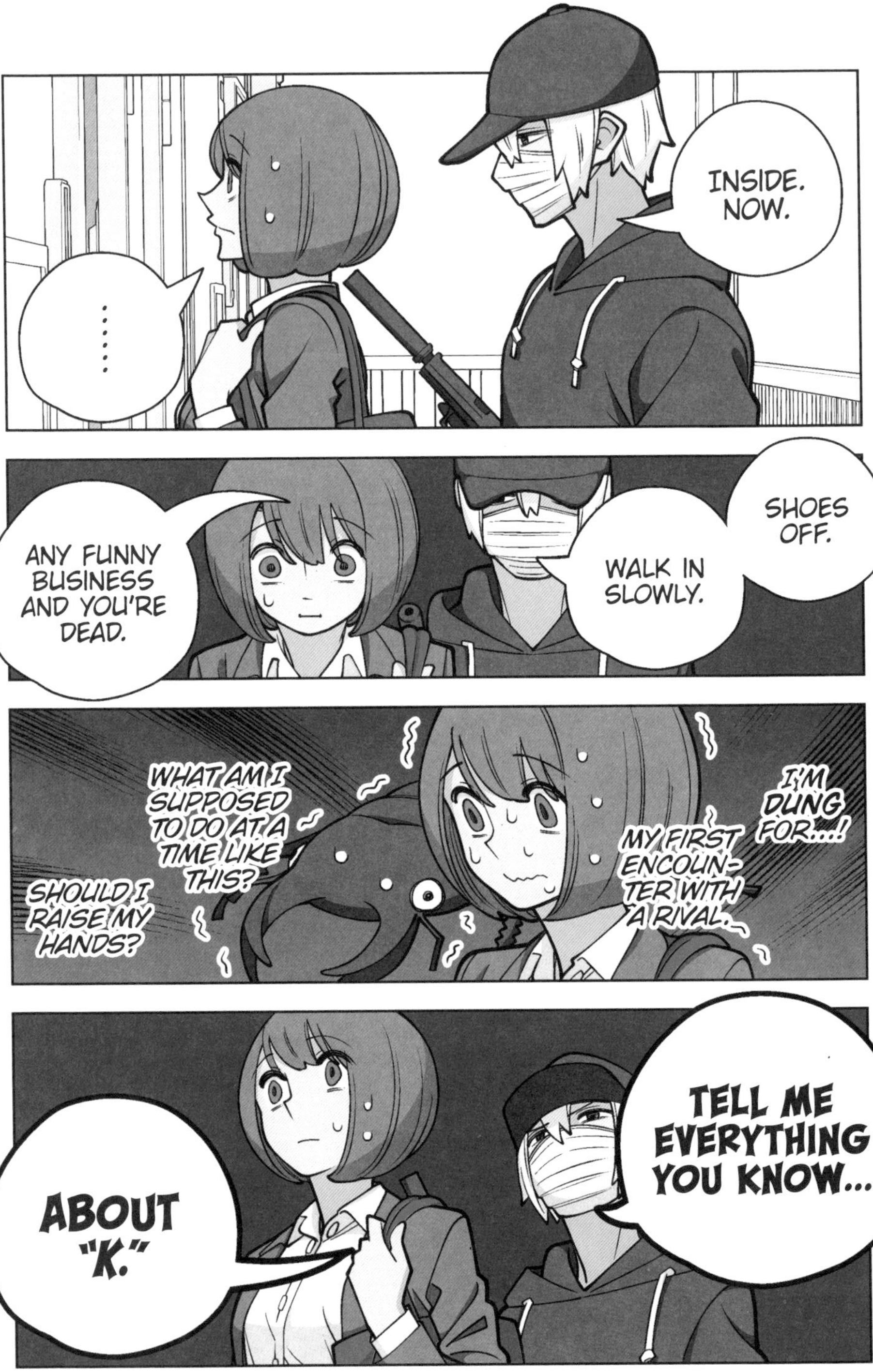
INSIDE. NOW.
......
SHOES OFF.
WALK IN SLOWLY.
ANY FUNNY BUSINESS AND YOU'RE DEAD.
I'M DUNG FOR...!
MY FIRST ENCOUN-TER WITH A RIVAL...
WHAT AM I SUPPOSED TO DO AT A TIME LIKE THIS?
SHOULD I RAISE MY HANDS?
TELL ME EVERYTHING YOU KNOW...
ABOUT "K."

☆ ——— **Would you like my business card?**

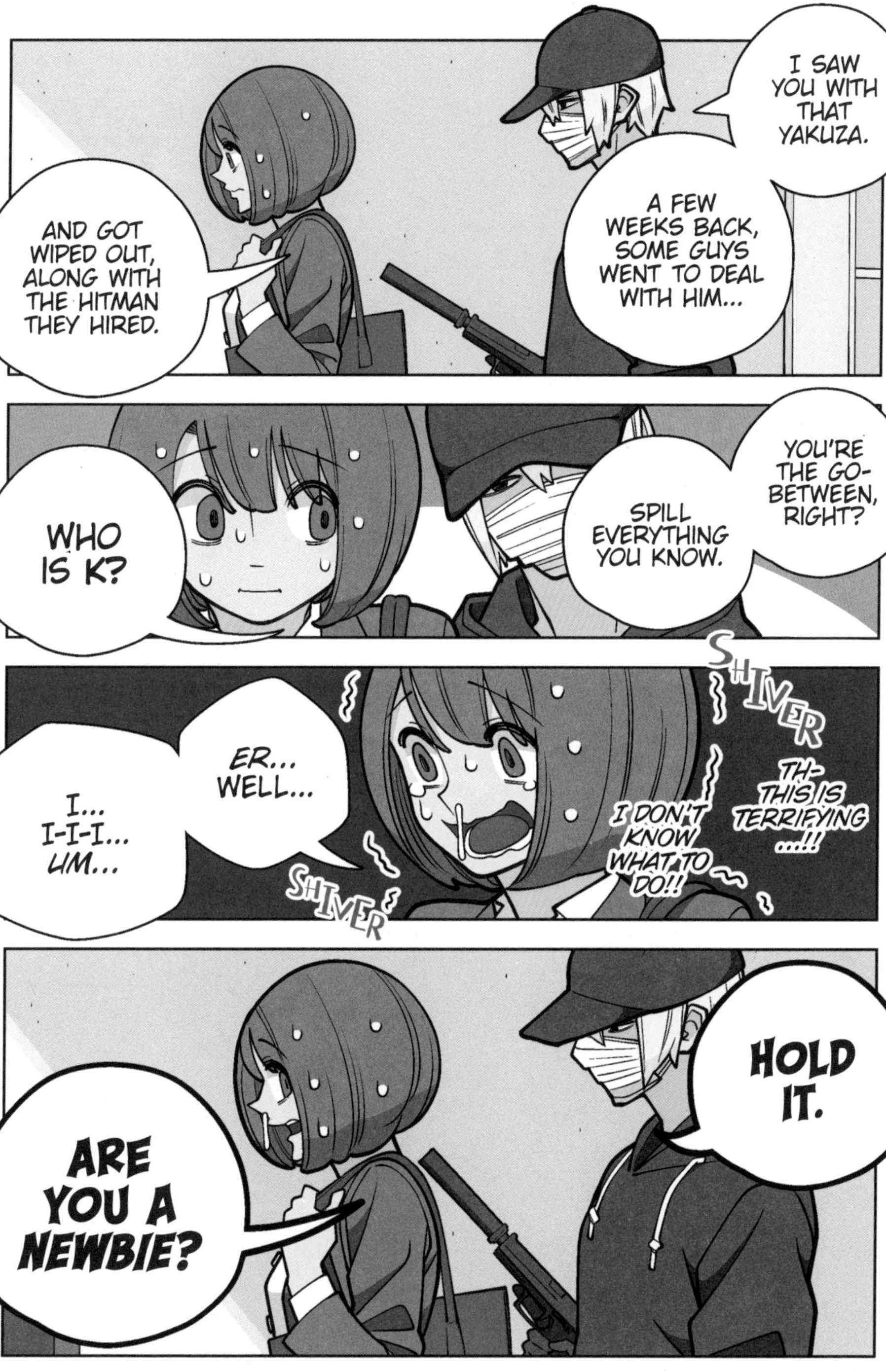
I SAW YOU WITH THAT YAKUZA.
A FEW WEEKS BACK, SOME GUYS WENT TO DEAL WITH HIM...
AND GOT WIPED OUT, ALONG WITH THE HITMAN THEY HIRED.
YOU'RE THE GO-BETWEEN, RIGHT?
SPILL EVERYTHING YOU KNOW.
WHO IS K?
SHIVER
TH- THIS IS TERRIFYING ...!!
I DON'T KNOW WHAT TO DO!!
ER... WELL...
I... I-I-I... UM...
SHIVER
HOLD IT.
ARE YOU A NEWBIE?

Just started this spring.—☆

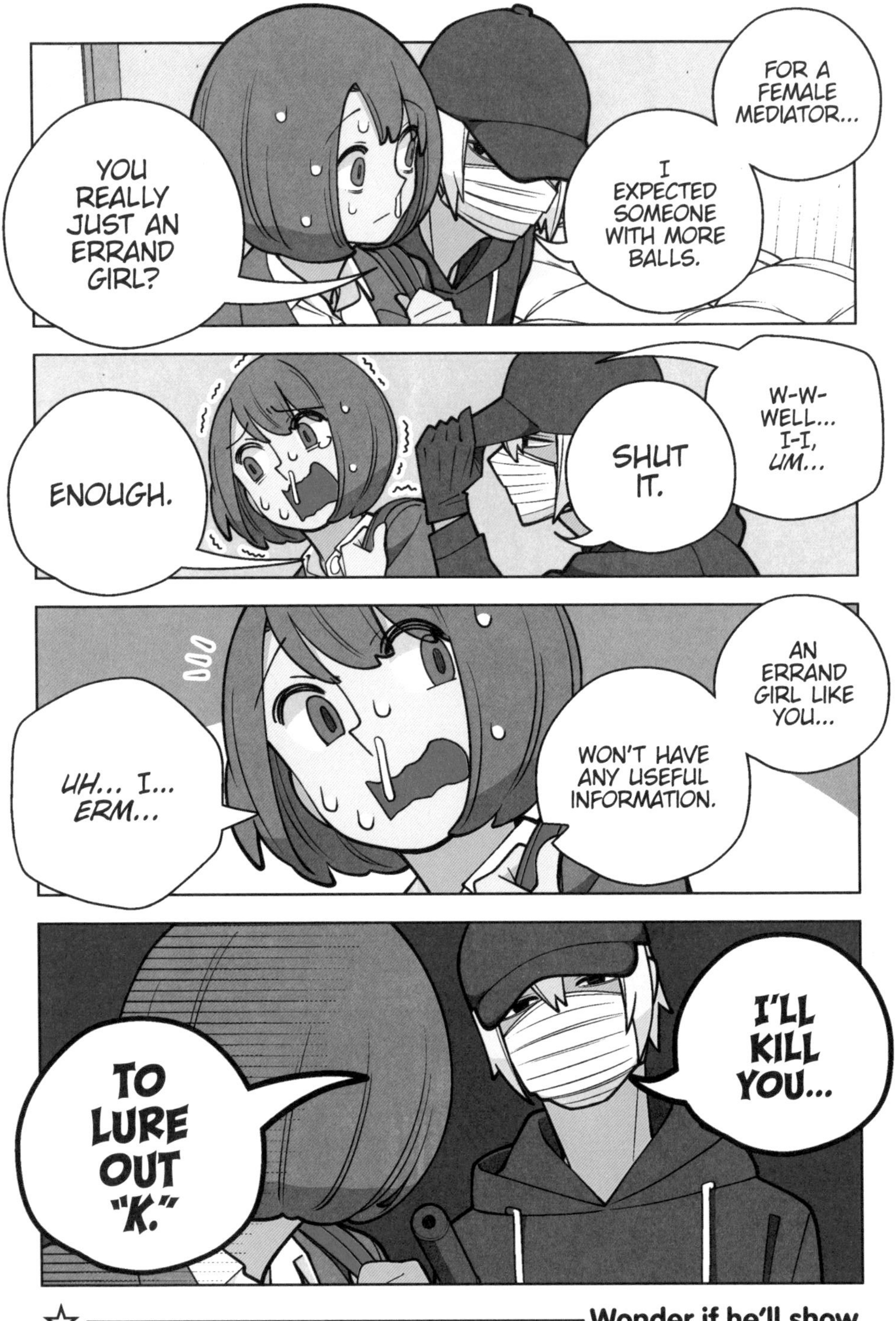
FOR A FEMALE MEDIATOR...
I EXPECTED SOMEONE WITH MORE BALLS.
YOU REALLY JUST AN ERRAND GIRL?
W-W-WELL... I-I, UM...
SHUT IT.
ENOUGH.
AN ERRAND GIRL LIKE YOU...
WON'T HAVE ANY USEFUL INFORMATION.
UH... I... ERM...
I'LL KILL YOU...
TO LURE OUT "K."

☆ ——— Wonder if he'll show.

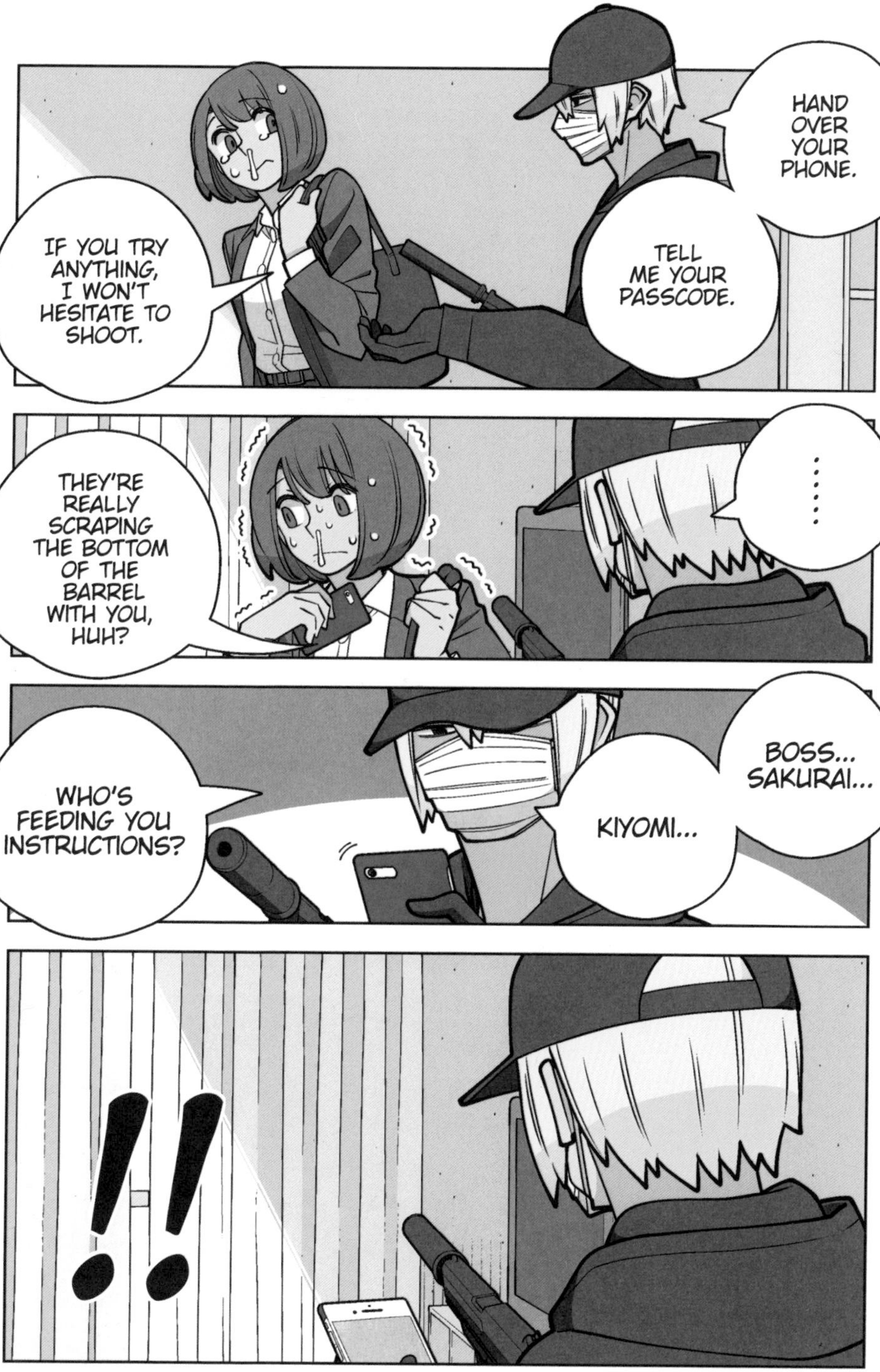
HAND OVER YOUR PHONE.
TELL ME YOUR PASSCODE.
IF YOU TRY ANYTHING, I WON'T HESITATE TO SHOOT.
......
THEY'RE REALLY SCRAPING THE BOTTOM OF THE BARREL WITH YOU, HUH?
BOSS... SAKURAI...
KIYOMI...
WHO'S FEEDING YOU INSTRUCTIONS?
!!

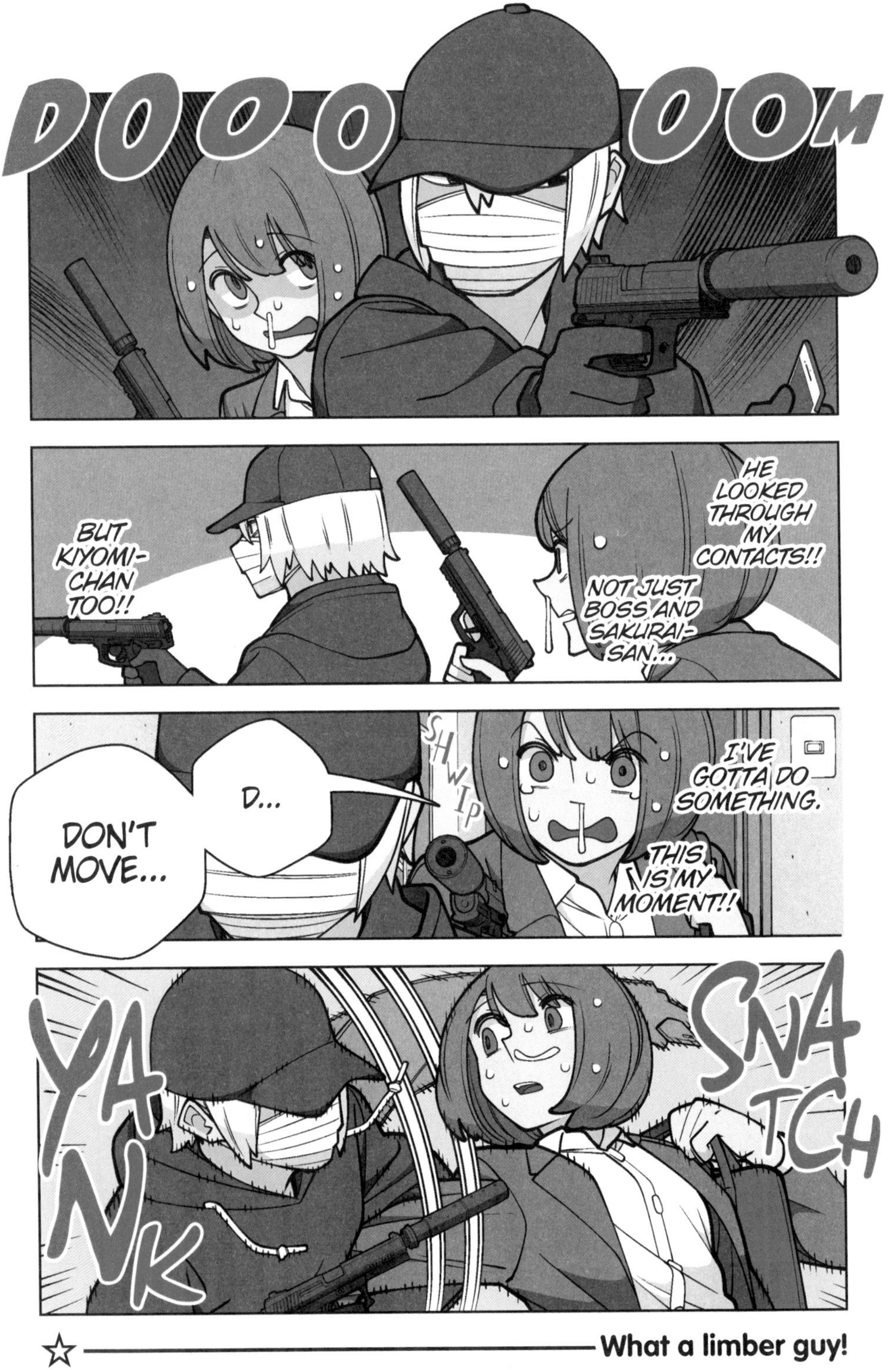
DOOOOOOOM
HE LOOKED THROUGH MY CONTACTS!!
NOT JUST BOSS AND SAKURAI-SAN...
BUT KIYOMI-CHAN TOO!!
I'VE GOTTA DO SOMETHING.
THIS IS MY MOMENT!!
SHWIP
D...
DON'T MOVE...
SNATCH
YANK

☆ ——— What a limber guy!

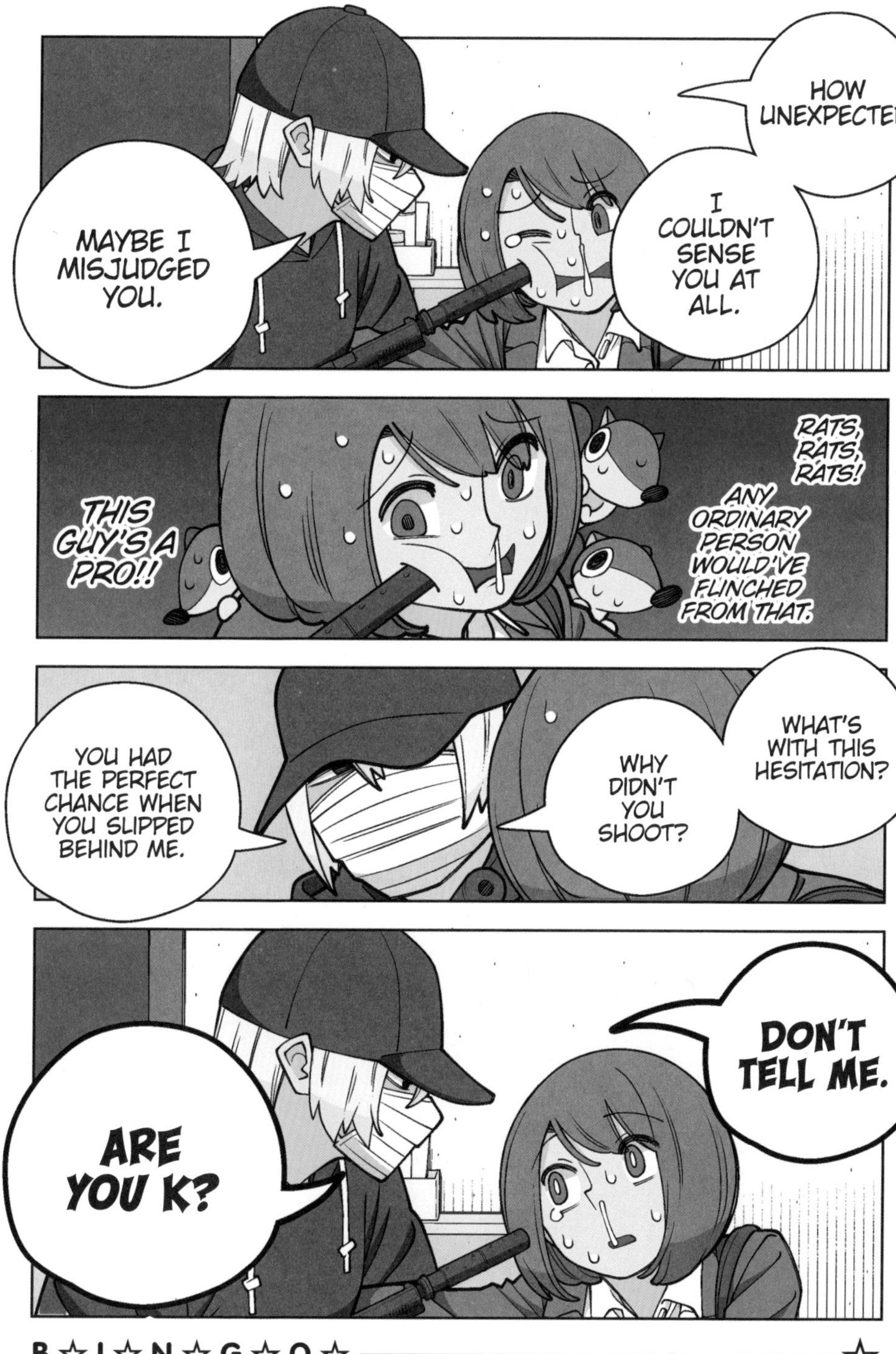
HOW UNEXPECTED.
I COULDN'T SENSE YOU AT ALL.
MAYBE I MISJUDGED YOU.
RATS, RATS, RATS!
ANY ORDINARY PERSON WOULD'VE FLINCHED FROM THAT.
THIS GUY'S A PRO!!
WHAT'S WITH THIS HESITATION?
WHY DIDN'T YOU SHOOT?
YOU HAD THE PERFECT CHANCE WHEN YOU SLIPPED BEHIND ME.
DON'T TELL ME.
ARE YOU K?

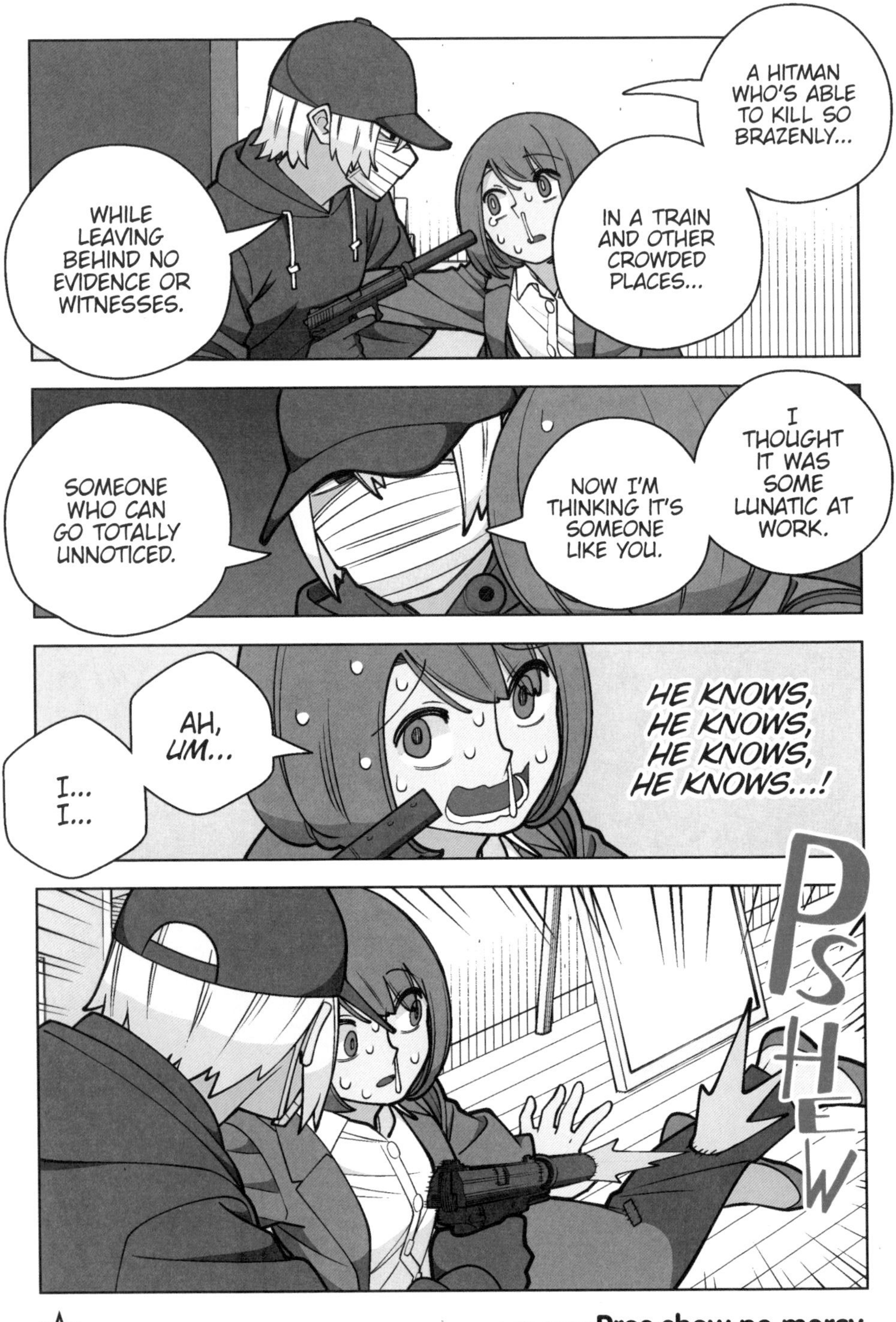
A HITMAN WHO'S ABLE TO KILL SO BRAZENLY...
IN A TRAIN AND OTHER CROWDED PLACES...
WHILE LEAVING BEHIND NO EVIDENCE OR WITNESSES.
I THOUGHT IT WAS SOME LUNATIC AT WORK.
NOW I'M THINKING IT'S SOMEONE LIKE YOU.
SOMEONE WHO CAN GO TOTALLY UNNOTICED.
HE KNOWS, HE KNOWS, HE KNOWS, HE KNOWS...!
AH, UM...
I... I...
PSHEW

☆ —— Pros show no mercy.

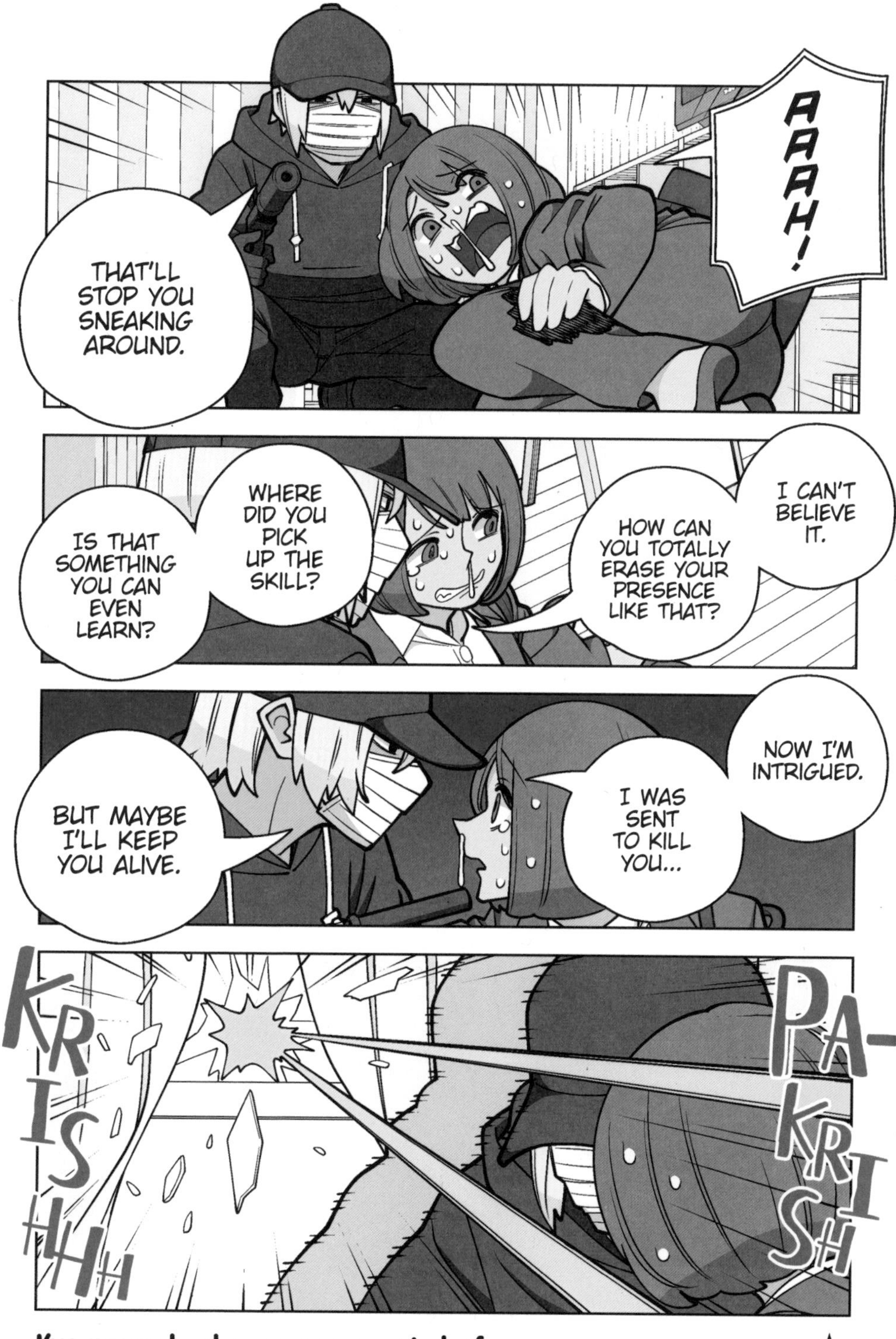
AAAAH!
THAT'LL STOP YOU SNEAKING AROUND.
I CAN'T BELIEVE IT.
HOW CAN YOU TOTALLY ERASE YOUR PRESENCE LIKE THAT?
WHERE DID YOU PICK UP THE SKILL?
IS THAT SOMETHING YOU CAN EVEN LEARN?
NOW I'M INTRIGUED.
I WAS SENT TO KILL YOU...
BUT MAYBE I'LL KEEP YOU ALIVE.
PA-KRISH
KRISHHHH

I've never had so many guests before.——————☆

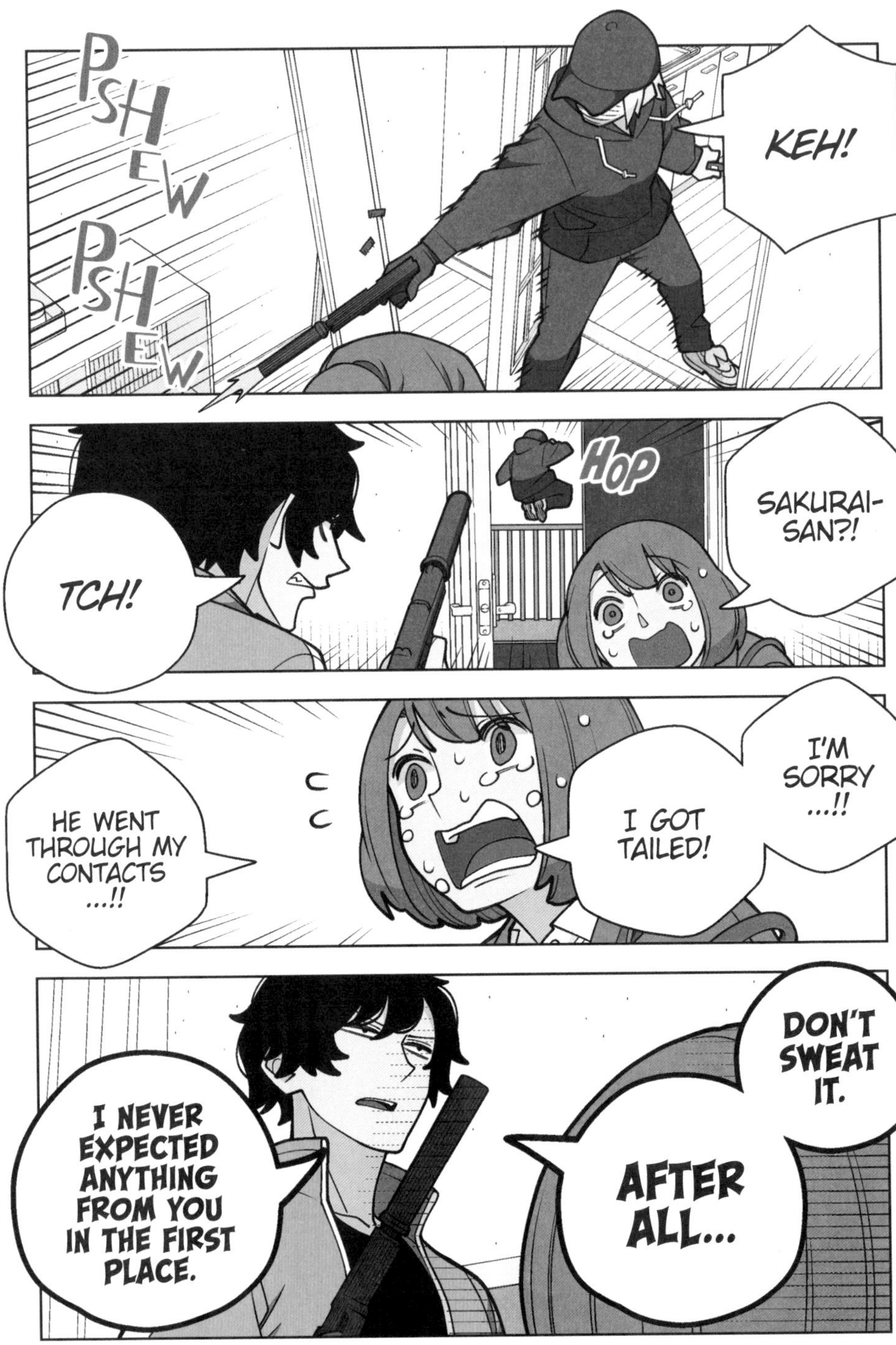
KEH!
PSHEW
PSHEW
SAKURAI-SAN?!
HOP
TCH!
I'M SORRY ...!!
I GOT TAILED!
HE WENT THROUGH MY CONTACTS ...!!
DON'T SWEAT IT.
AFTER ALL...
I NEVER EXPECTED ANYTHING FROM YOU IN THE FIRST PLACE.

☆ — Gut Punch.

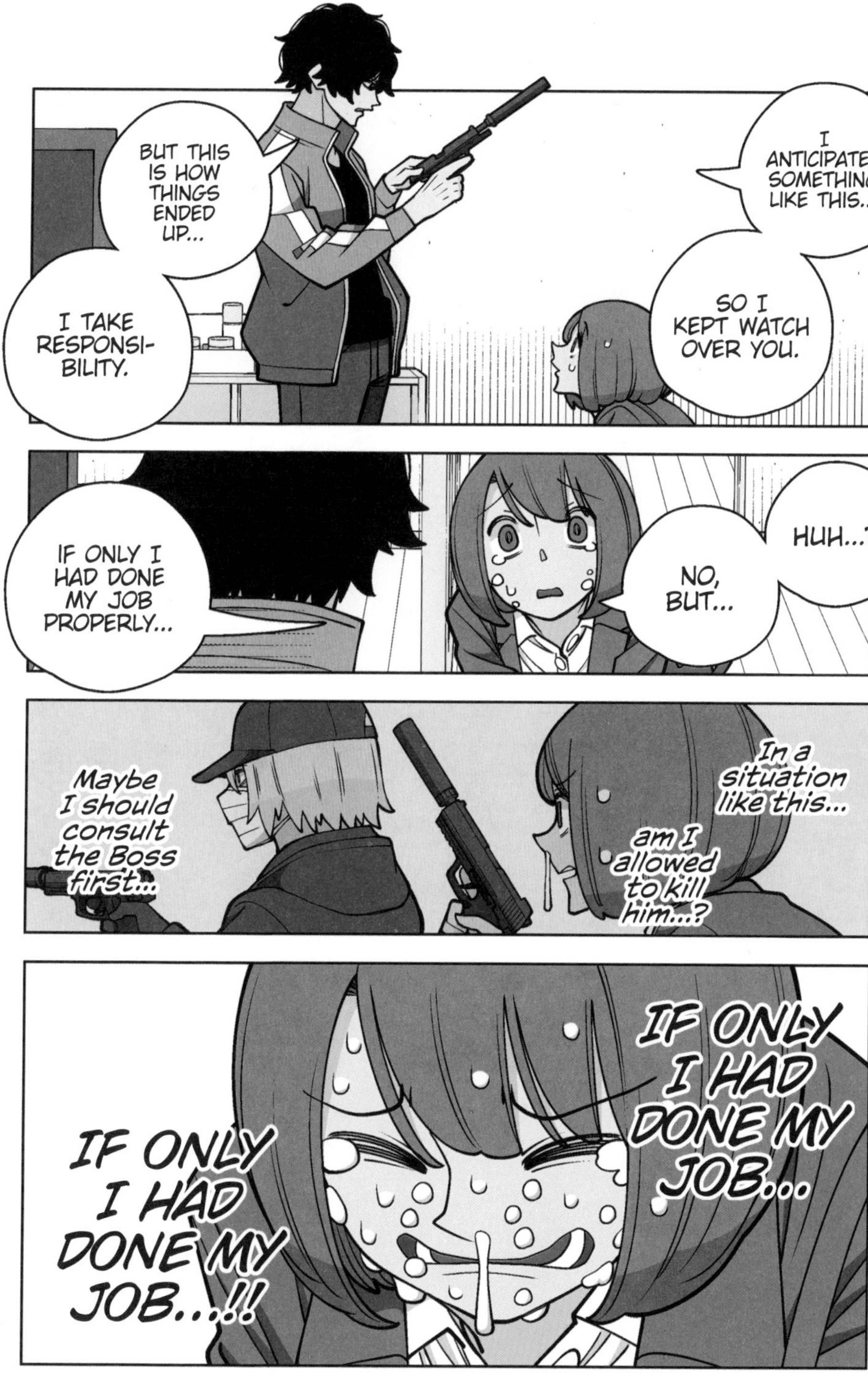
I ANTICIPATED SOMETHING LIKE THIS...
SO I KEPT WATCH OVER YOU.
BUT THIS IS HOW THINGS ENDED UP...
I TAKE RESPONSI-BILITY.
HUH...?
NO, BUT...
IF ONLY I HAD DONE MY JOB PROPERLY...
In a situation like this...
am I allowed to kill him...?
Maybe I should consult the Boss first...
IF ONLY I HAD DONE MY JOB...
IF ONLY I HAD DONE MY JOB...!!

When are you going to grow up and stop being a rookie? – ☆

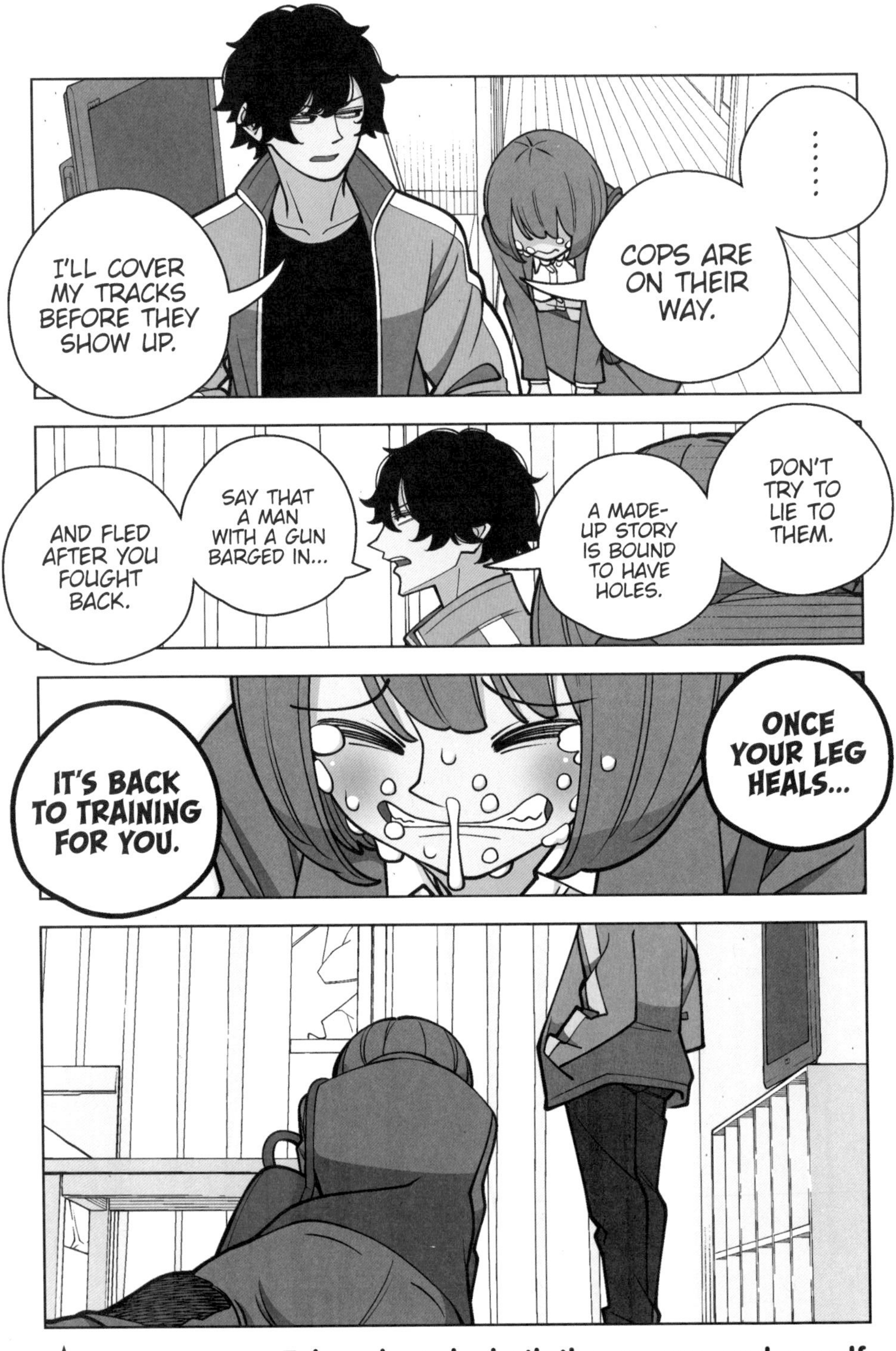
......
COPS ARE ON THEIR WAY.
I'LL COVER MY TRACKS BEFORE THEY SHOW UP.
DON'T TRY TO LIE TO THEM.
A MADE-UP STORY IS BOUND TO HAVE HOLES.
SAY THAT A MAN WITH A GUN BARGED IN...
AND FLED AFTER YOU FOUGHT BACK.
ONCE YOUR LEG HEALS...
IT'S BACK TO TRAINING FOR YOU.

☆ ——Taken down by both the enemy...and myself.

Happy Kanako's
Killer Life

I'm waiting for your request!!

Happy Kanako's
Killer Life

041

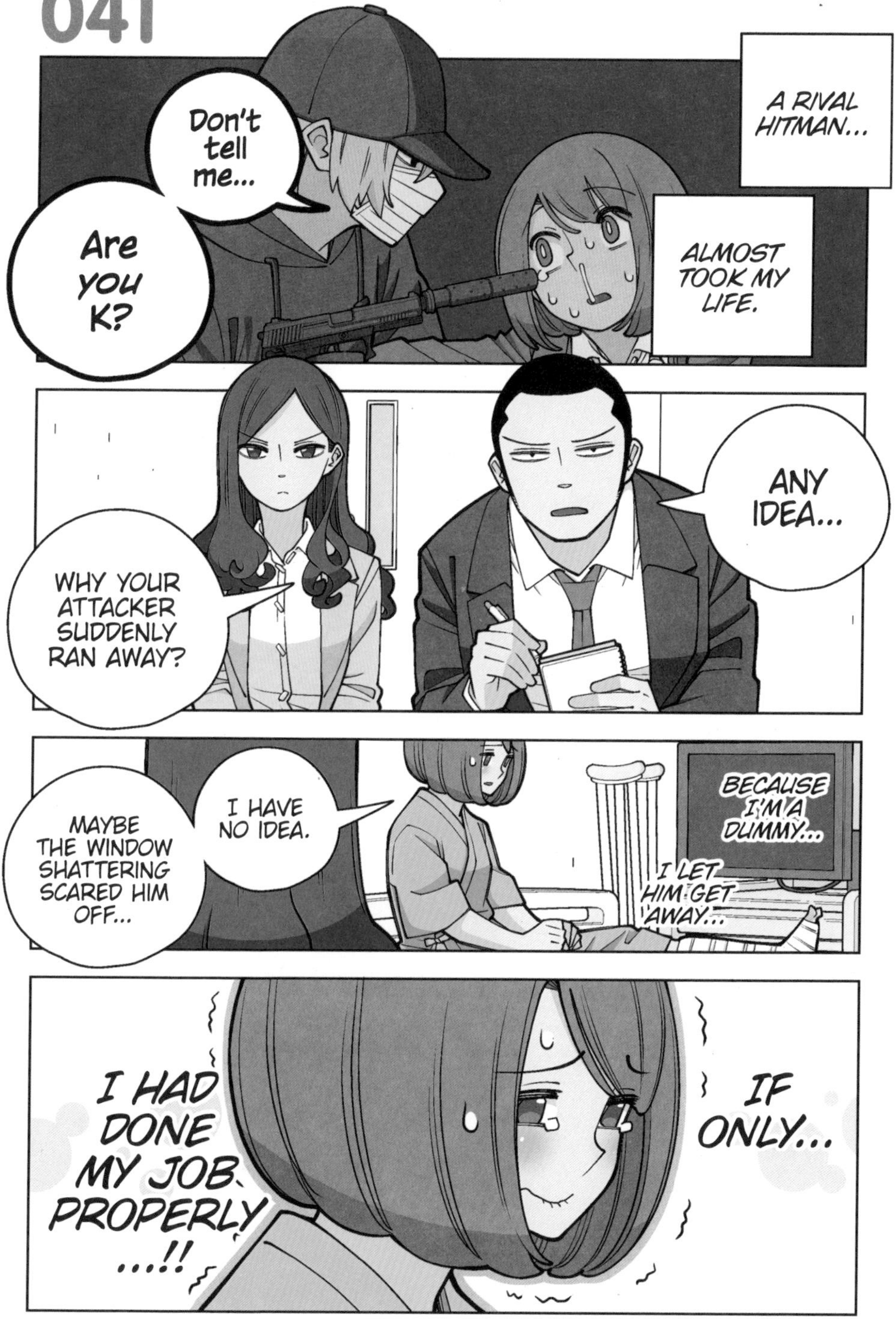
A RIVAL HITMAN...
ALMOST TOOK MY LIFE.
Don't tell me...
Are you K?
ANY IDEA...
WHY YOUR ATTACKER SUDDENLY RAN AWAY?
BECAUSE I'M A DUMMY...
I LET HIM GET AWAY...
I HAVE NO IDEA.
MAYBE THE WINDOW SHATTERING SCARED HIM OFF...
IF ONLY...
I HAD DONE MY JOB PROPERLY ...!!

Don't blame yourself. ☆

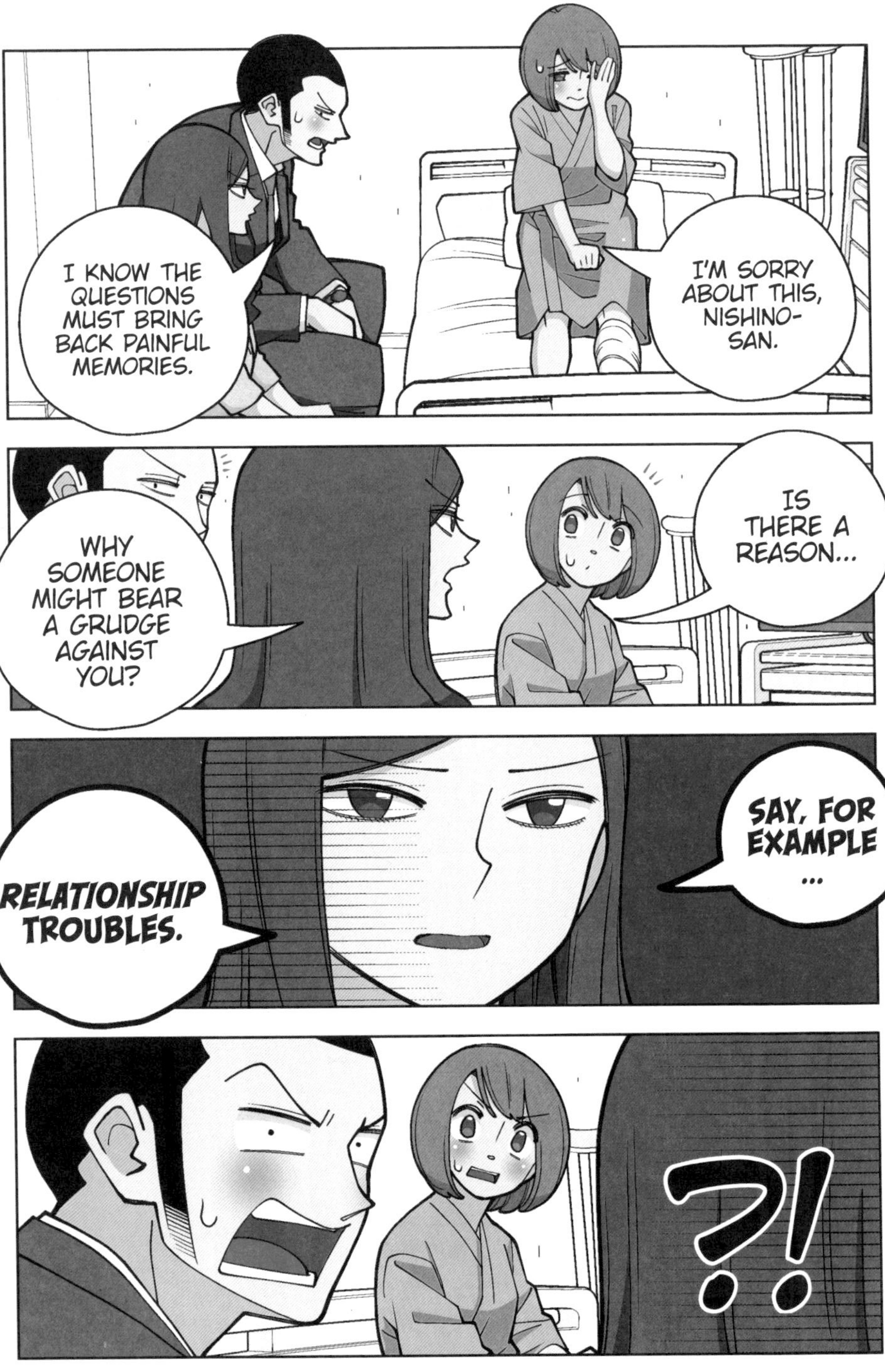
I'M SORRY ABOUT THIS, NISHINO-SAN.
I KNOW THE QUESTIONS MUST BRING BACK PAINFUL MEMORIES.
IS THERE A REASON...
WHY SOMEONE MIGHT BEAR A GRUDGE AGAINST YOU?
SAY, FOR EXAMPLE...
RELATIONSHIP TROUBLES.
?!

☆ It's a loooove triangle!

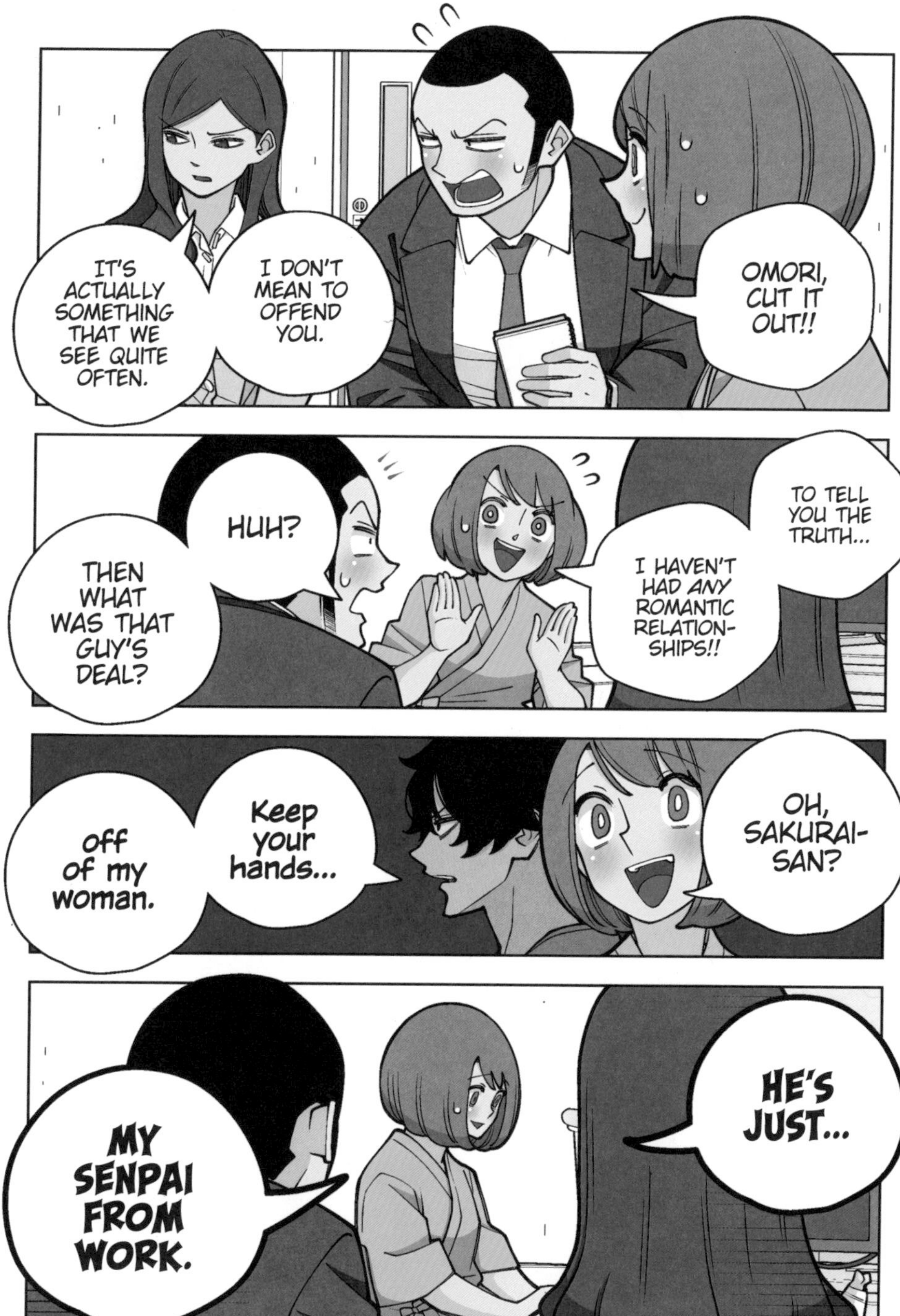
OMORI, CUT IT OUT!!
I DON'T MEAN TO OFFEND YOU.
IT'S ACTUALLY SOMETHING THAT WE SEE QUITE OFTEN.
TO TELL YOU THE TRUTH...
I HAVEN'T HAD ANY ROMANTIC RELATIONSHIPS!!
HUH?
THEN WHAT WAS THAT GUY'S DEAL?
OH, SAKURAI-SAN?
Keep your hands...
off of my woman.
HE'S JUST...
MY SENPAI FROM WORK.

That's all I can say. ☆

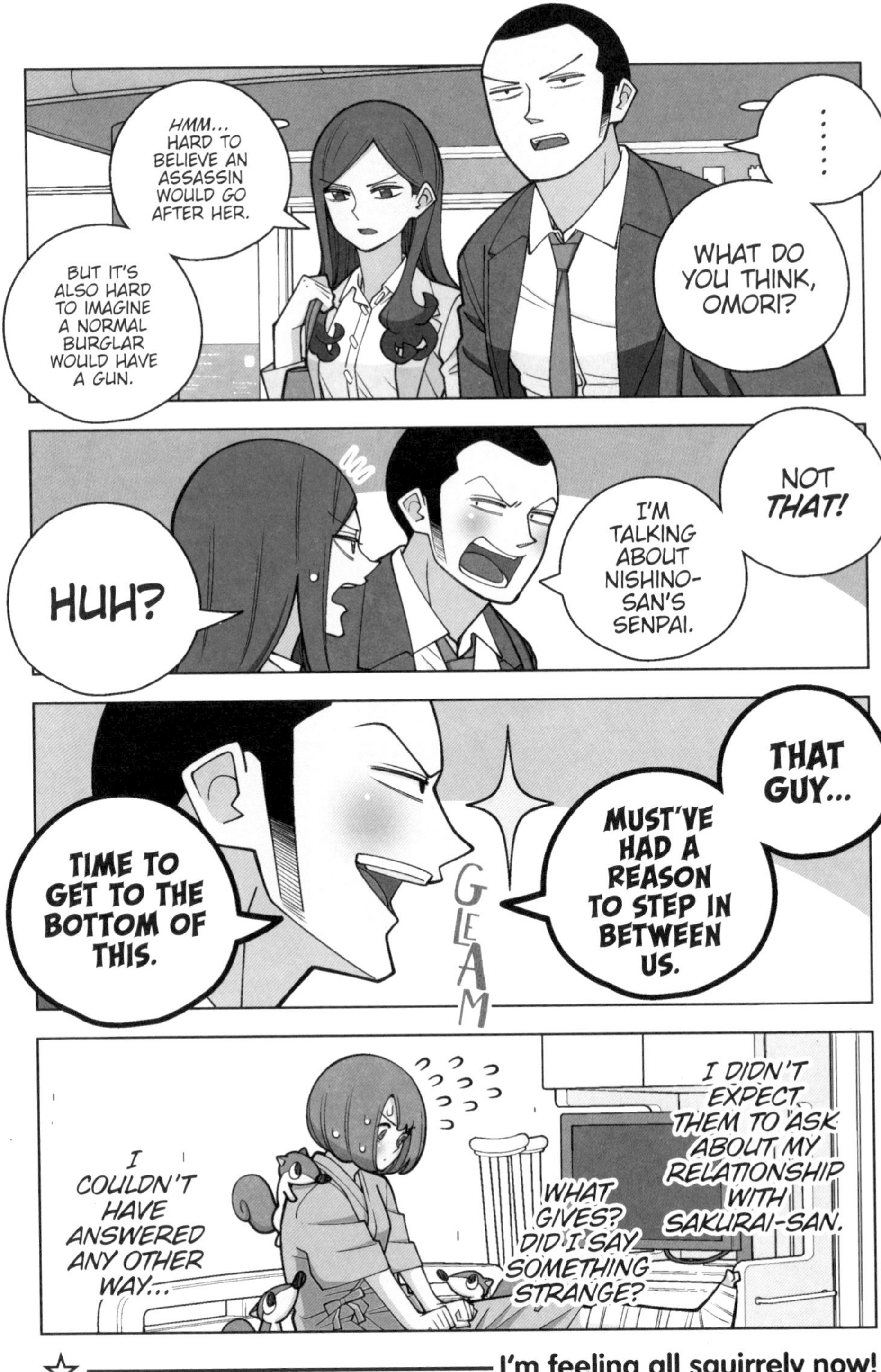
......
WHAT DO YOU THINK, OMORI?
HMM... HARD TO BELIEVE AN ASSASSIN WOULD GO AFTER HER.
BUT IT'S ALSO HARD TO IMAGINE A NORMAL BURGLAR WOULD HAVE A GUN.
NOT THAT!
I'M TALKING ABOUT NISHINO-SAN'S SENPAI.
HUH?
THAT GUY...
MUST'VE HAD A REASON TO STEP IN BETWEEN US.
GLEAM
TIME TO GET TO THE BOTTOM OF THIS.
I DIDN'T EXPECT THEM TO ASK ABOUT MY RELATIONSHIP WITH SAKURAI-SAN.
WHAT GIVES? DID I SAY SOMETHING STRANGE?
I COULDN'T HAVE ANSWERED ANY OTHER WAY...

☆ —— I'm feeling all squirrely now!

042

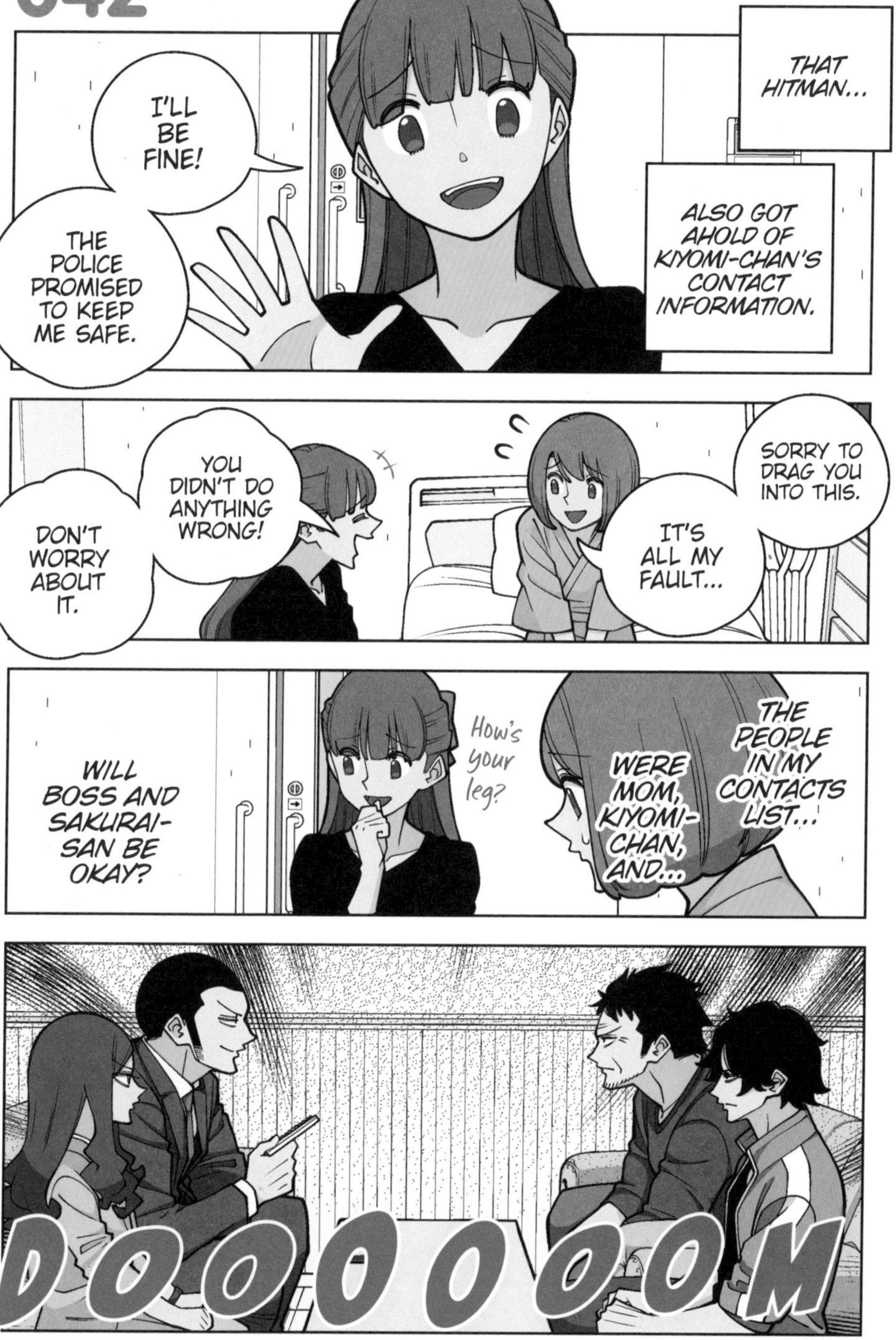
THAT HITMAN...
ALSO GOT AHOLD OF KIYOMI-CHAN'S CONTACT INFORMATION.
I'LL BE FINE!
THE POLICE PROMISED TO KEEP ME SAFE.
SORRY TO DRAG YOU INTO THIS.
IT'S ALL MY FAULT...
YOU DIDN'T DO ANYTHING WRONG!
DON'T WORRY ABOUT IT.
THE PEOPLE IN MY CONTACTS LIST...
WERE MOM, KIYOMI-CHAN, AND...
How's your leg?
WILL BOSS AND SAKURAI-SAN BE OKAY?
DOOOOOOOM

A fun little conversation. ☆

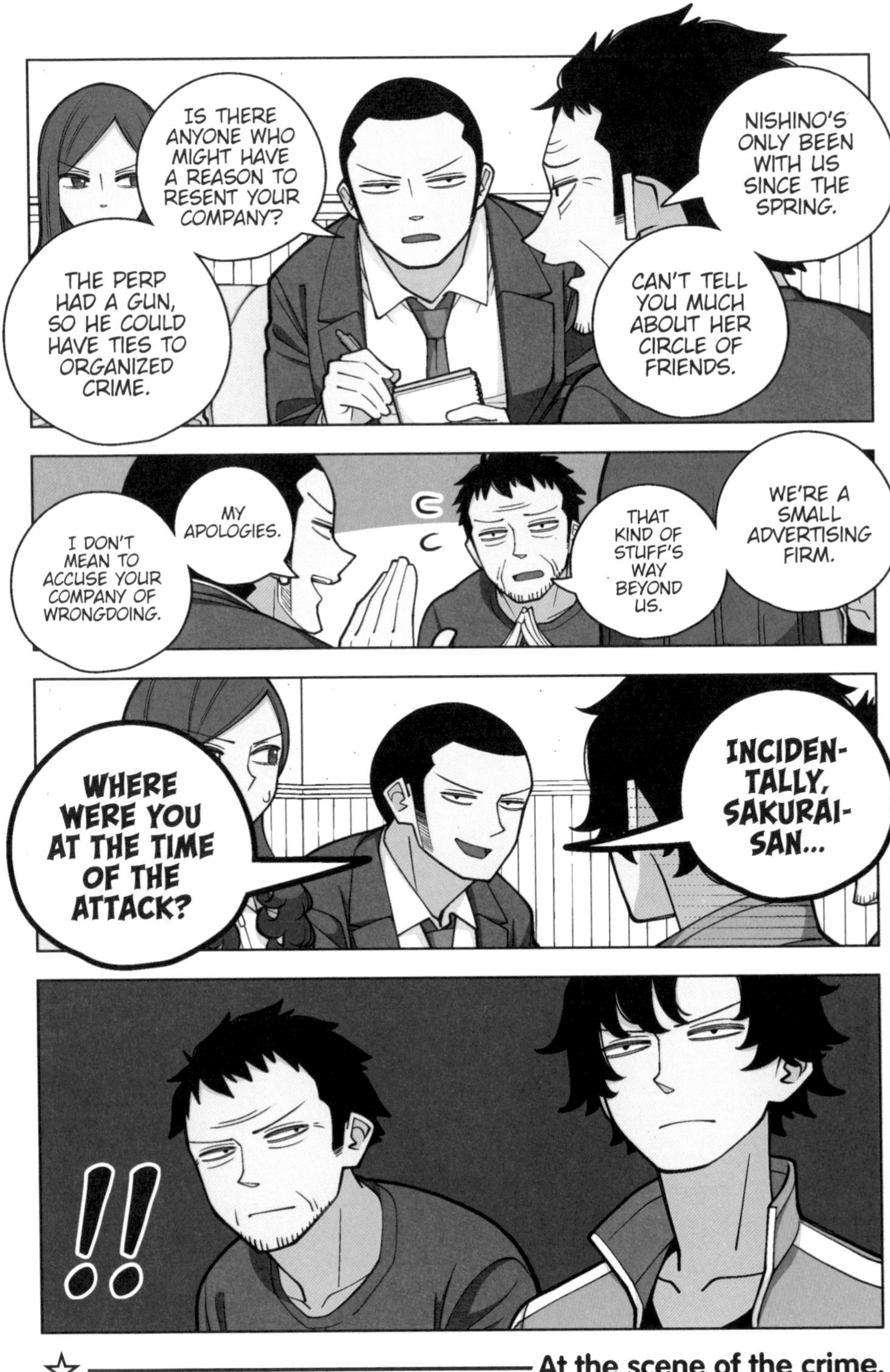
NISHINO'S ONLY BEEN WITH US SINCE THE SPRING.
CAN'T TELL YOU MUCH ABOUT HER CIRCLE OF FRIENDS.
IS THERE ANYONE WHO MIGHT HAVE A REASON TO RESENT YOUR COMPANY?
THE PERP HAD A GUN, SO HE COULD HAVE TIES TO ORGANIZED CRIME.
WE'RE A SMALL ADVERTISING FIRM.
THAT KIND OF STUFF'S WAY BEYOND US.
MY APOLOGIES.
I DON'T MEAN TO ACCUSE YOUR COMPANY OF WRONGDOING.
INCIDENTALLY, SAKURAI-SAN...
WHERE WERE YOU AT THE TIME OF THE ATTACK?
!!

☆ — At the scene of the crime.

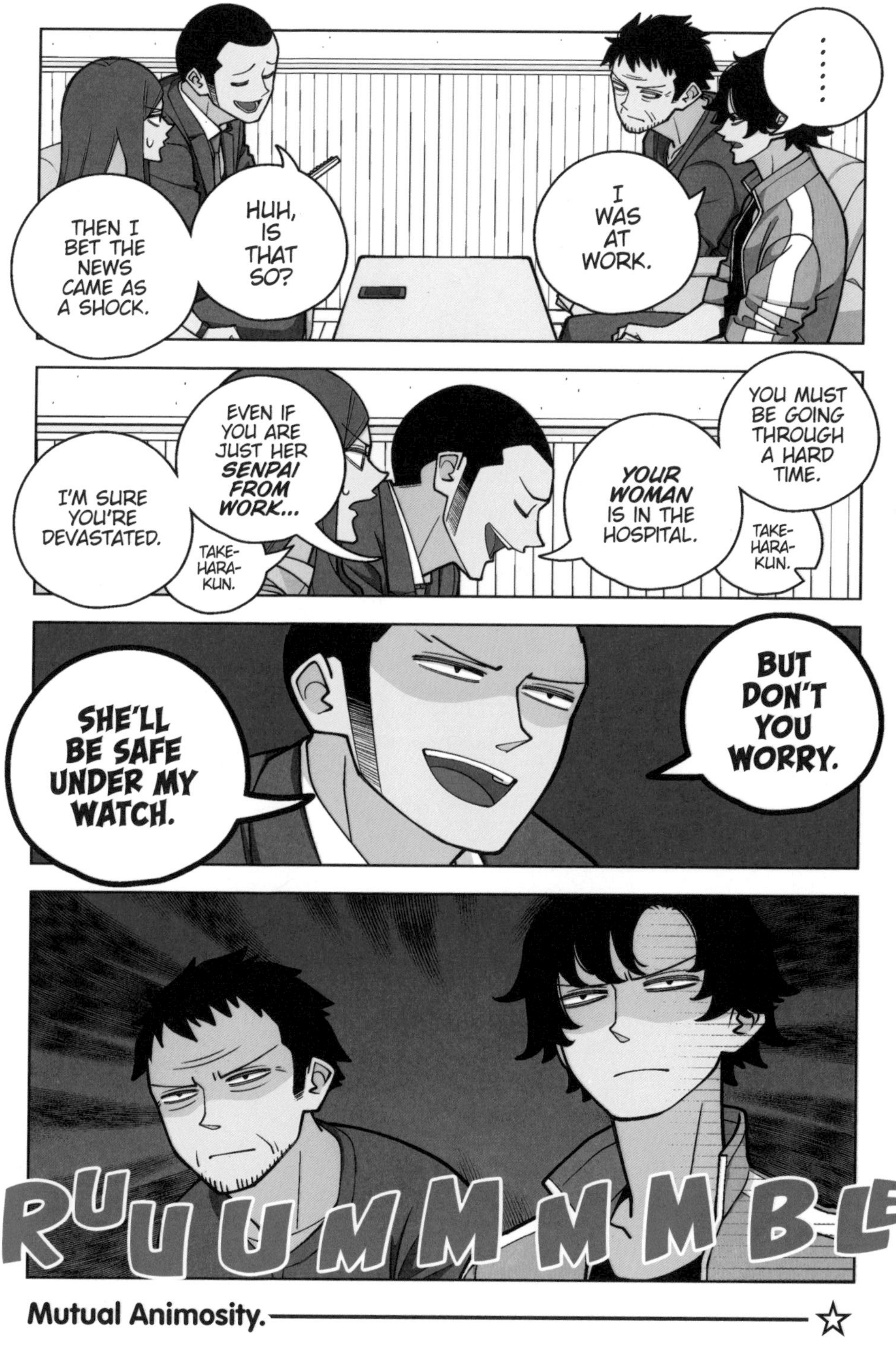
......
I WAS AT WORK.
HUH, IS THAT SO?
THEN I BET THE NEWS CAME AS A SHOCK.
YOU MUST BE GOING THROUGH A HARD TIME.
TAKE-HARA-KUN.
YOUR WOMAN IS IN THE HOSPITAL.
EVEN IF YOU ARE JUST HER *SENPAI FROM WORK...*
TAKE-HARA-KUN.
I'M SURE YOU'RE DEVASTATED.
BUT DON'T YOU WORRY.
SHE'LL BE SAFE UNDER MY WATCH.
RUUUMMMMMBLE

Mutual Animosity. ☆

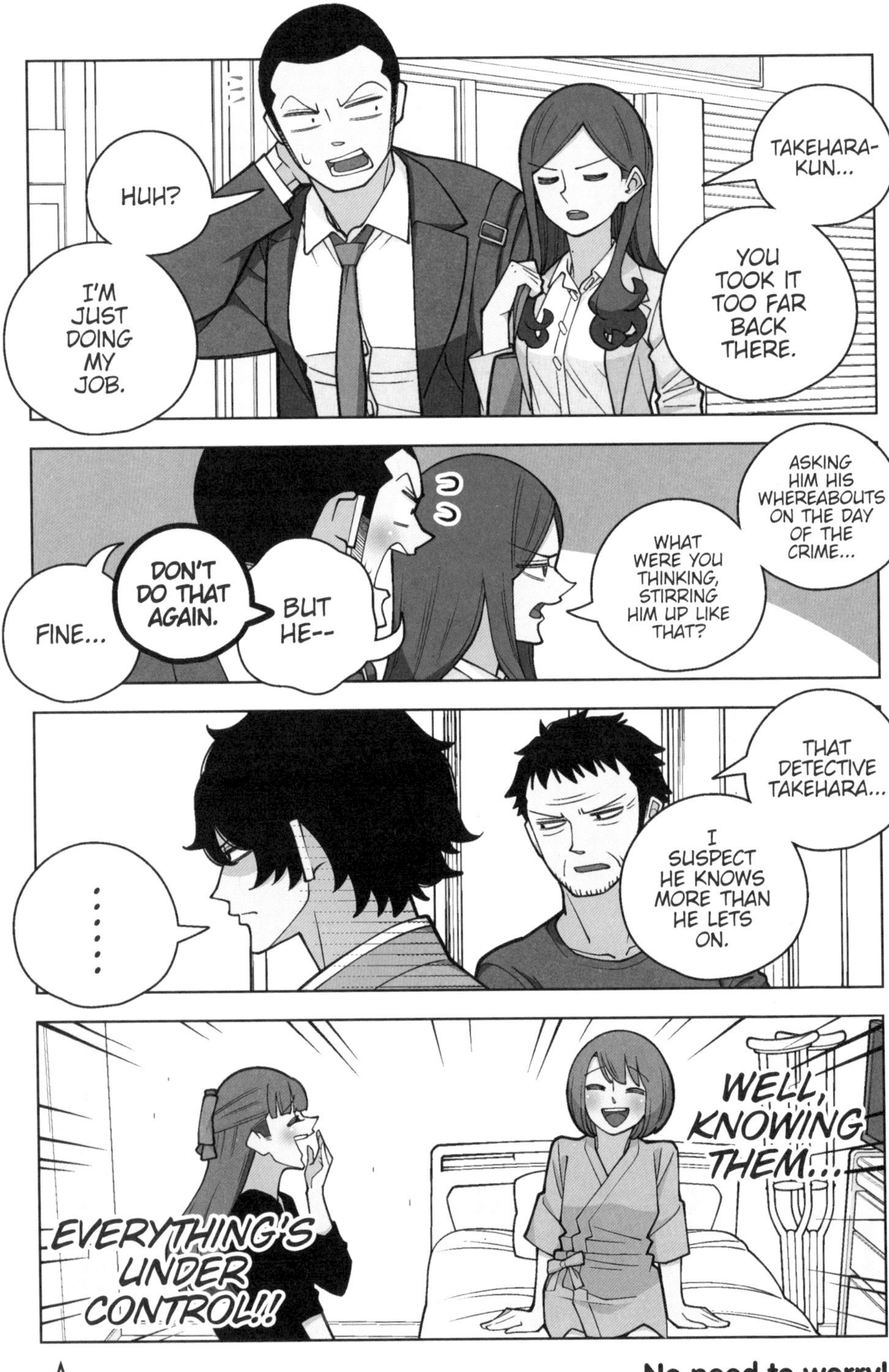
TAKEHARA-KUN...
YOU TOOK IT TOO FAR BACK THERE.
HUH?
I'M JUST DOING MY JOB.
ASKING HIM HIS WHEREABOUTS ON THE DAY OF THE CRIME...
WHAT WERE YOU THINKING, STIRRING HIM UP LIKE THAT?
BUT HE--
DON'T DO THAT AGAIN.
FINE...
THAT DETECTIVE TAKEHARA...
I SUSPECT HE KNOWS MORE THAN HE LETS ON.
......
WELL, KNOWING THEM...
EVERYTHING'S UNDER CONTROL!!

☆ — **No need to worry!**

043

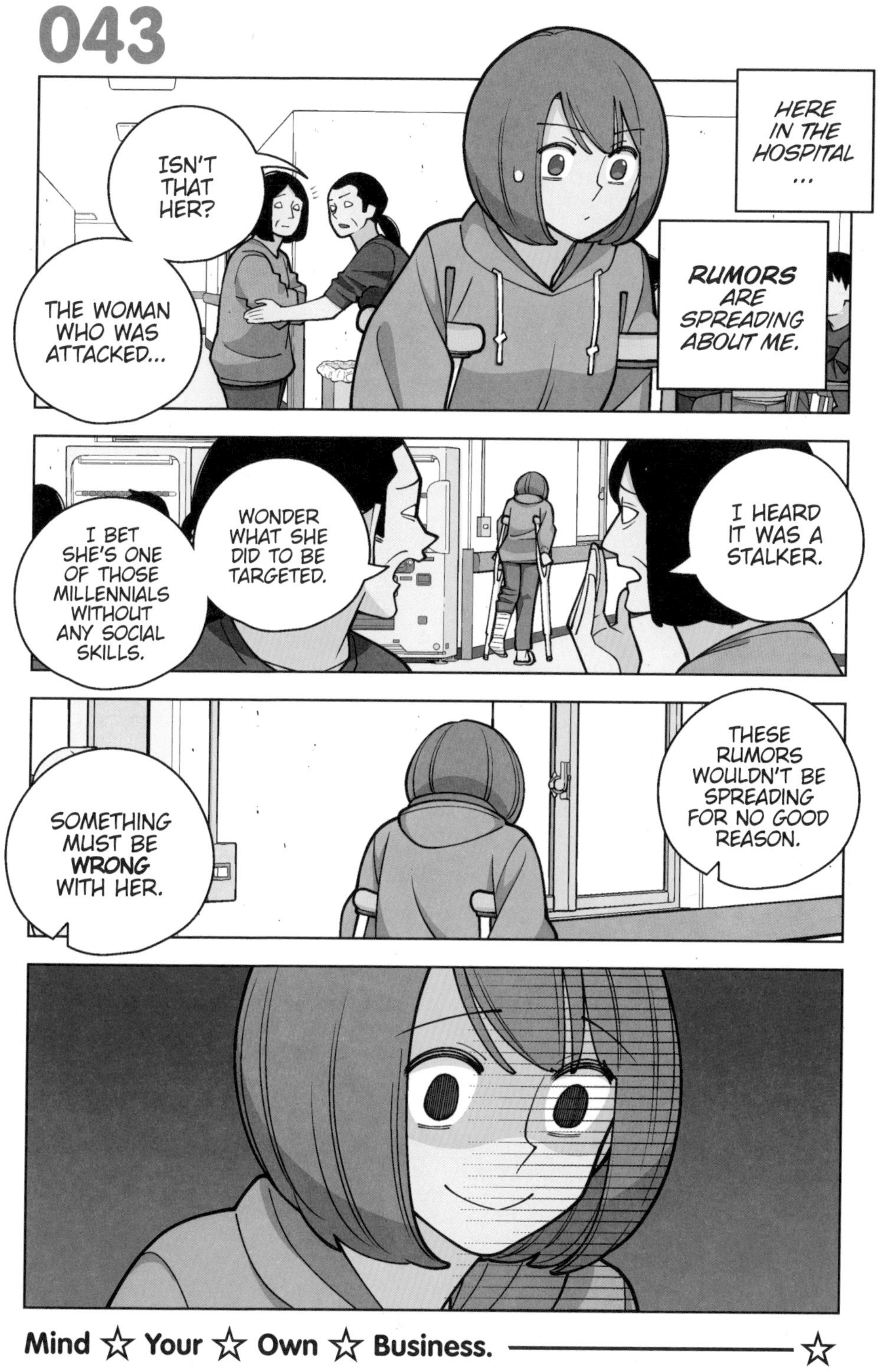
HERE IN THE HOSPITAL...
RUMORS ARE SPREADING ABOUT ME.
ISN'T THAT HER?
THE WOMAN WHO WAS ATTACKED...
I HEARD IT WAS A STALKER.
WONDER WHAT SHE DID TO BE TARGETED.
I BET SHE'S ONE OF THOSE MILLENNIALS WITHOUT ANY SOCIAL SKILLS.
THESE RUMORS WOULDN'T BE SPREADING FOR NO GOOD REASON.
SOMETHING MUST BE WRONG WITH HER.

Mind ☆ Your ☆ Own ☆ Business. ☆

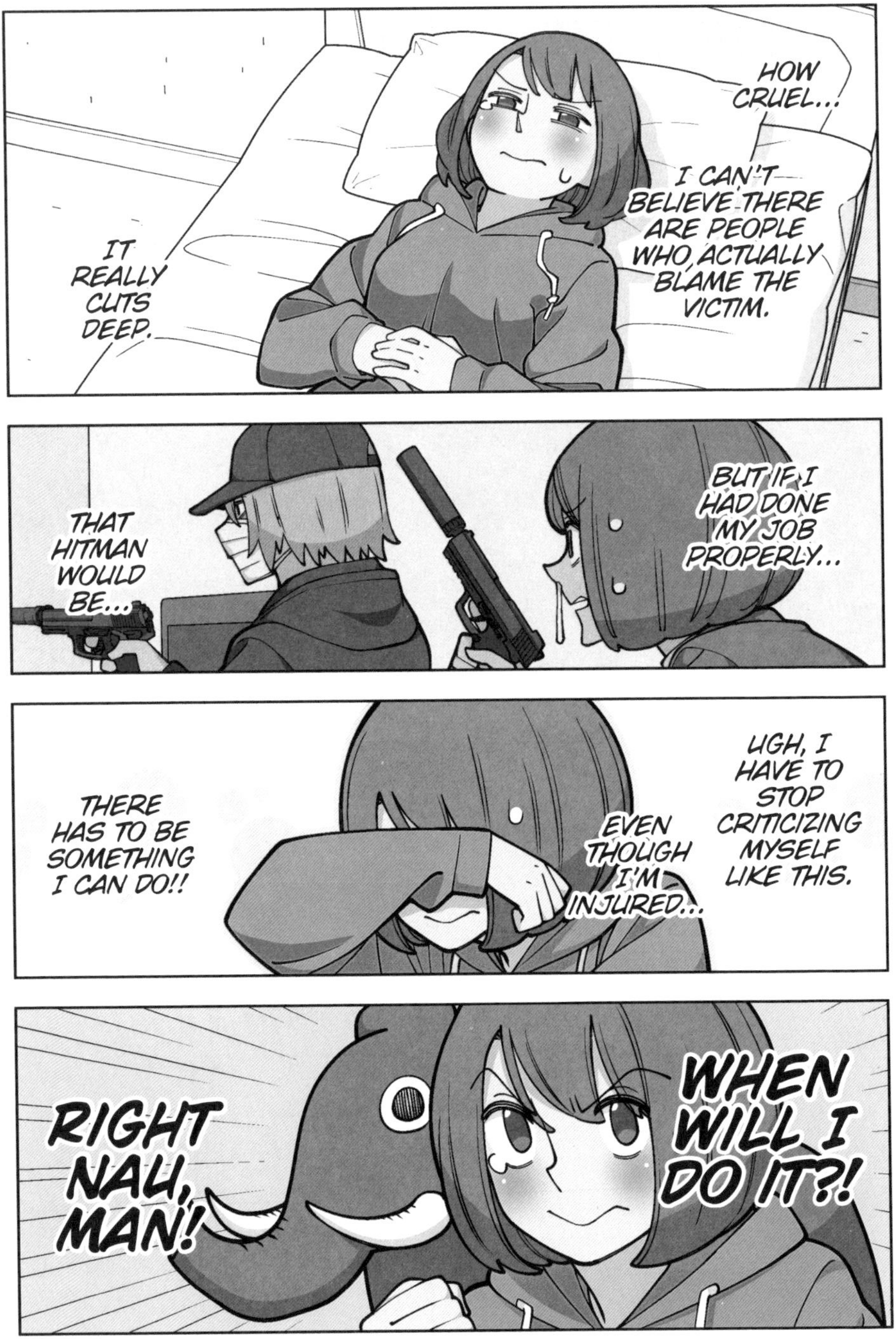
HOW CRUEL...
I CAN'T BELIEVE THERE ARE PEOPLE WHO ACTUALLY BLAME THE VICTIM.
IT REALLY CUTS DEEP.
BUT IF I HAD DONE MY JOB PROPERLY...
THAT HITMAN WOULD BE...
UGH, I HAVE TO STOP CRITICIZING MYSELF LIKE THIS.
EVEN THOUGH I'M INJURED...
THERE HAS TO BE SOMETHING I CAN DO!!
WHEN WILL I DO IT?!
RIGHT NAU, MAN!

☆ —— Because Naumann sounds like now, man!

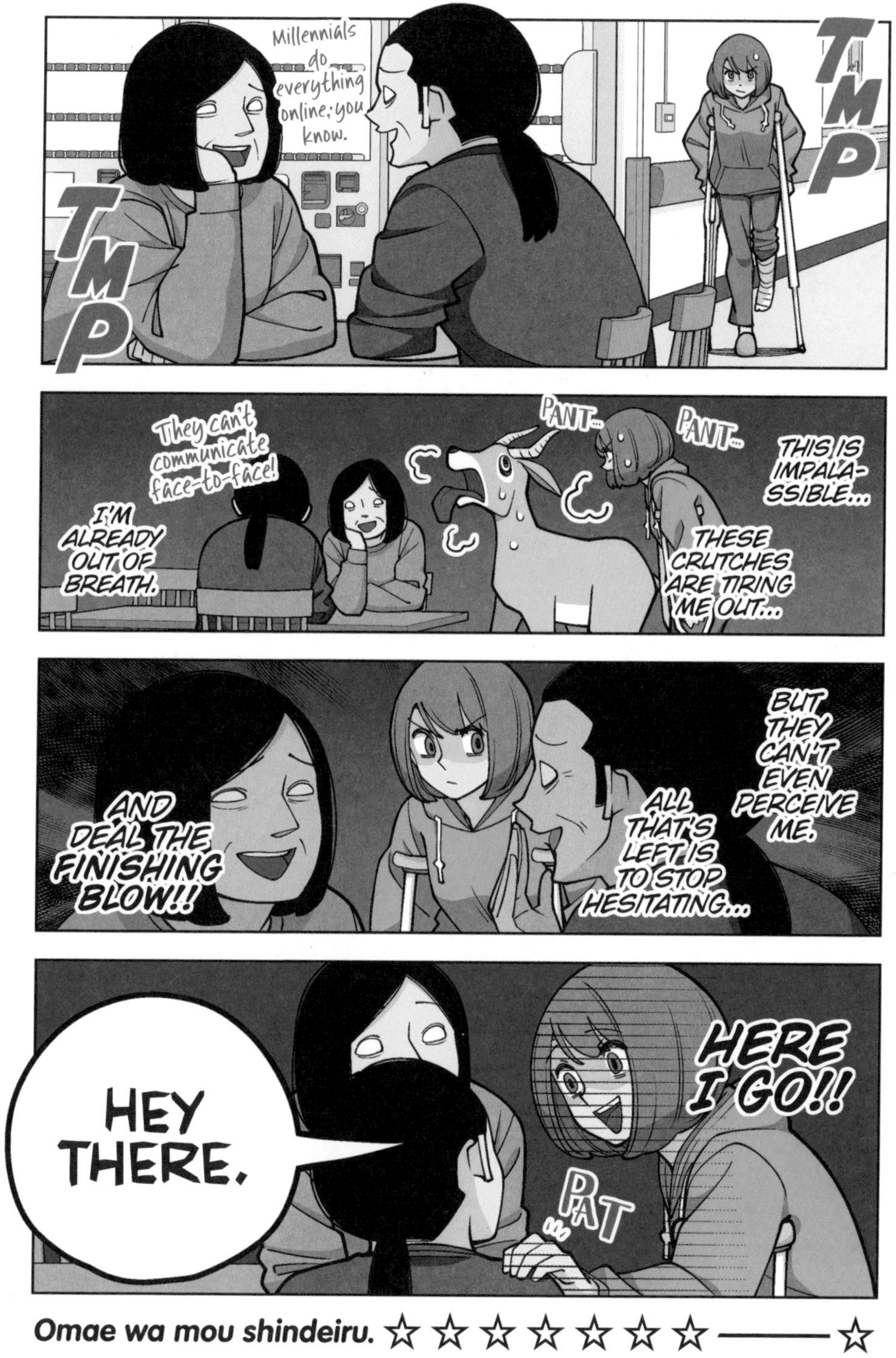
TMP
Millennials do everything online, you know.
TMP
THIS IS IMPALA-SSIBLE...
THESE CRUTCHES ARE TIRING ME OUT...
PANT...
PANT...
They can't communicate face-to-face!
I'M ALREADY OUT OF BREATH.
BUT THEY CAN'T EVEN PERCEIVE ME.
ALL THAT'S LEFT IS TO STOP HESITATING...
AND DEAL THE FINISHING BLOW!!
HERE I GO!!
PAT
HEY THERE.

Omae wa mou shindeiru. ☆☆☆☆☆☆☆———☆

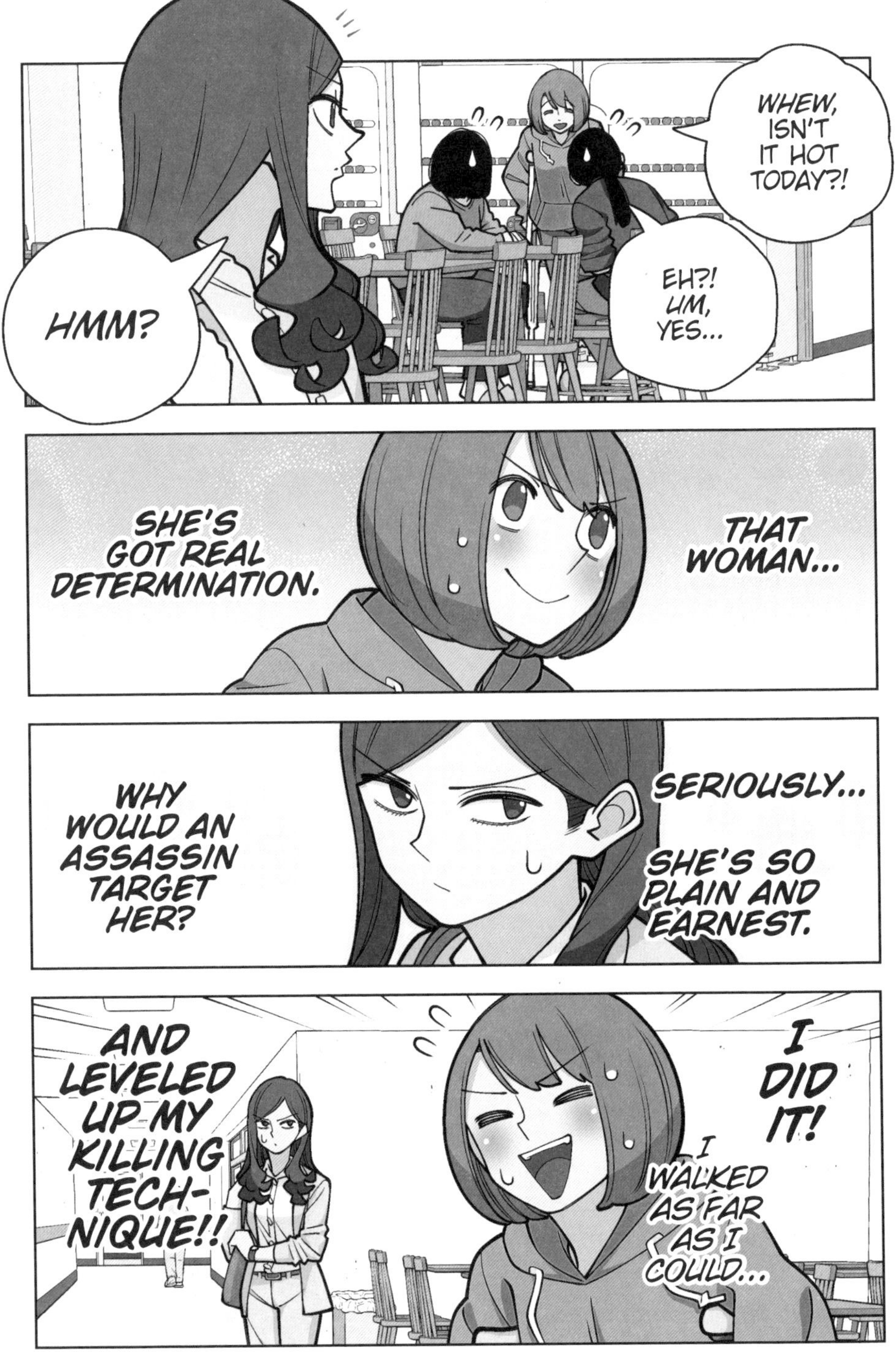
WHEW, ISN'T IT HOT TODAY?!
EH?! UM, YES...
HMM?
THAT WOMAN...
SHE'S GOT REAL DETERMINATION.
SERIOUSLY...
SHE'S SO PLAIN AND EARNEST.
WHY WOULD AN ASSASSIN TARGET HER?
I DID IT!
I WALKED AS FAR AS I COULD...
AND LEVELED UP MY KILLING TECH-NIQUE!!

☆ — Dashing into the sunset!

044

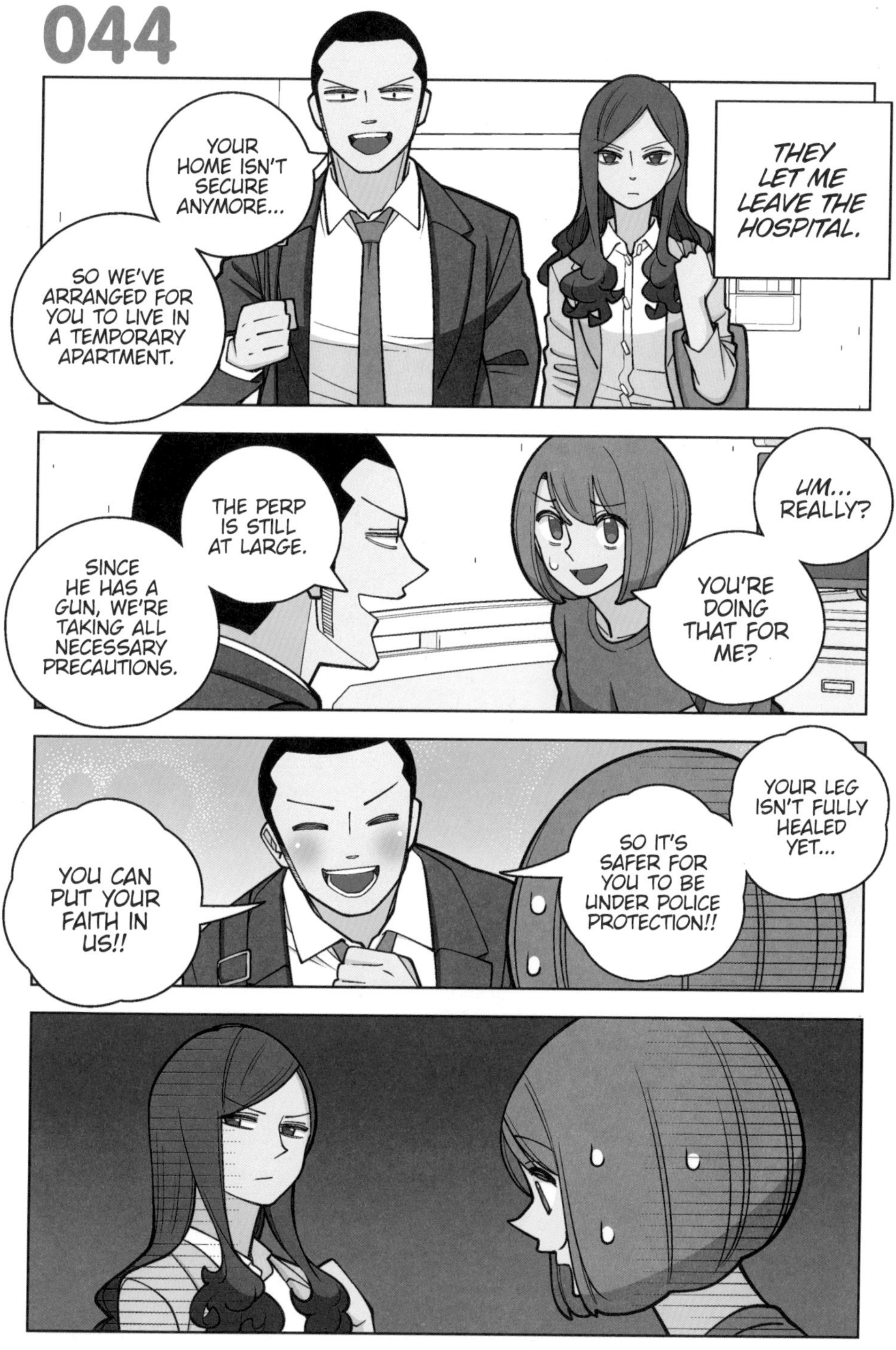
THEY LET ME LEAVE THE HOSPITAL.
YOUR HOME ISN'T SECURE ANYMORE...
SO WE'VE ARRANGED FOR YOU TO LIVE IN A TEMPORARY APARTMENT.
UM... REALLY?
YOU'RE DOING THAT FOR ME?
THE PERP IS STILL AT LARGE.
SINCE HE HAS A GUN, WE'RE TAKING ALL NECESSARY PRECAUTIONS.
YOUR LEG ISN'T FULLY HEALED YET...
SO IT'S SAFER FOR YOU TO BE UNDER POLICE PROTECTION!!
YOU CAN PUT YOUR FAITH IN US!!

Feels more like police surveillance. ☆

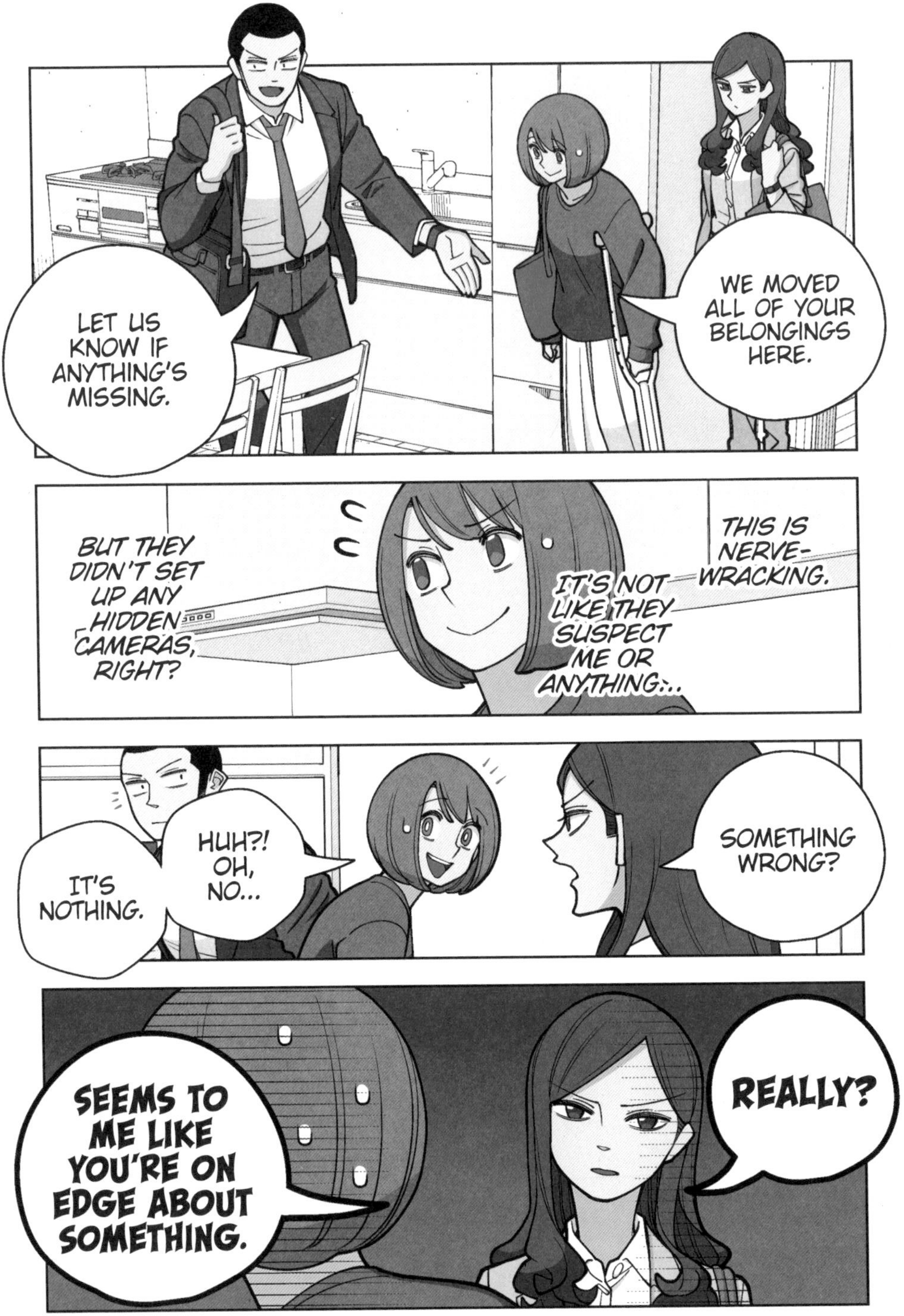
WE MOVED ALL OF YOUR BELONGINGS HERE.
LET US KNOW IF ANYTHING'S MISSING.
THIS IS NERVE-WRACKING.
IT'S NOT LIKE THEY SUSPECT ME OR ANYTHING...
BUT THEY DIDN'T SET UP ANY HIDDEN CAMERAS, RIGHT?
SOMETHING WRONG?
HUH?! OH, NO...
IT'S NOTHING.
REALLY?
SEEMS TO ME LIKE YOU'RE ON EDGE ABOUT SOMETHING.

☆ ——————You could stop glaring at me, for starters!

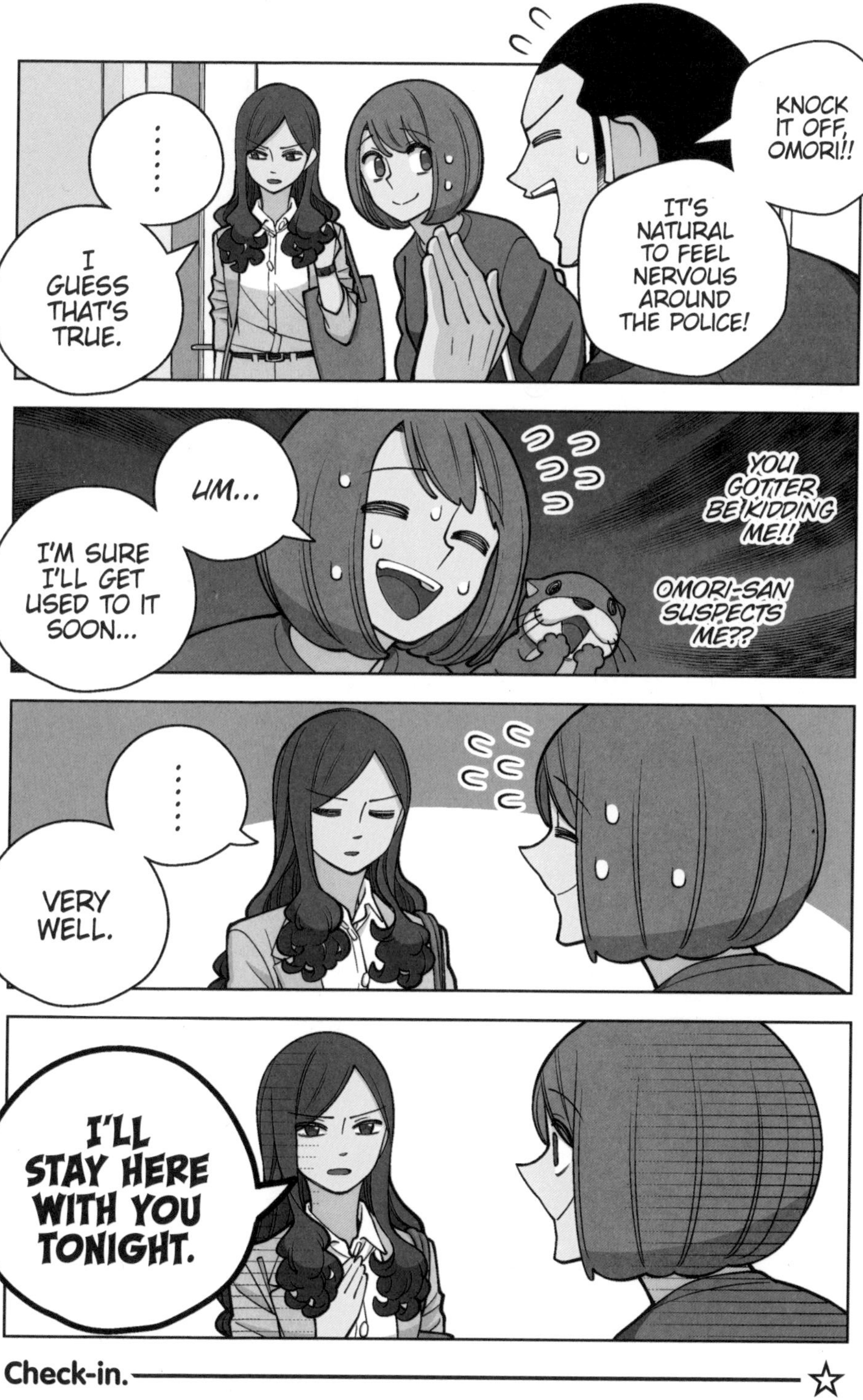
KNOCK IT OFF, OMORI!!
IT'S NATURAL TO FEEL NERVOUS AROUND THE POLICE!
......
I GUESS THAT'S TRUE.
YOU GOTTER BE KIDDING ME!!
OMORI-SAN SUSPECTS ME??
UM...
I'M SURE I'LL GET USED TO IT SOON...
......
VERY WELL.
I'LL STAY HERE WITH YOU TONIGHT.

Check-in. ☆

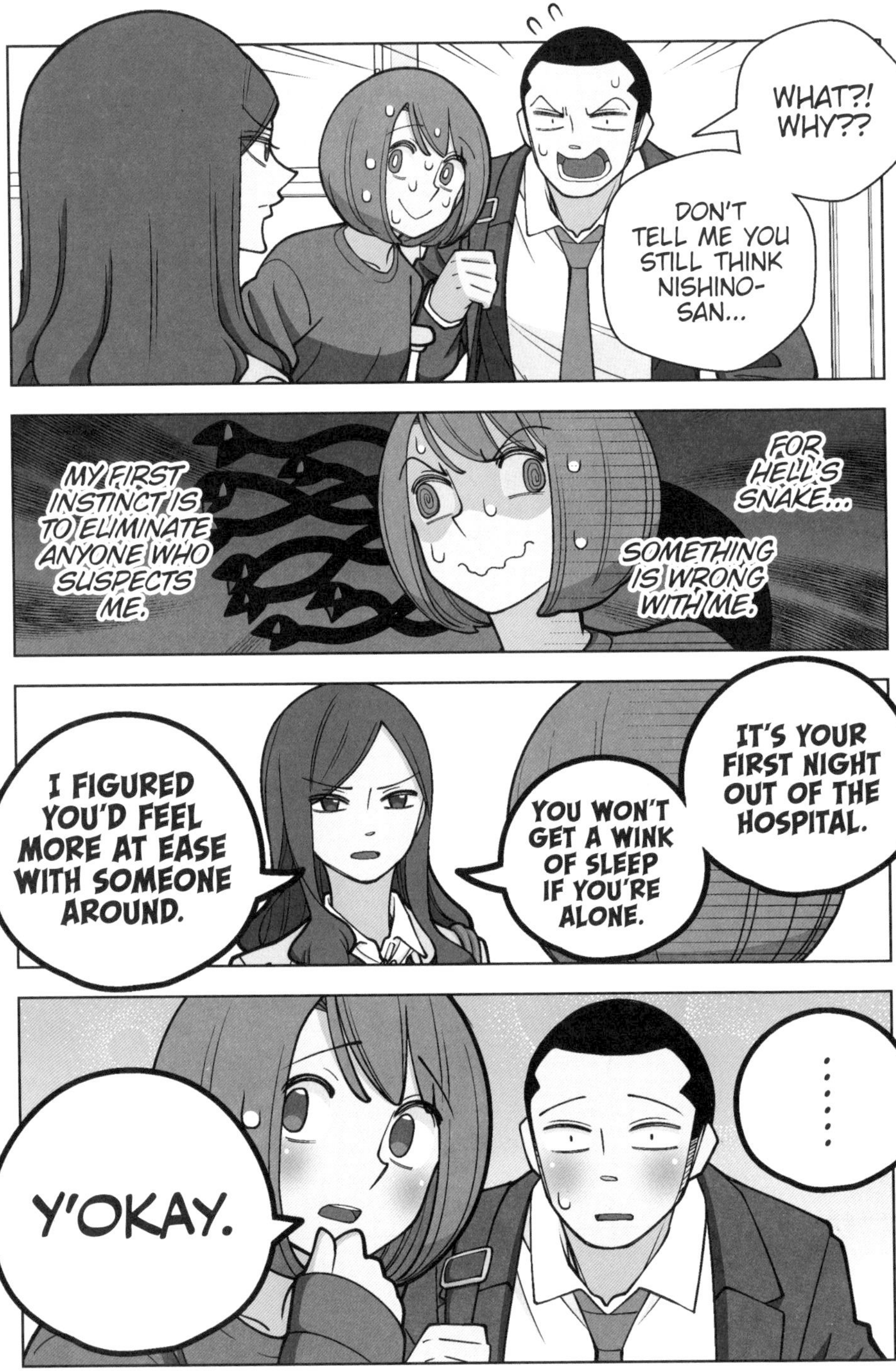
WHAT?! WHY??
DON'T TELL ME YOU STILL THINK NISHINO-SAN...
FOR HELL'S SNAKE...
SOMETHING IS WRONG WITH ME.
MY FIRST INSTINCT IS TO ELIMINATE ANYONE WHO SUSPECTS ME.
IT'S YOUR FIRST NIGHT OUT OF THE HOSPITAL.
YOU WON'T GET A WINK OF SLEEP IF YOU'RE ALONE.
I FIGURED YOU'D FEEL MORE AT EASE WITH SOMEONE AROUND.
......
Y'OKAY.

Happy Kanako's
Killer Life

It's a
Secret
!!

Happy Kanako's Killer Life

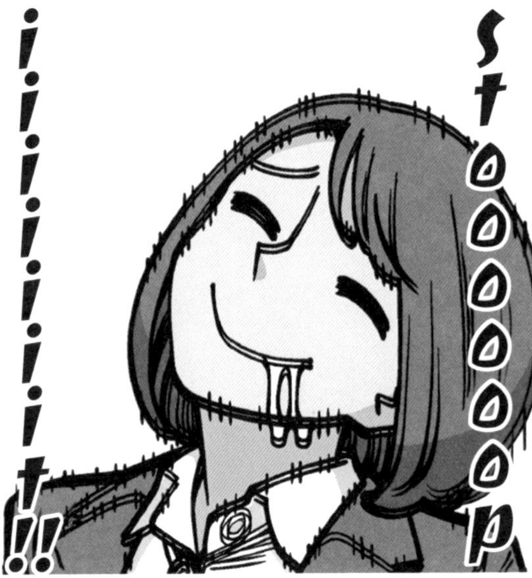
stoooooooop
iiiiiiit!!

Bonus

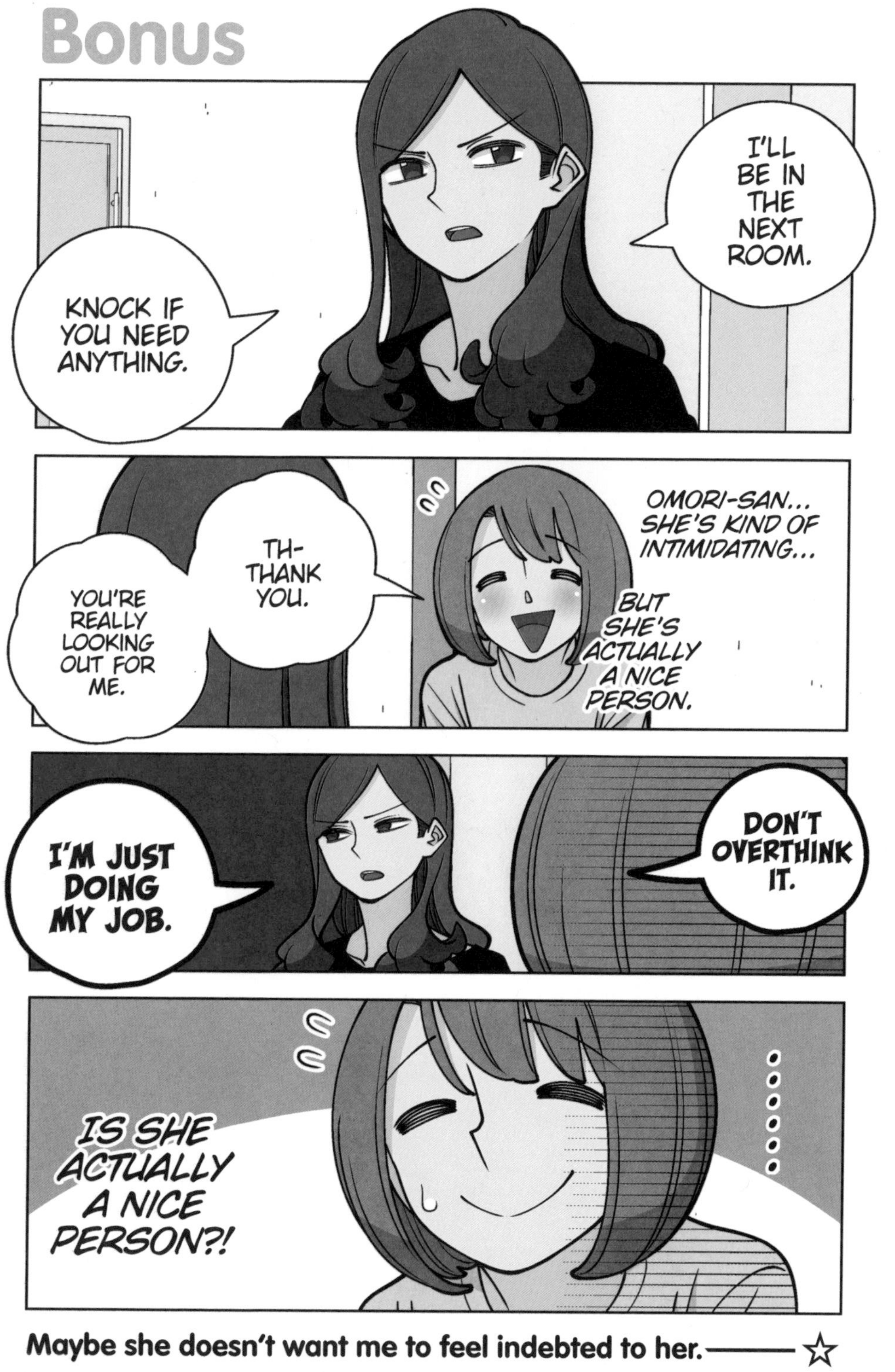
I'LL BE IN THE NEXT ROOM.
KNOCK IF YOU NEED ANYTHING.
OMORI-SAN... SHE'S KIND OF INTIMIDATING...
BUT SHE'S ACTUALLY A NICE PERSON.
TH-THANK YOU.
YOU'RE REALLY LOOKING OUT FOR ME.
DON'T OVERTHINK IT.
I'M JUST DOING MY JOB.
......
IS SHE ACTUALLY A NICE PERSON?!

Maybe she doesn't want me to feel indebted to her.——☆

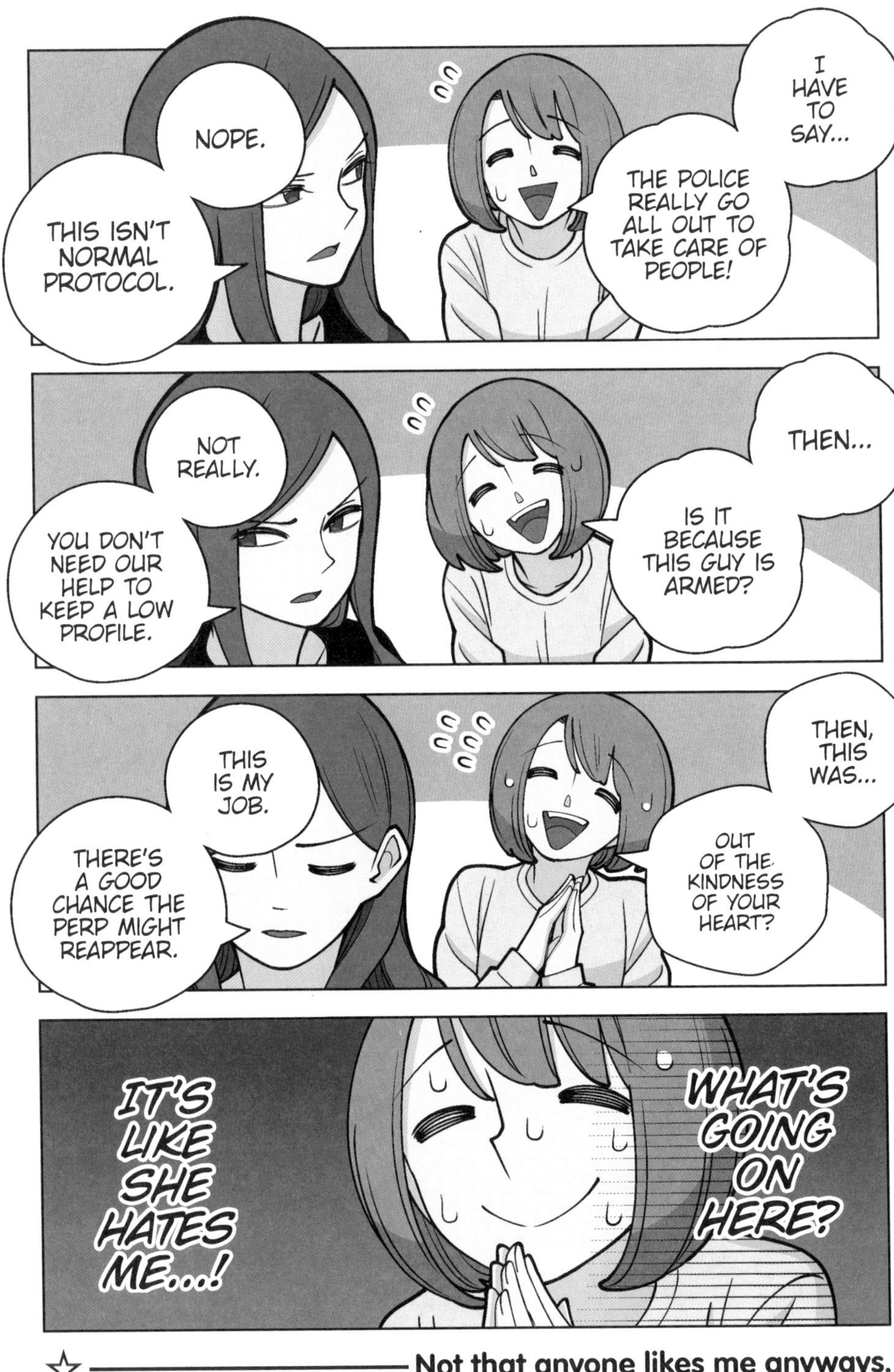
I HAVE TO SAY...
THE POLICE REALLY GO ALL OUT TO TAKE CARE OF PEOPLE!
NOPE.
THIS ISN'T NORMAL PROTOCOL.
THEN...
IS IT BECAUSE THIS GUY IS ARMED?
NOT REALLY.
YOU DON'T NEED OUR HELP TO KEEP A LOW PROFILE.
THEN, THIS WAS...
OUT OF THE KINDNESS OF YOUR HEART?
THIS IS MY JOB.
THERE'S A GOOD CHANCE THE PERP MIGHT REAPPEAR.
WHAT'S GOING ON HERE?
IT'S LIKE SHE HATES ME...!

☆ —— **Not that anyone likes me anyways.**

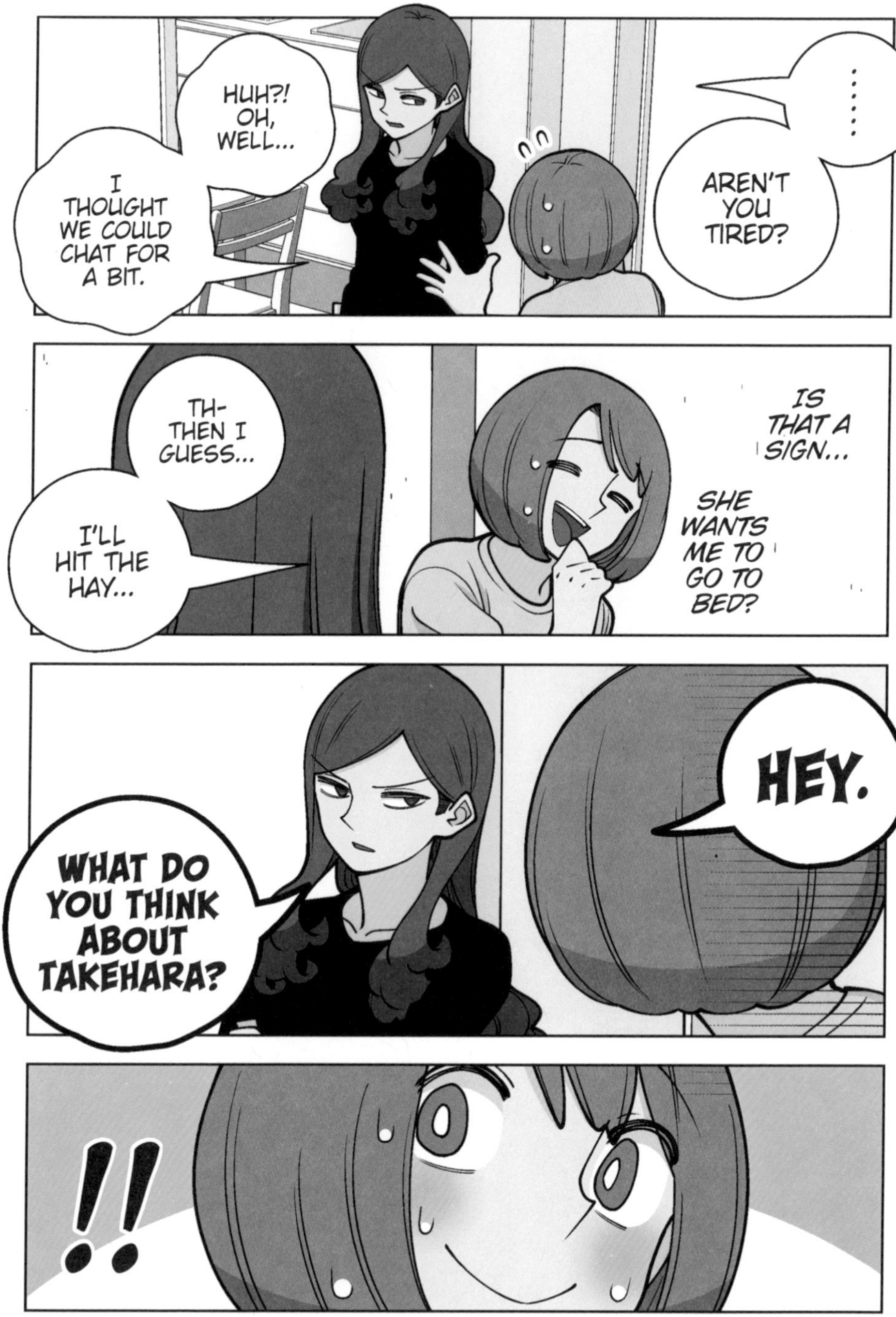
......
AREN'T YOU TIRED?
HUH?! OH, WELL...
I THOUGHT WE COULD CHAT FOR A BIT.
IS THAT A SIGN...
SHE WANTS ME TO GO TO BED?
TH- THEN I GUESS...
I'LL HIT THE HAY...
HEY.
WHAT DO YOU THINK ABOUT TAKEHARA?
!!

Of all the topics... ☆

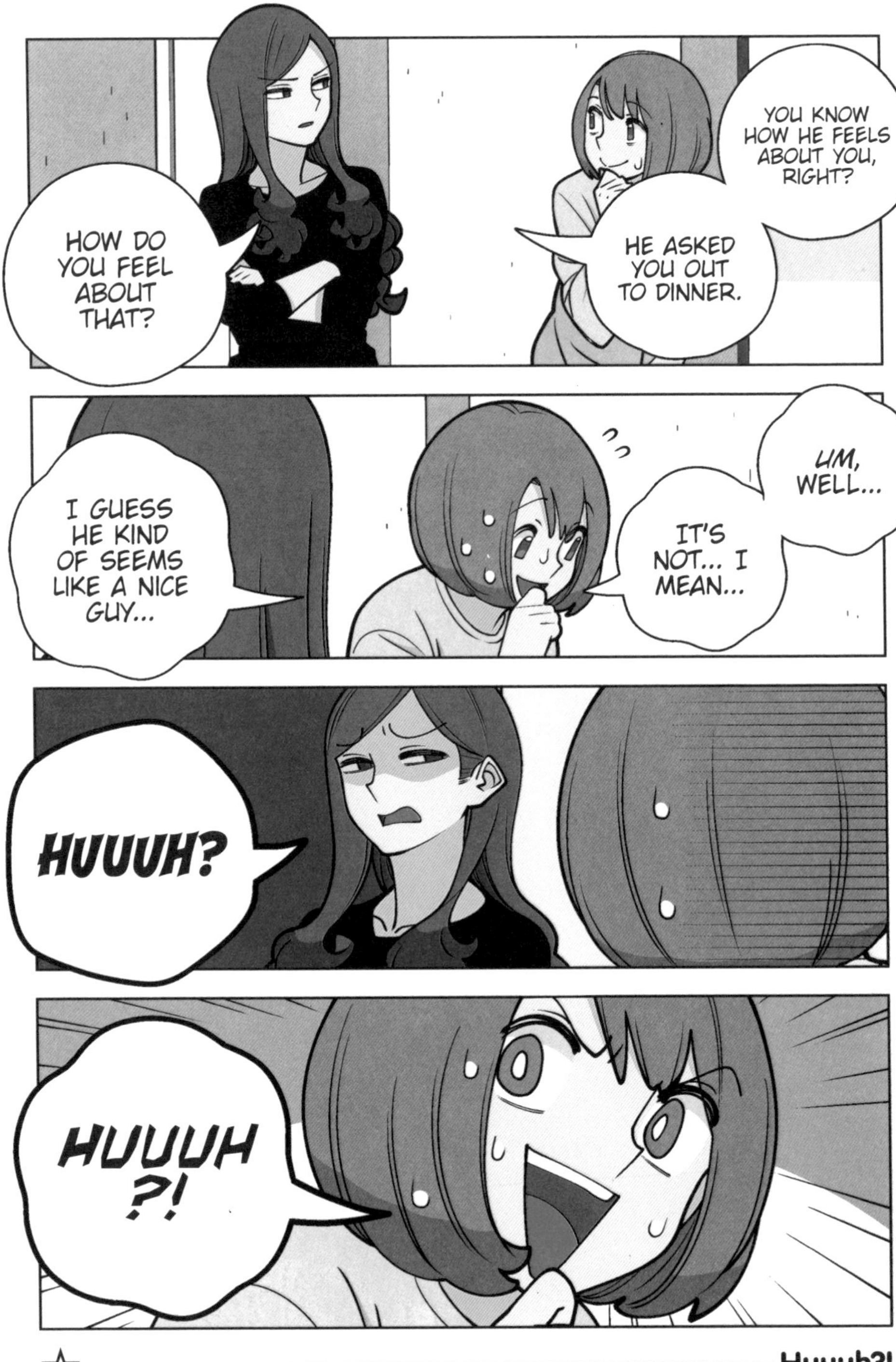
YOU KNOW HOW HE FEELS ABOUT YOU, RIGHT?
HE ASKED YOU OUT TO DINNER.
HOW DO YOU FEEL ABOUT THAT?
UM, WELL...
IT'S NOT... I MEAN...
I GUESS HE KIND OF SEEMS LIKE A NICE GUY...
HUUUH?
HUUUH ?!

☆ Huuuh?!

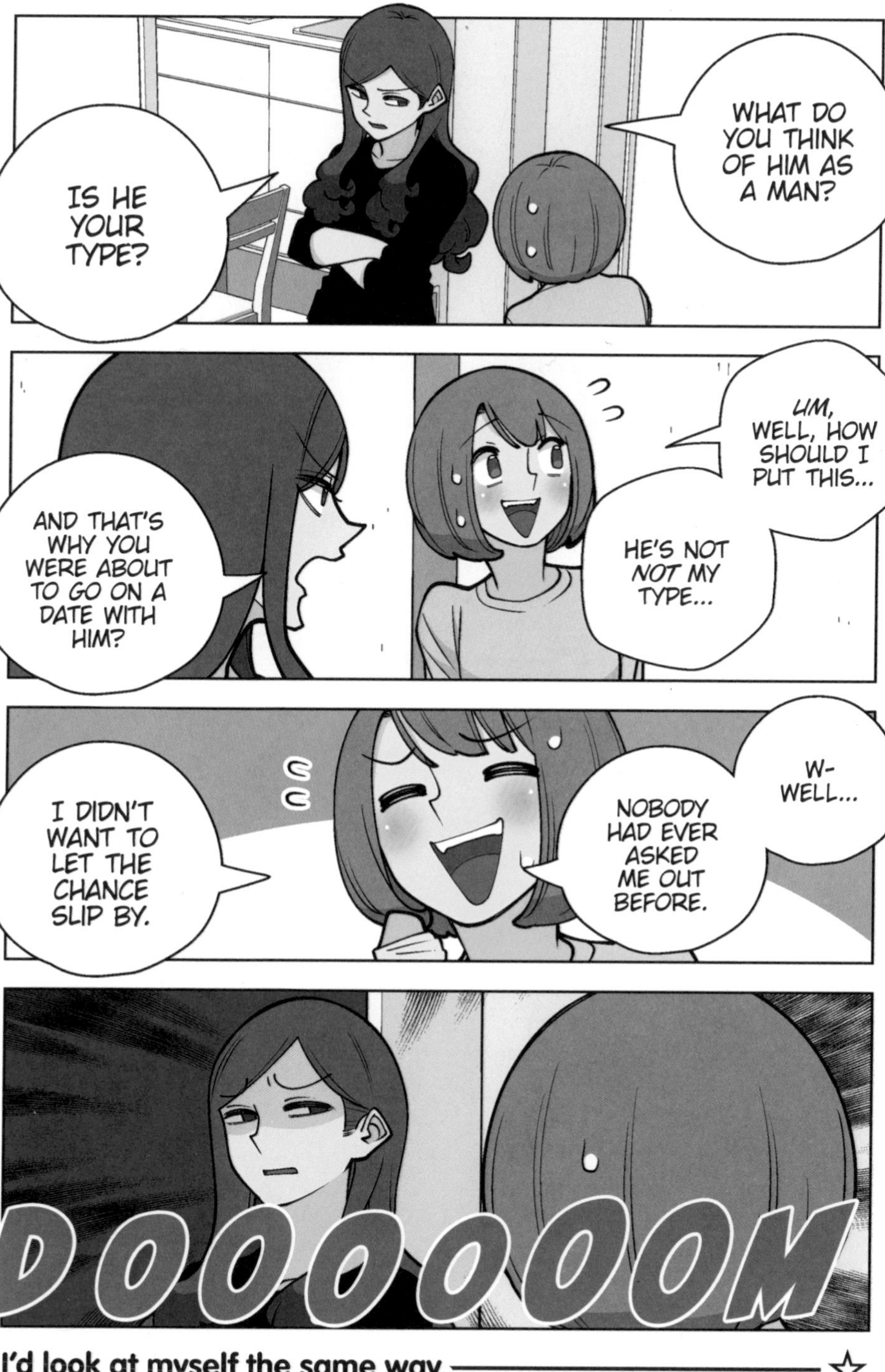
WHAT DO YOU THINK OF HIM AS A MAN?
IS HE YOUR TYPE?
UM, WELL, HOW SHOULD I PUT THIS...
HE'S NOT *NOT* MY TYPE...
AND THAT'S WHY YOU WERE ABOUT TO GO ON A DATE WITH HIM?
W-WELL...
NOBODY HAD EVER ASKED ME OUT BEFORE.
I DIDN'T WANT TO LET THE CHANCE SLIP BY.
DOOOOOOM

I'd look at myself the same way. ☆

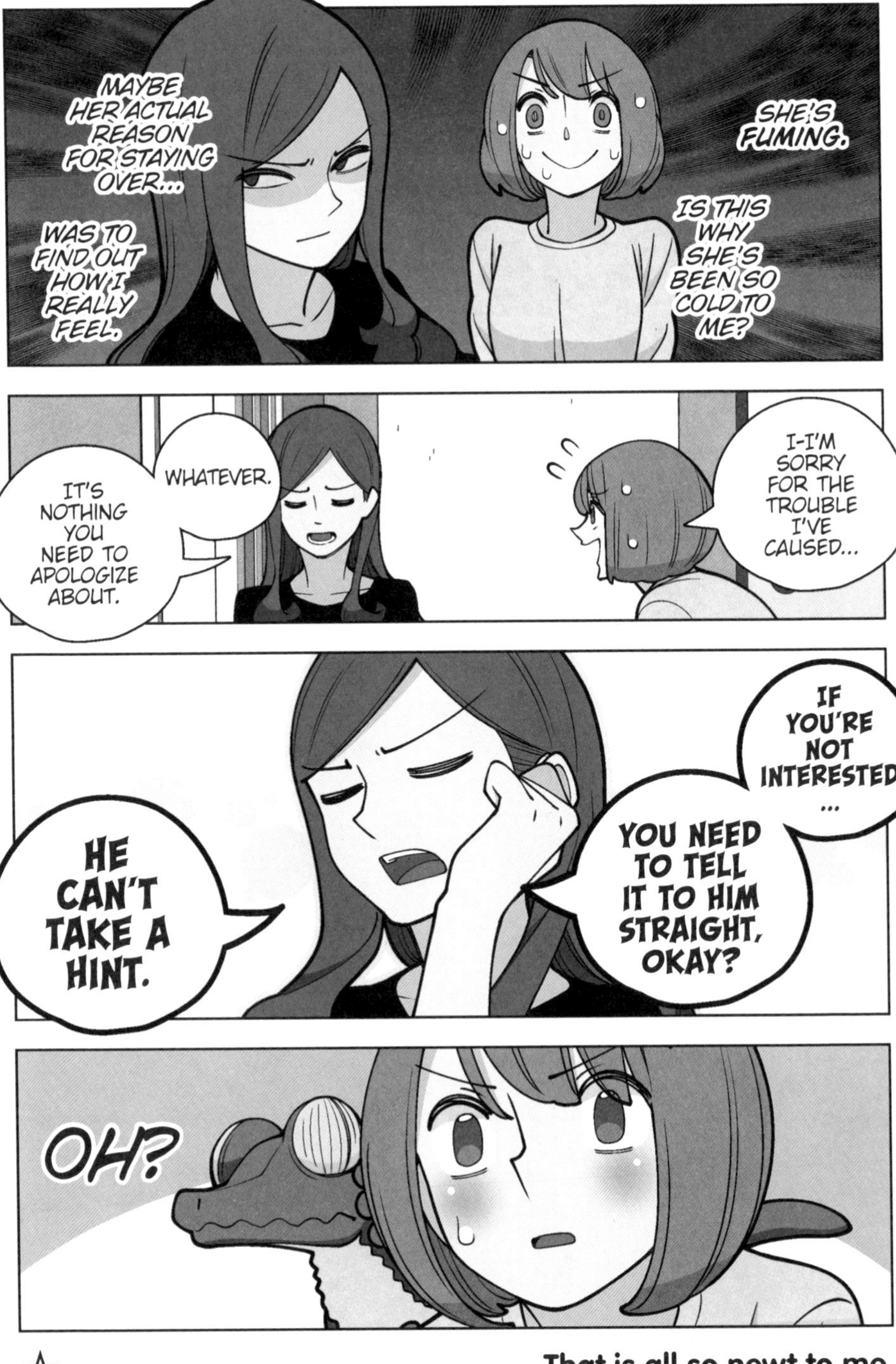
SHE'S FUMING.
IS THIS WHY SHE'S BEEN SO COLD TO ME?
MAYBE HER ACTUAL REASON FOR STAYING OVER...
WAS TO FIND OUT HOW I REALLY FEEL.
I-I'M SORRY FOR THE TROUBLE I'VE CAUSED...
WHATEVER.
IT'S NOTHING YOU NEED TO APOLOGIZE ABOUT.
IF YOU'RE NOT INTERESTED...
YOU NEED TO TELL IT TO HIM STRAIGHT, OKAY?
HE CAN'T TAKE A HINT.
OH?

☆ ———That is all so newt to me.

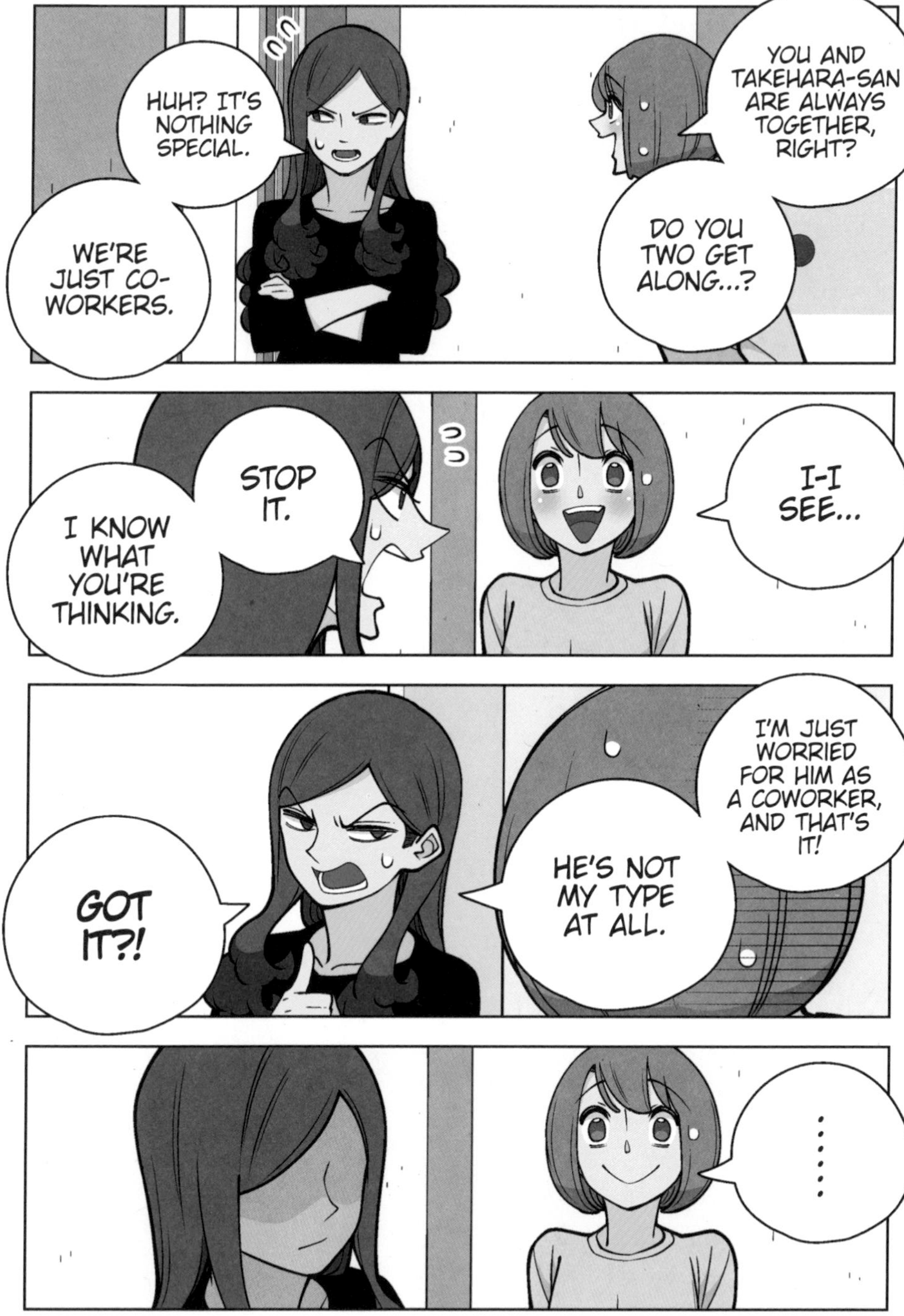
YOU AND TAKEHARA-SAN ARE ALWAYS TOGETHER, RIGHT?
DO YOU TWO GET ALONG...?
HUH? IT'S NOTHING SPECIAL.
WE'RE JUST CO-WORKERS.
I-I SEE...
STOP IT.
I KNOW WHAT YOU'RE THINKING.
I'M JUST WORRIED FOR HIM AS A COWORKER, AND THAT'S IT!
HE'S NOT MY TYPE AT ALL.
GOT IT?!
......

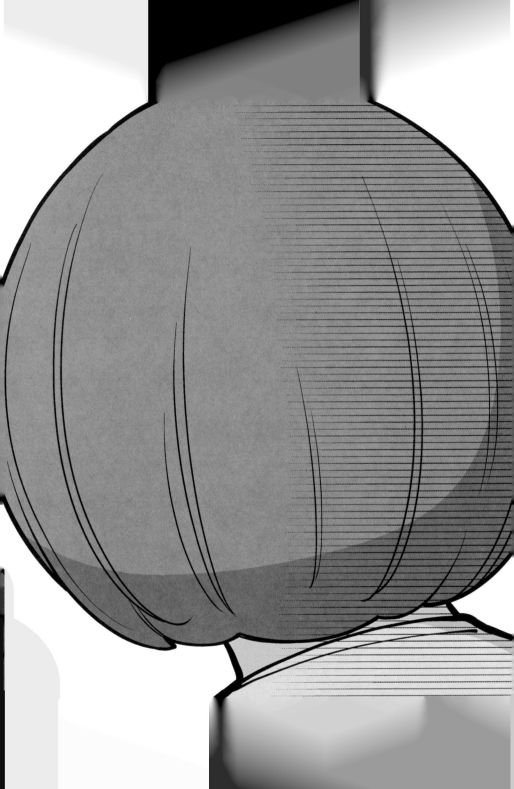

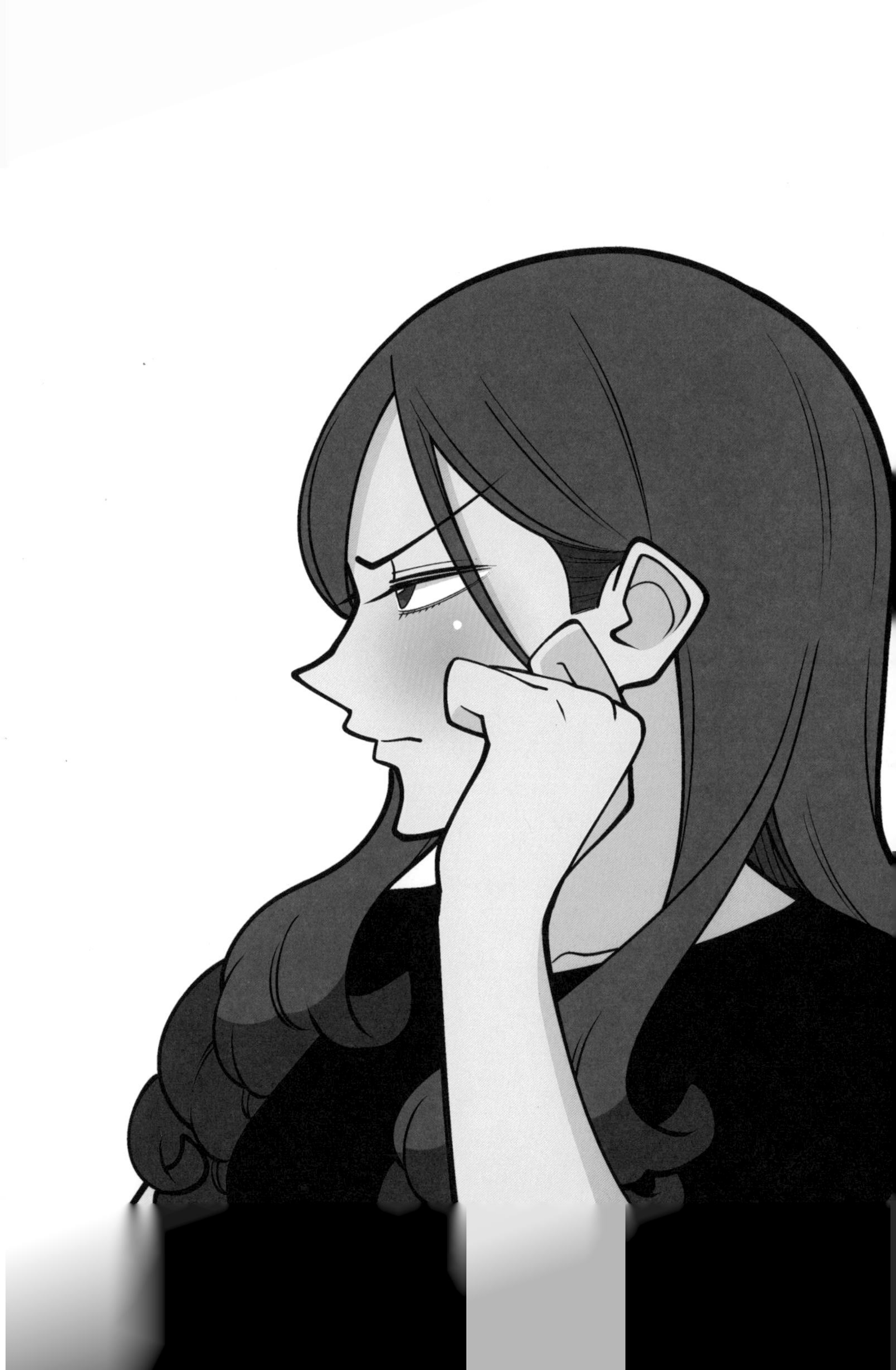

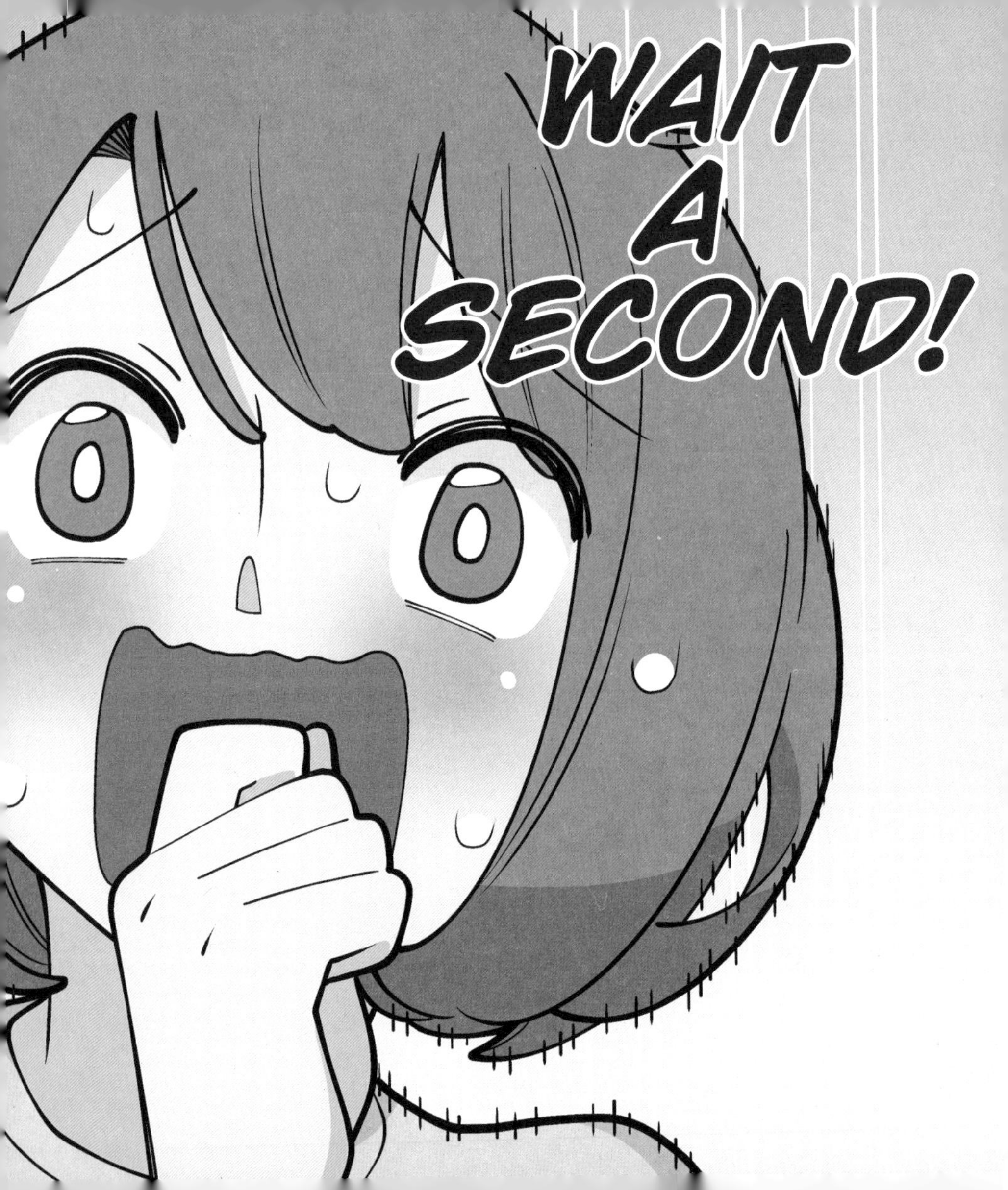
WAIT A SECOND!

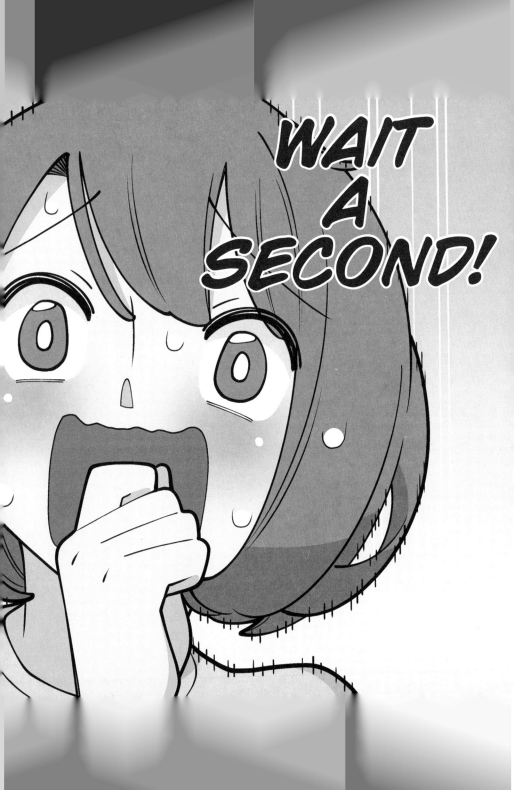

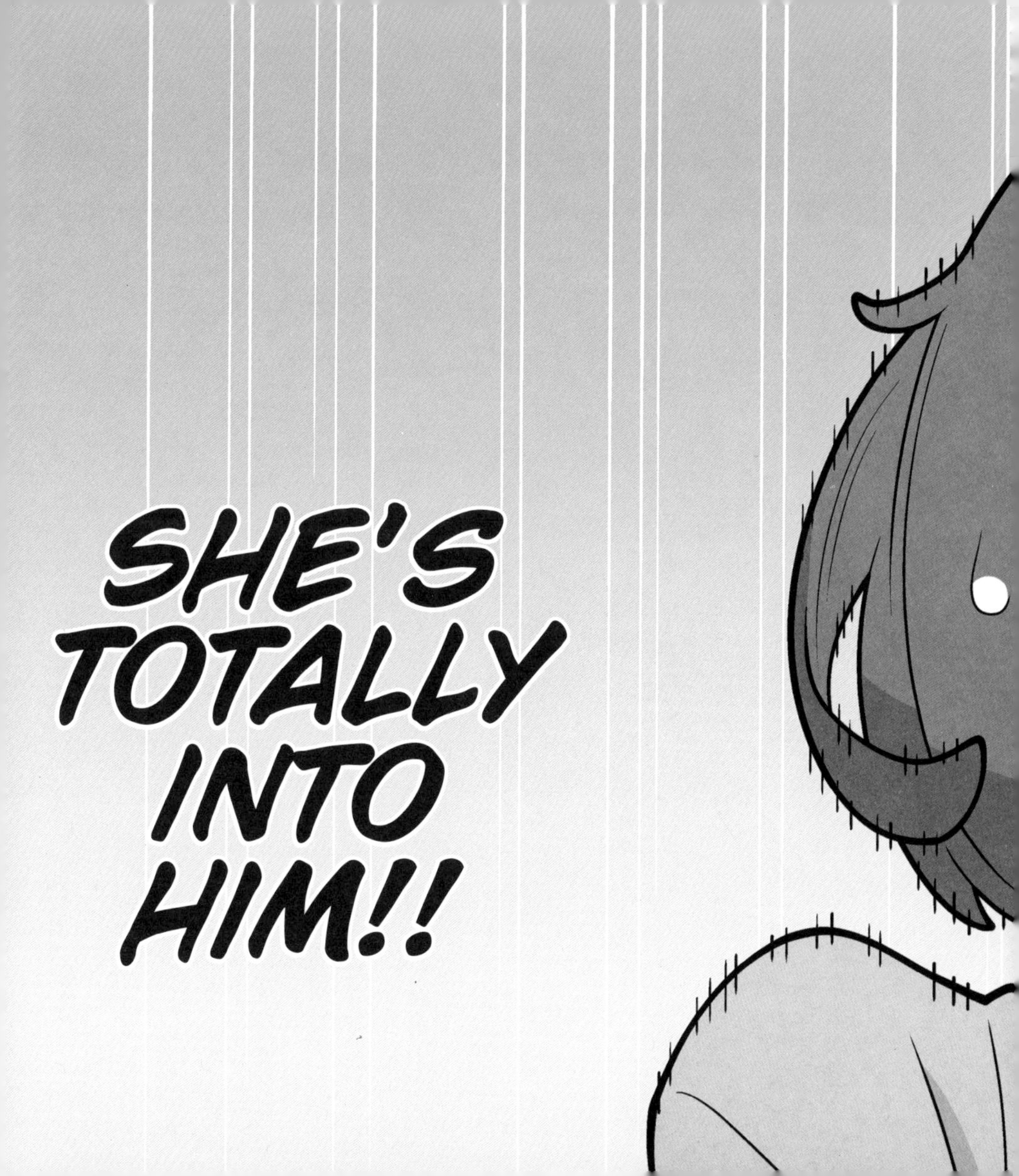
SHE'S TOTALLY INTO HIM!!

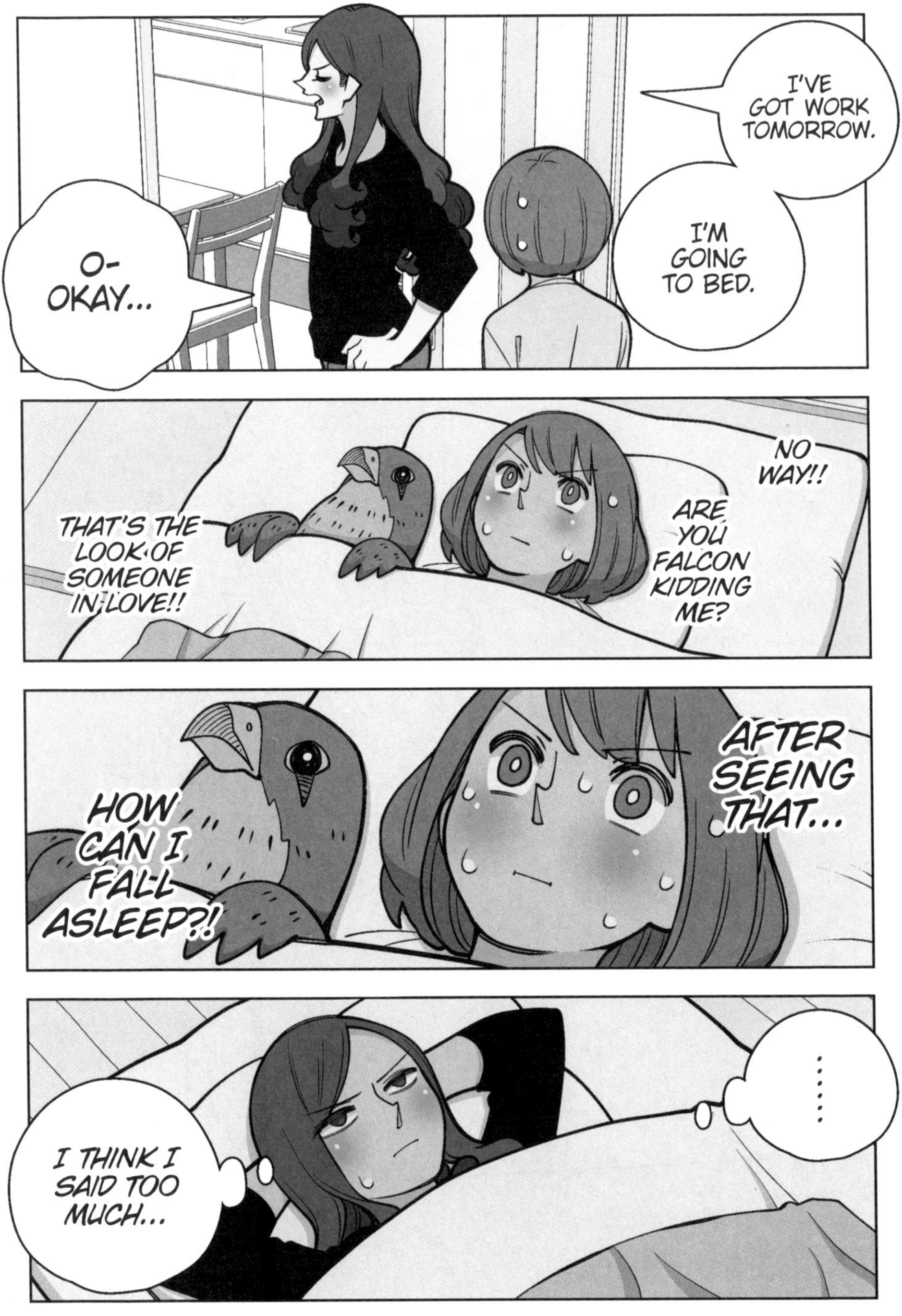
I'VE GOT WORK TOMORROW.
I'M GOING TO BED.
O-OKAY...
NO WAY!!
ARE YOU FALCON KIDDING ME?
THAT'S THE LOOK OF SOMEONE IN LOVE!!
AFTER SEEING THAT...
HOW CAN I FALL ASLEEP?!
......
I THINK I SAID TOO MUCH...

☆ —— **A sleepless night.**

Happy Kanako's
Killer Life

THE HELL
ARE YOU
SAYING?

Happy Kanako's
Killer Life

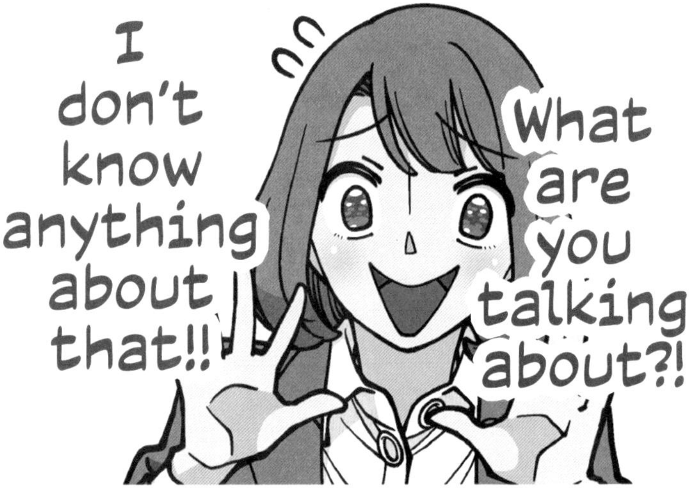
What are you talking about?!
I don't know anything about that!!

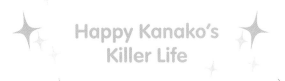

045

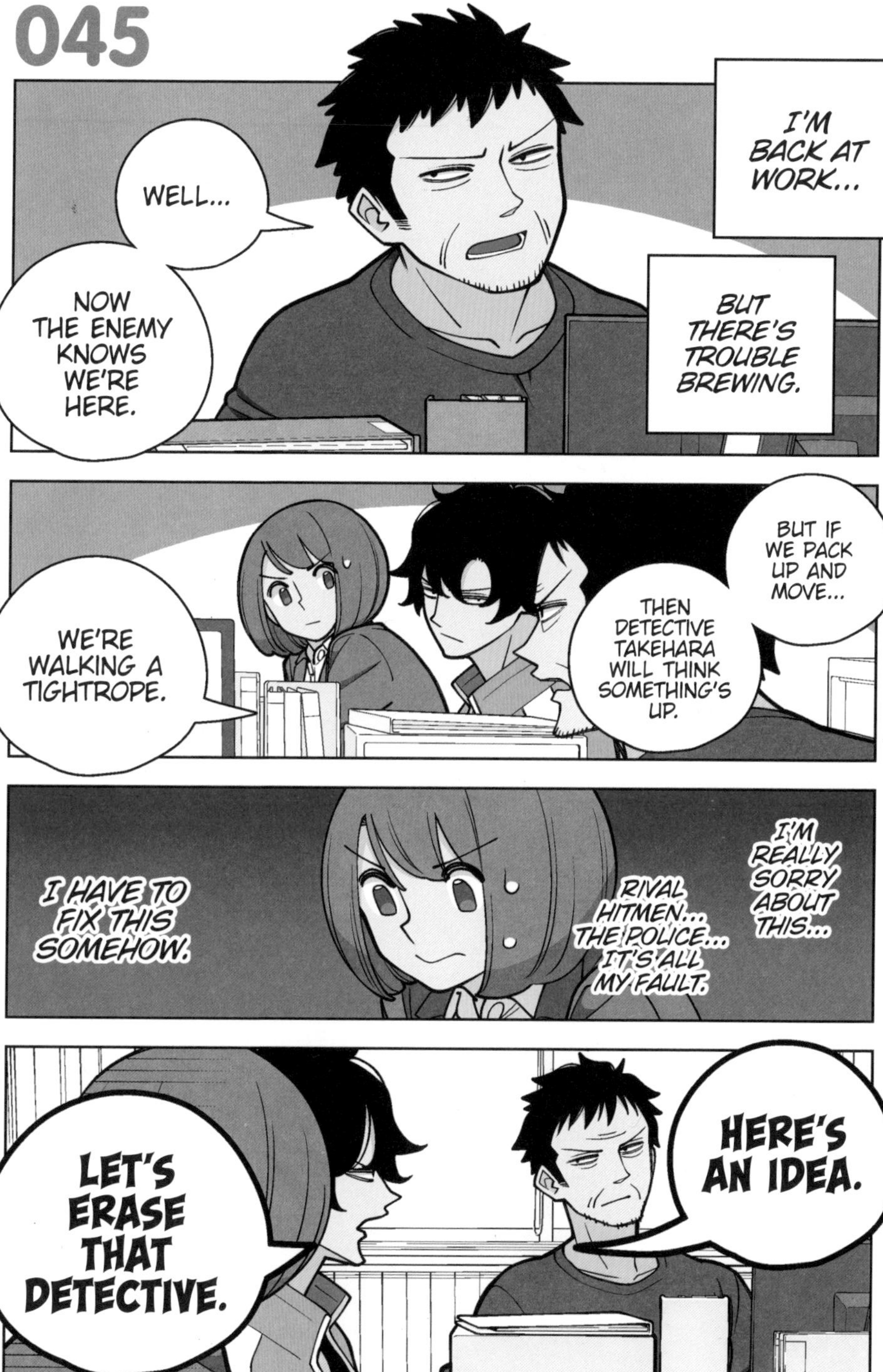
I'M BACK AT WORK...
BUT THERE'S TROUBLE BREWING.
WELL...
NOW THE ENEMY KNOWS WE'RE HERE.
BUT IF WE PACK UP AND MOVE...
THEN DETECTIVE TAKEHARA WILL THINK SOMETHING'S UP.
WE'RE WALKING A TIGHTROPE.
I'M REALLY SORRY ABOUT THIS...
RIVAL HITMEN... THE POLICE... IT'S ALL MY FAULT.
I HAVE TO FIX THIS SOMEHOW.
HERE'S AN IDEA.
LET'S ERASE THAT DETECTIVE.

No mercy. ☆

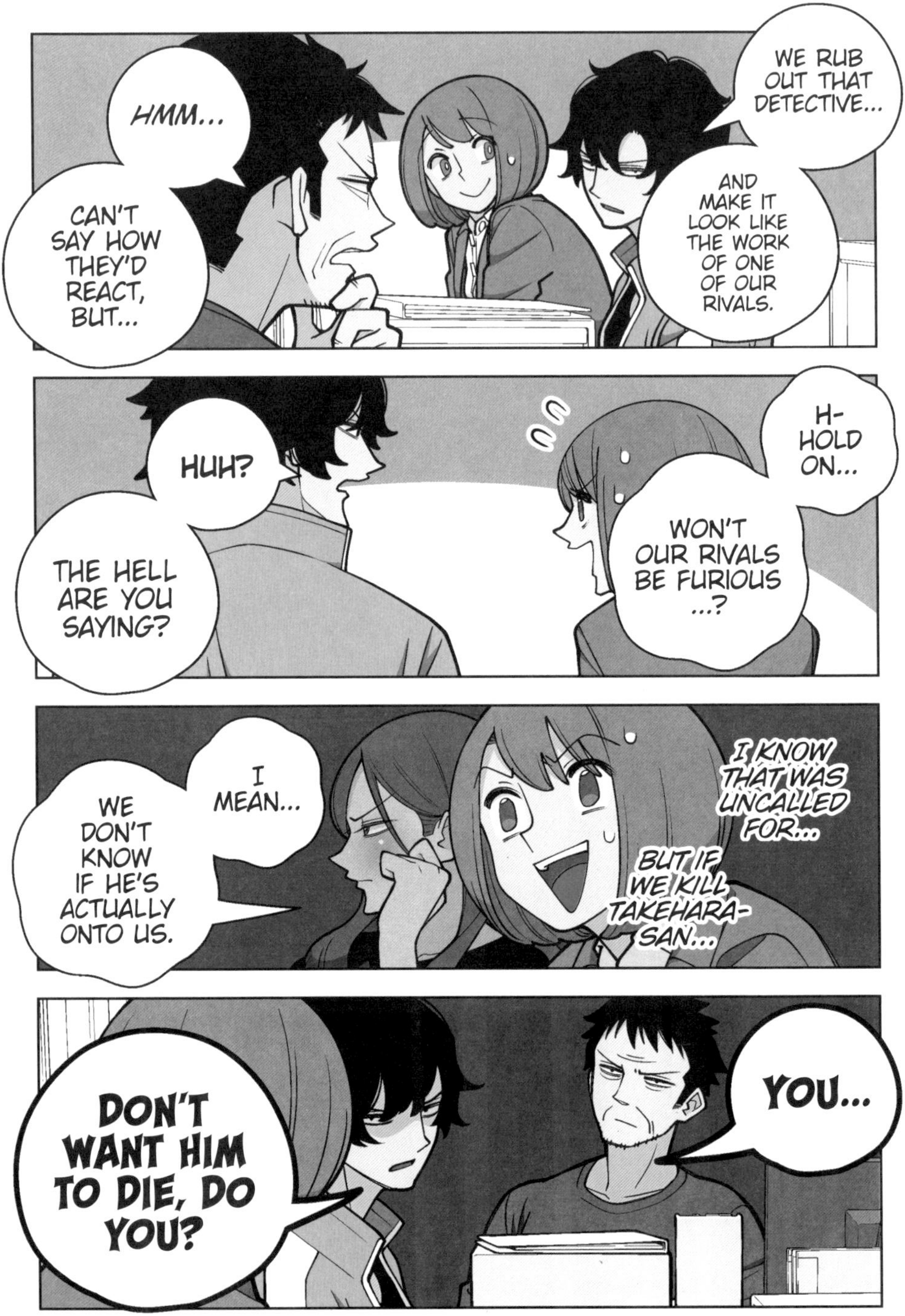
WE RUB OUT THAT DETECTIVE...
AND MAKE IT LOOK LIKE THE WORK OF ONE OF OUR RIVALS.
HMM...
CAN'T SAY HOW THEY'D REACT, BUT...
H-HOLD ON...
WON'T OUR RIVALS BE FURIOUS ...?
HUH?
THE HELL ARE YOU SAYING?
I KNOW THAT WAS UNCALLED FOR...
BUT IF WE KILL TAKEHARA-SAN...
I MEAN...
WE DON'T KNOW IF HE'S ACTUALLY ONTO US.
YOU...
DON'T WANT HIM TO DIE, DO YOU?

☆——There's some kind of misunderstanding here.

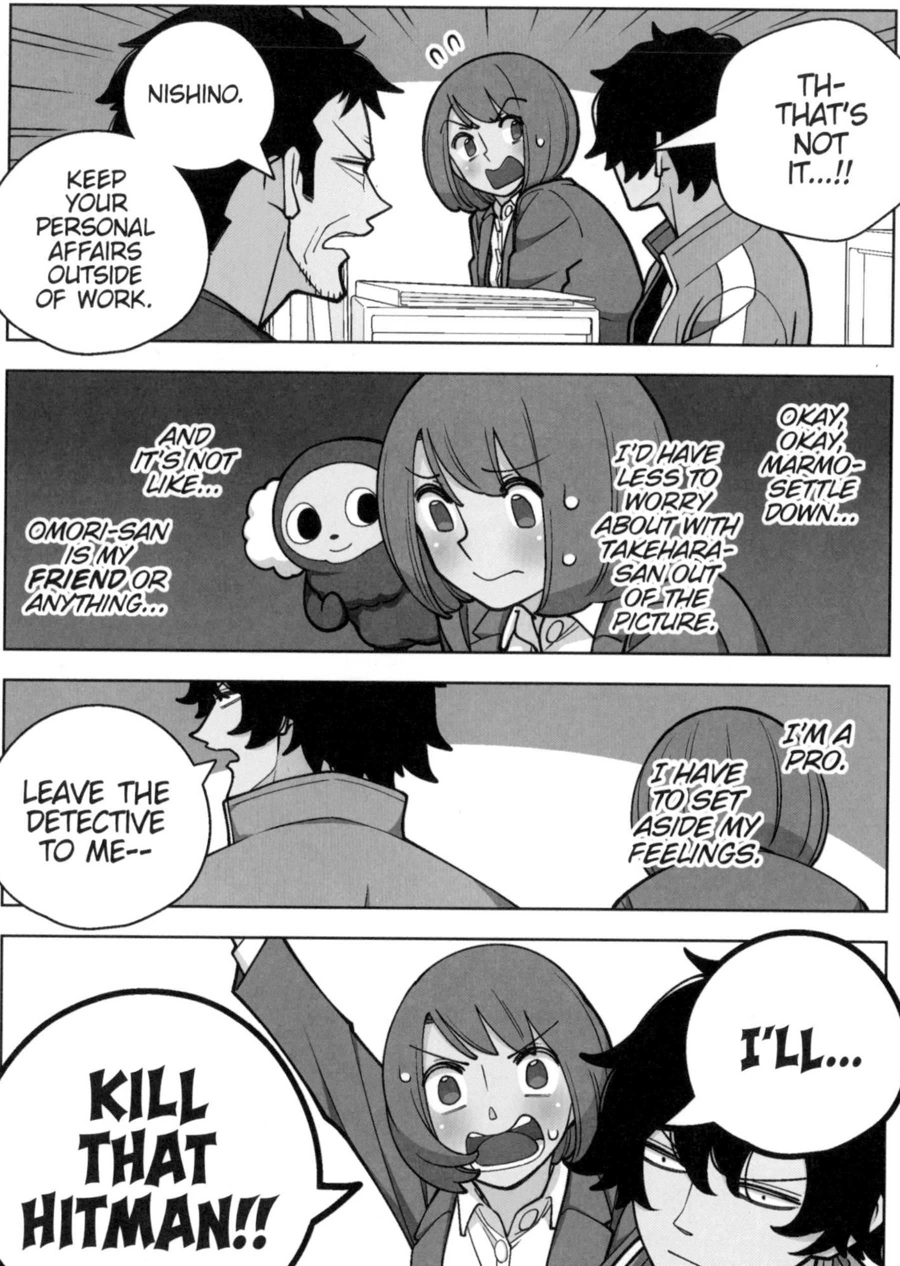

TH-THAT'S NOT IT...!!
NISHINO.
KEEP YOUR PERSONAL AFFAIRS OUTSIDE OF WORK.
OKAY, OKAY, MARMO-SETTLE DOWN...
I'D HAVE LESS TO WORRY ABOUT WITH TAKEHARA-SAN OUT OF THE PICTURE.
AND IT'S NOT LIKE...
OMORI-SAN IS MY FRIEND OR ANYTHING...
I'M A PRO.
I HAVE TO SET ASIDE MY FEELINGS.
LEAVE THE DETECTIVE TO ME--
I'LL...
KILL THAT HITMAN!!

I'll do it. ☆

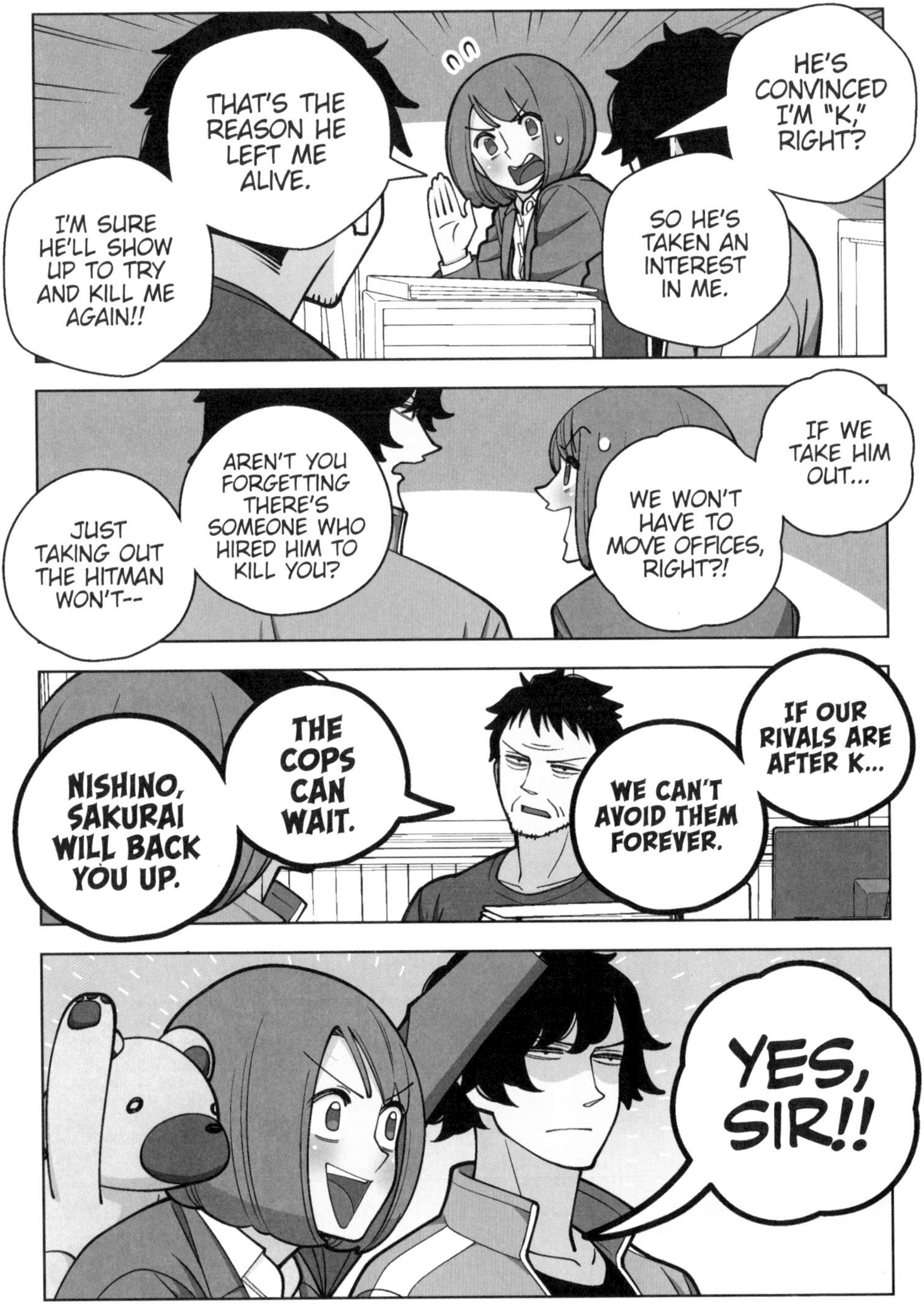
HE'S CONVINCED I'M "K," RIGHT?
SO HE'S TAKEN AN INTEREST IN ME.
THAT'S THE REASON HE LEFT ME ALIVE.
I'M SURE HE'LL SHOW UP TO TRY AND KILL ME AGAIN!!
IF WE TAKE HIM OUT...
WE WON'T HAVE TO MOVE OFFICES, RIGHT?!
AREN'T YOU FORGETTING THERE'S SOMEONE WHO HIRED HIM TO KILL YOU?
JUST TAKING OUT THE HITMAN WON'T--
IF OUR RIVALS ARE AFTER K...
WE CAN'T AVOID THEM FOREVER.
THE COPS CAN WAIT.
NISHINO, SAKURAI WILL BACK YOU UP.
YES, SIR!!

☆ —— I'm so beary beary excited!

046

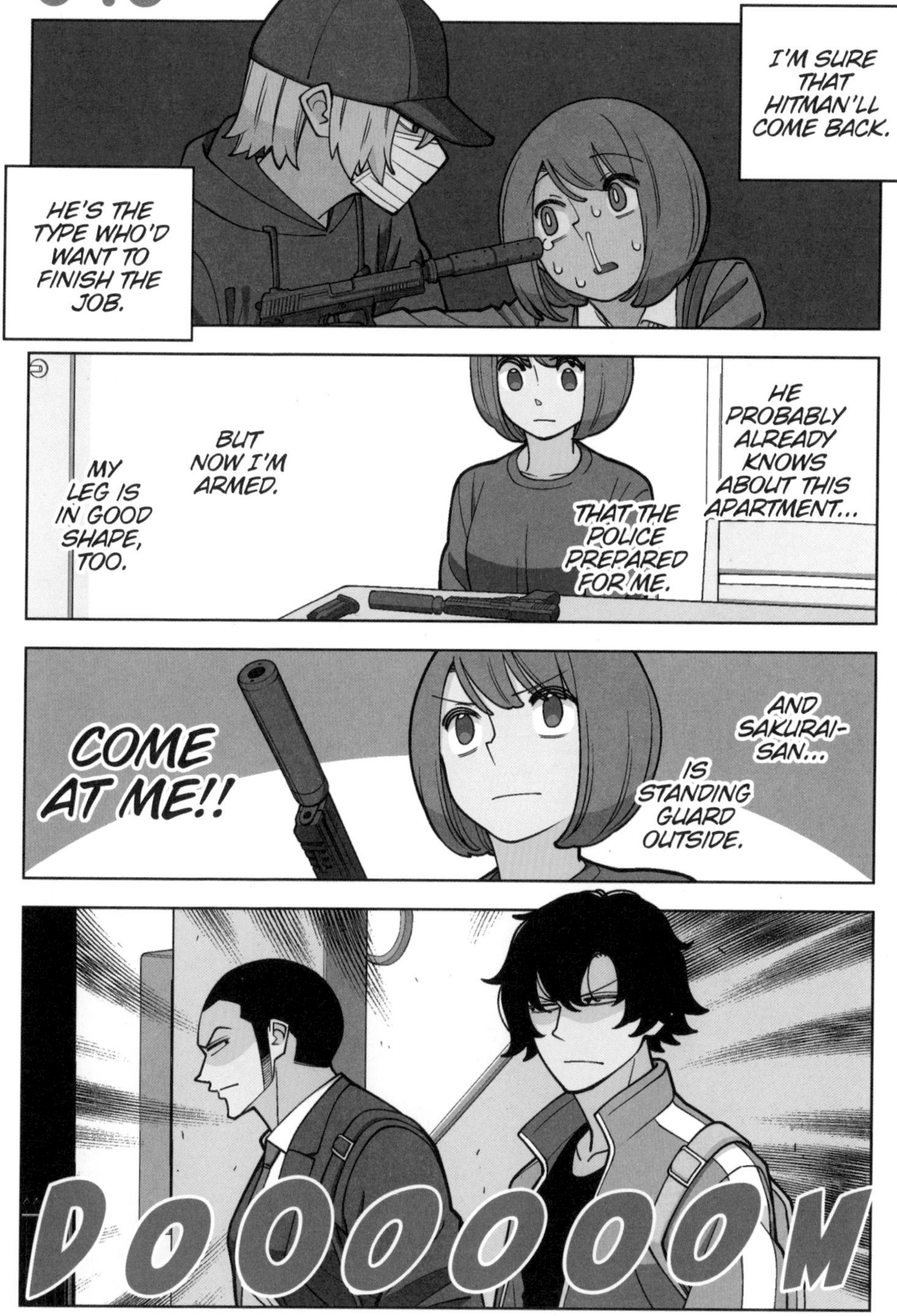
I'M SURE THAT HITMAN'LL COME BACK.
HE'S THE TYPE WHO'D WANT TO FINISH THE JOB.
HE PROBABLY ALREADY KNOWS ABOUT THIS APARTMENT...
THAT THE POLICE PREPARED FOR ME.
BUT NOW I'M ARMED.
MY LEG IS IN GOOD SHAPE, TOO.
AND SAKURAI-SAN...
IS STANDING GUARD OUTSIDE.
COME AT ME!!
DOOOOOOOM

An explosive situation! ☆

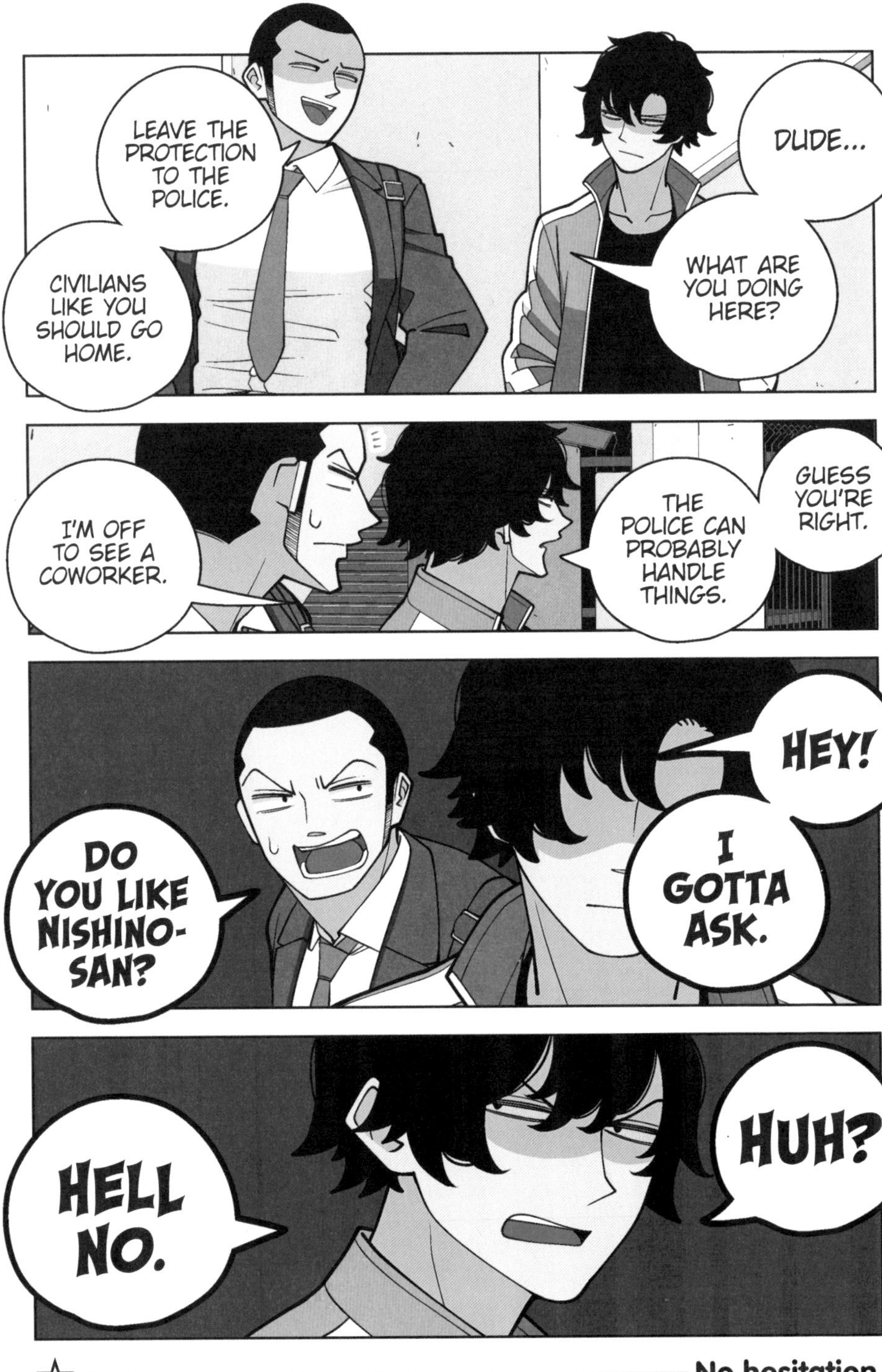
DUDE...
WHAT ARE YOU DOING HERE?
LEAVE THE PROTECTION TO THE POLICE.
CIVILIANS LIKE YOU SHOULD GO HOME.
GUESS YOU'RE RIGHT.
THE POLICE CAN PROBABLY HANDLE THINGS.
I'M OFF TO SEE A COWORKER.
HEY!
I GOTTA ASK.
DO YOU LIKE NISHINO-SAN?
HUH?
HELL NO.

☆ —— **No hesitation.**

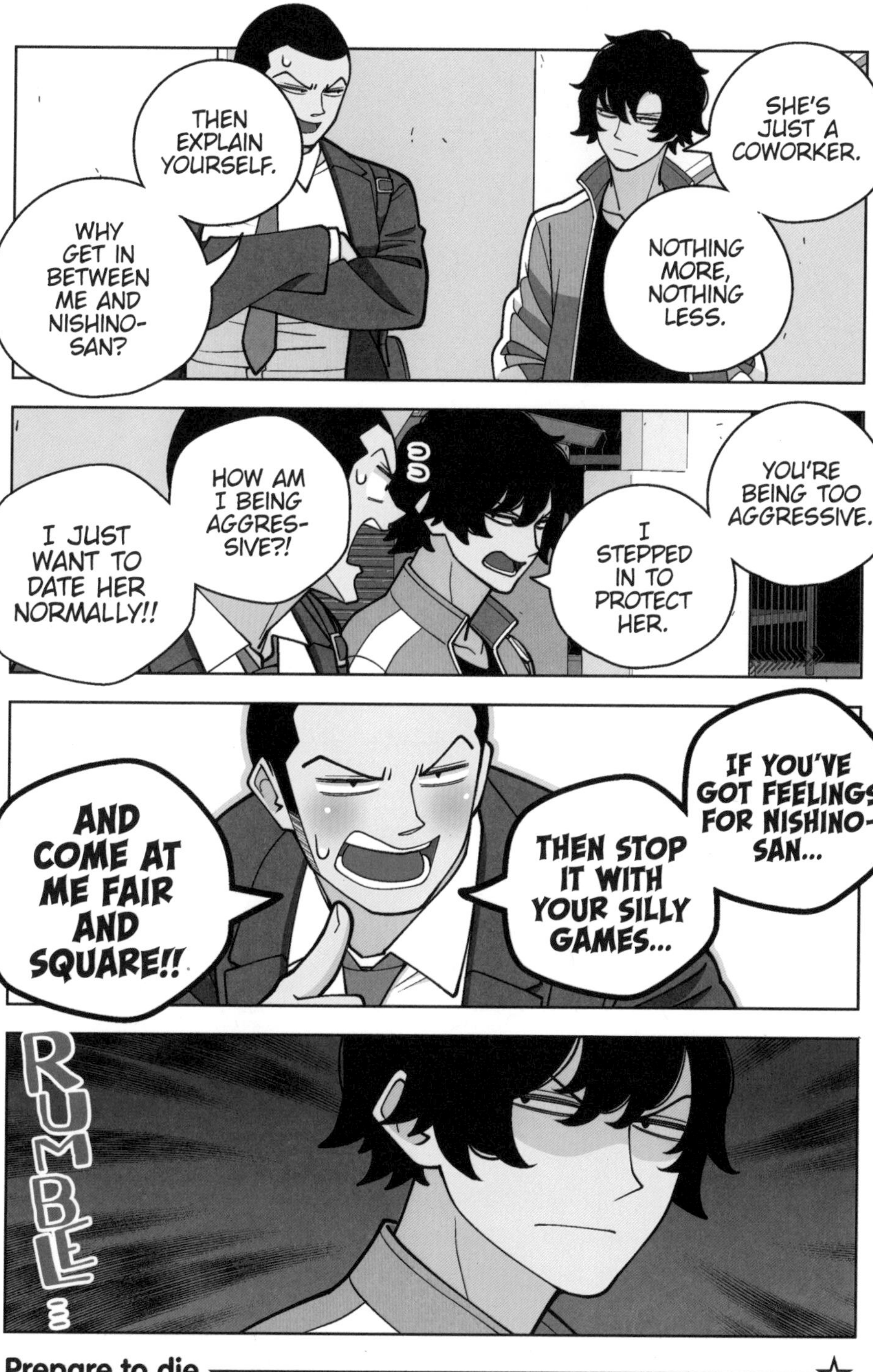
SHE'S JUST A COWORKER.
NOTHING MORE, NOTHING LESS.
THEN EXPLAIN YOURSELF.
WHY GET IN BETWEEN ME AND NISHINO-SAN?
YOU'RE BEING TOO AGGRESSIVE.
I STEPPED IN TO PROTECT HER.
HOW AM I BEING AGGRES-SIVE?!
I JUST WANT TO DATE HER NORMALLY!!
IF YOU'VE GOT FEELINGS FOR NISHINO-SAN...
THEN STOP IT WITH YOUR SILLY GAMES...
AND COME AT ME FAIR AND SQUARE!!
RUMBLE...

Prepare to die. ——— ☆

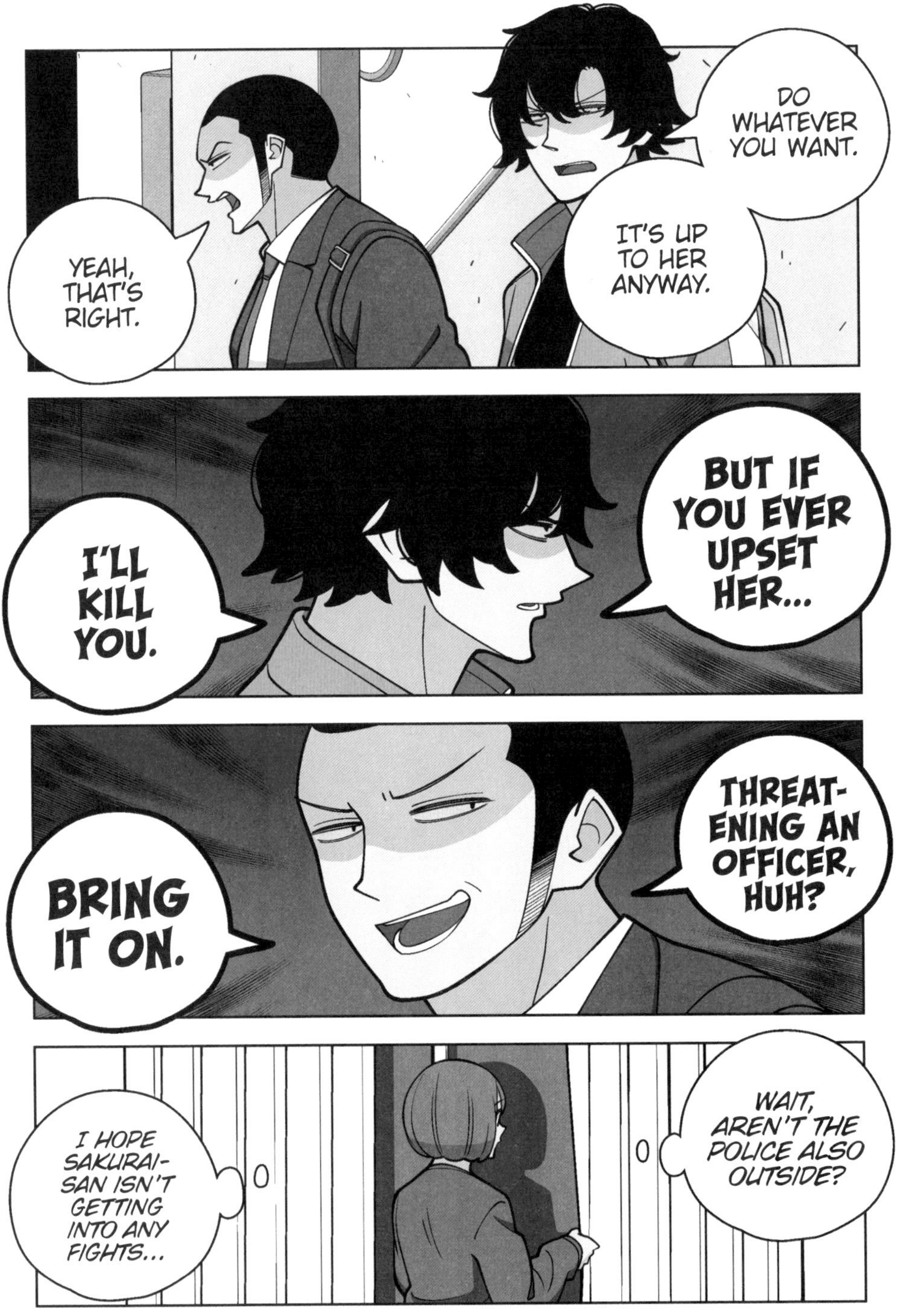
DO WHATEVER YOU WANT.
IT'S UP TO HER ANYWAY.
YEAH, THAT'S RIGHT.
BUT IF YOU EVER UPSET HER...
I'LL KILL YOU.
THREAT-ENING AN OFFICER, HUH?
BRING IT ON.
WAIT, AREN'T THE POLICE ALSO OUTSIDE?
I HOPE SAKURAI-SAN ISN'T GETTING INTO ANY FIGHTS...

☆ —They're really going at it.

047

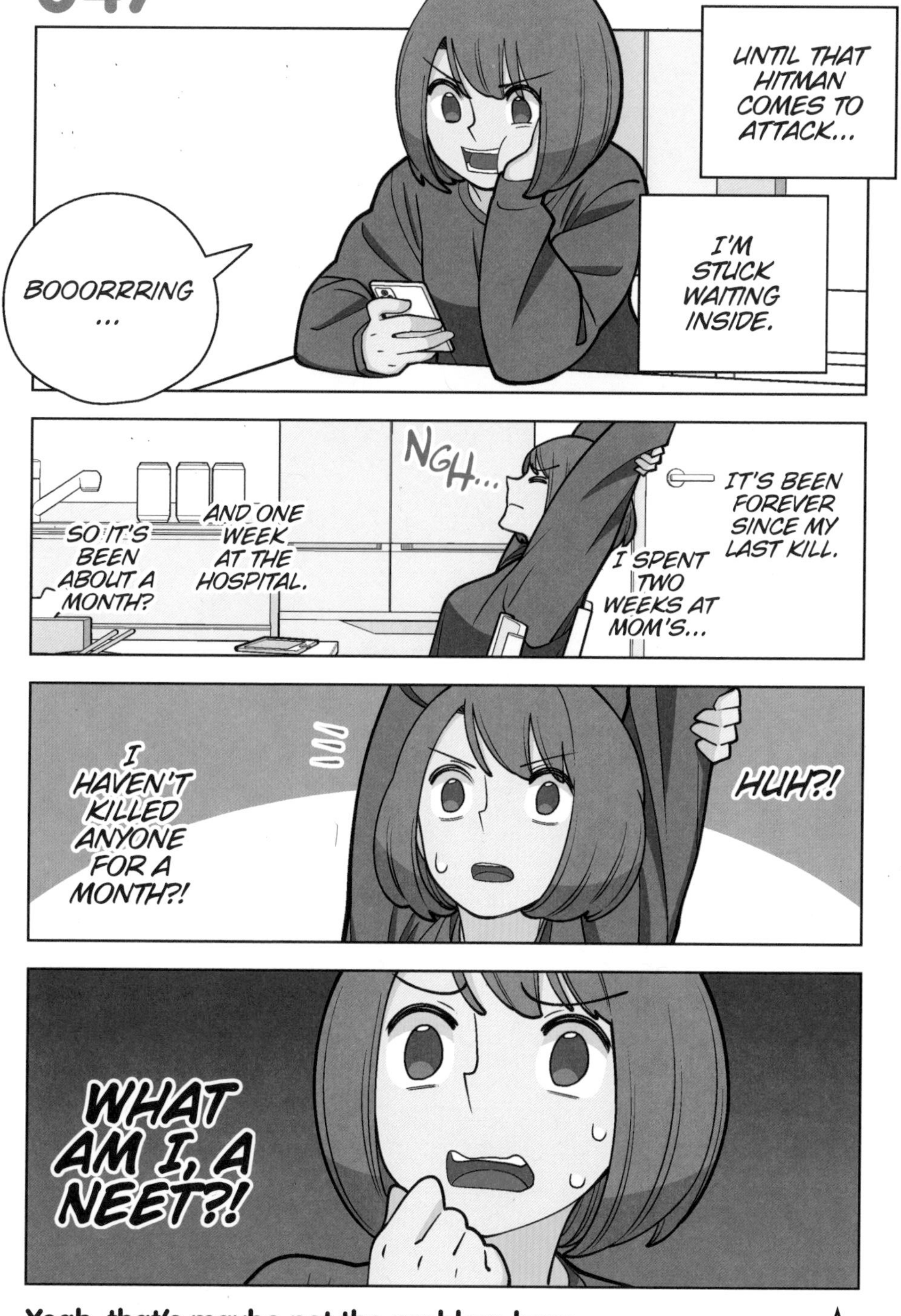
UNTIL THAT HITMAN COMES TO ATTACK...
I'M STUCK WAITING INSIDE.
BOOORRRING ...
IT'S BEEN FOREVER SINCE MY LAST KILL.
NGH...
I SPENT TWO WEEKS AT MOM'S...
AND ONE WEEK AT THE HOSPITAL.
SO IT'S BEEN ABOUT A MONTH?
HUH?!
I HAVEN'T KILLED ANYONE FOR A MONTH?!
WHAT AM I, A NEET?!

Yeah, that's maybe not the problem here... ☆

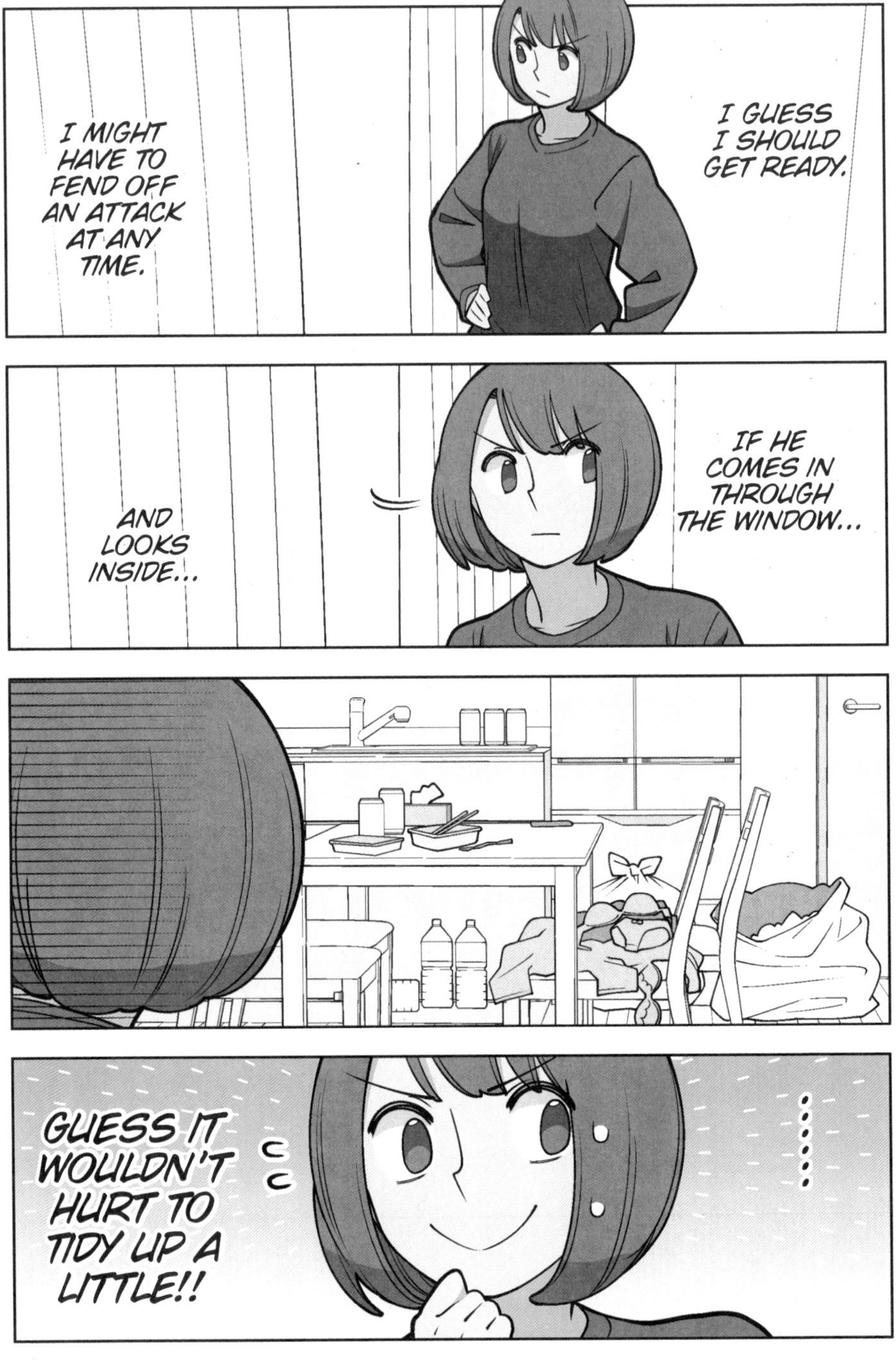
I GUESS I SHOULD GET READY.
I MIGHT HAVE TO FEND OFF AN ATTACK AT ANY TIME.
IF HE COMES IN THROUGH THE WINDOW...
AND LOOKS INSIDE...
......
GUESS IT WOULDN'T HURT TO TIDY UP A LITTLE!!

☆ —— **Not ready for guests.**

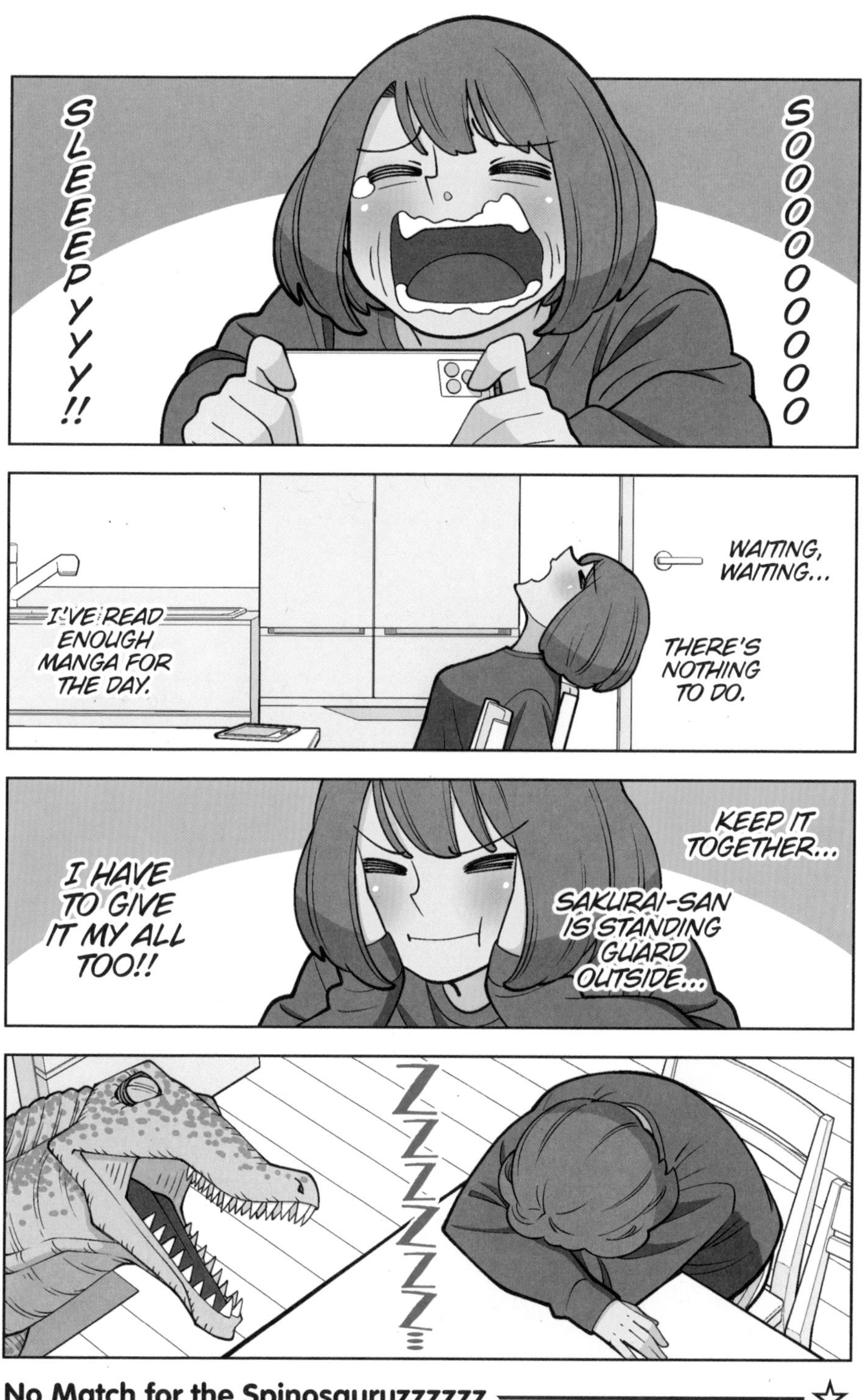
SOOOOOOOOOOO
SLEEEPYYY!!
WAITING, WAITING...
THERE'S NOTHING TO DO.
I'VE READ ENOUGH MANGA FOR THE DAY.
KEEP IT TOGETHER...
SAKURAI-SAN IS STANDING GUARD OUTSIDE...
I HAVE TO GIVE IT MY ALL TOO!!
ZZZZZ

No Match for the Spinosauruzzzzzz. ☆

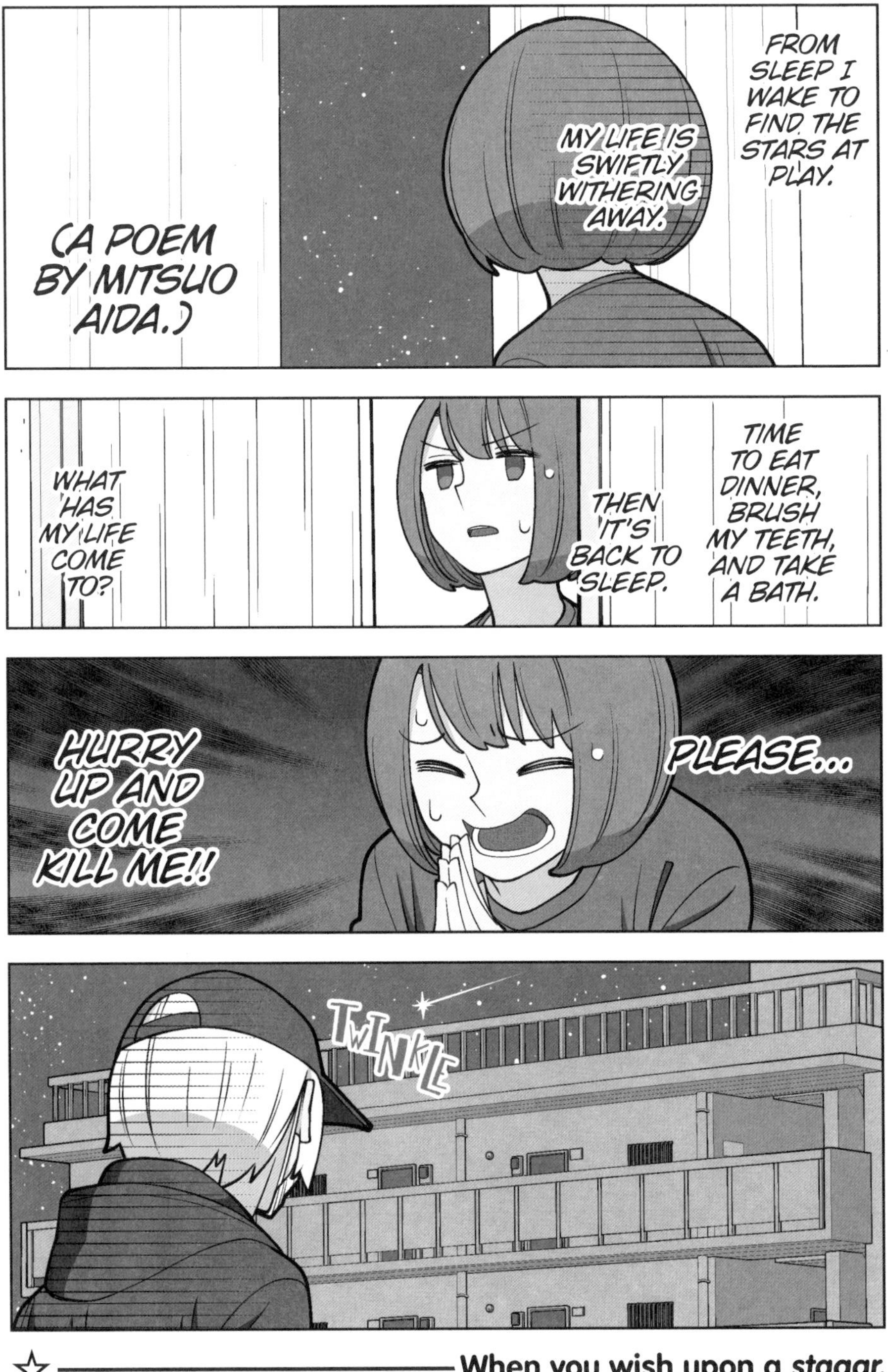
FROM SLEEP I WAKE TO FIND THE STARS AT PLAY.
MY LIFE IS SWIFTLY WITHERING AWAY.
(A POEM BY MITSUO AIDA.)
TIME TO EAT DINNER, BRUSH MY TEETH, AND TAKE A BATH.
THEN IT'S BACK TO SLEEP.
WHAT HAS MY LIFE COME TO?
PLEASE...
HURRY UP AND COME KILL ME!!
TWINKLE

☆ —— When you wish upon a *staaar.*

048

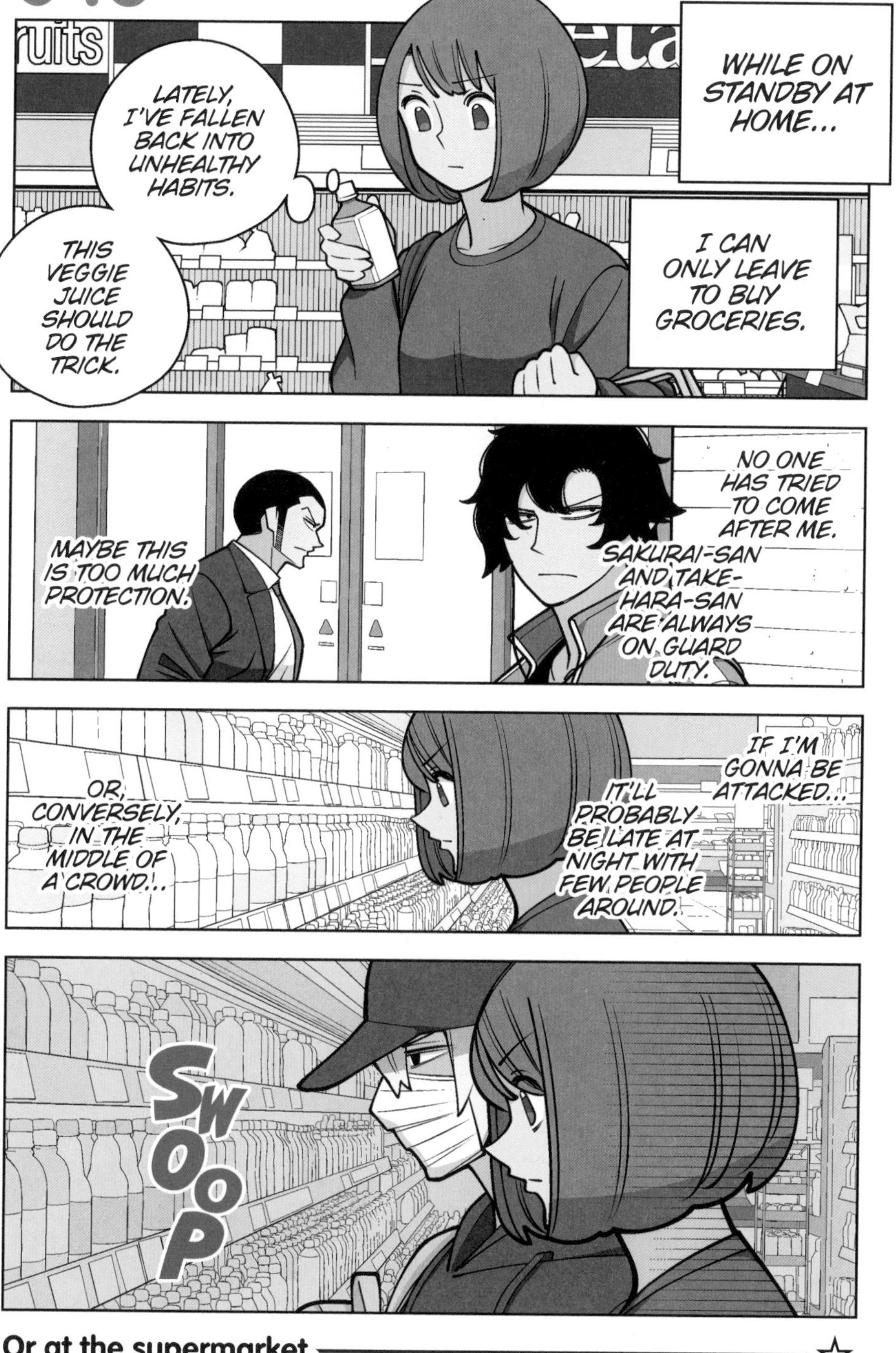
WHILE ON STANDBY AT HOME...
I CAN ONLY LEAVE TO BUY GROCERIES.
LATELY, I'VE FALLEN BACK INTO UNHEALTHY HABITS.
THIS VEGGIE JUICE SHOULD DO THE TRICK.
ruits
NO ONE HAS TRIED TO COME AFTER ME.
SAKURAI-SAN AND TAKE-HARA-SAN ARE ALWAYS ON GUARD DUTY.
MAYBE THIS IS TOO MUCH PROTECTION.
IF I'M GONNA BE ATTACKED...
IT'LL PROBABLY BE LATE AT NIGHT WITH FEW PEOPLE AROUND.
OR, CONVERSELY, IN THE MIDDLE OF A CROWD...
SWOOP

Or at the supermarket. ☆

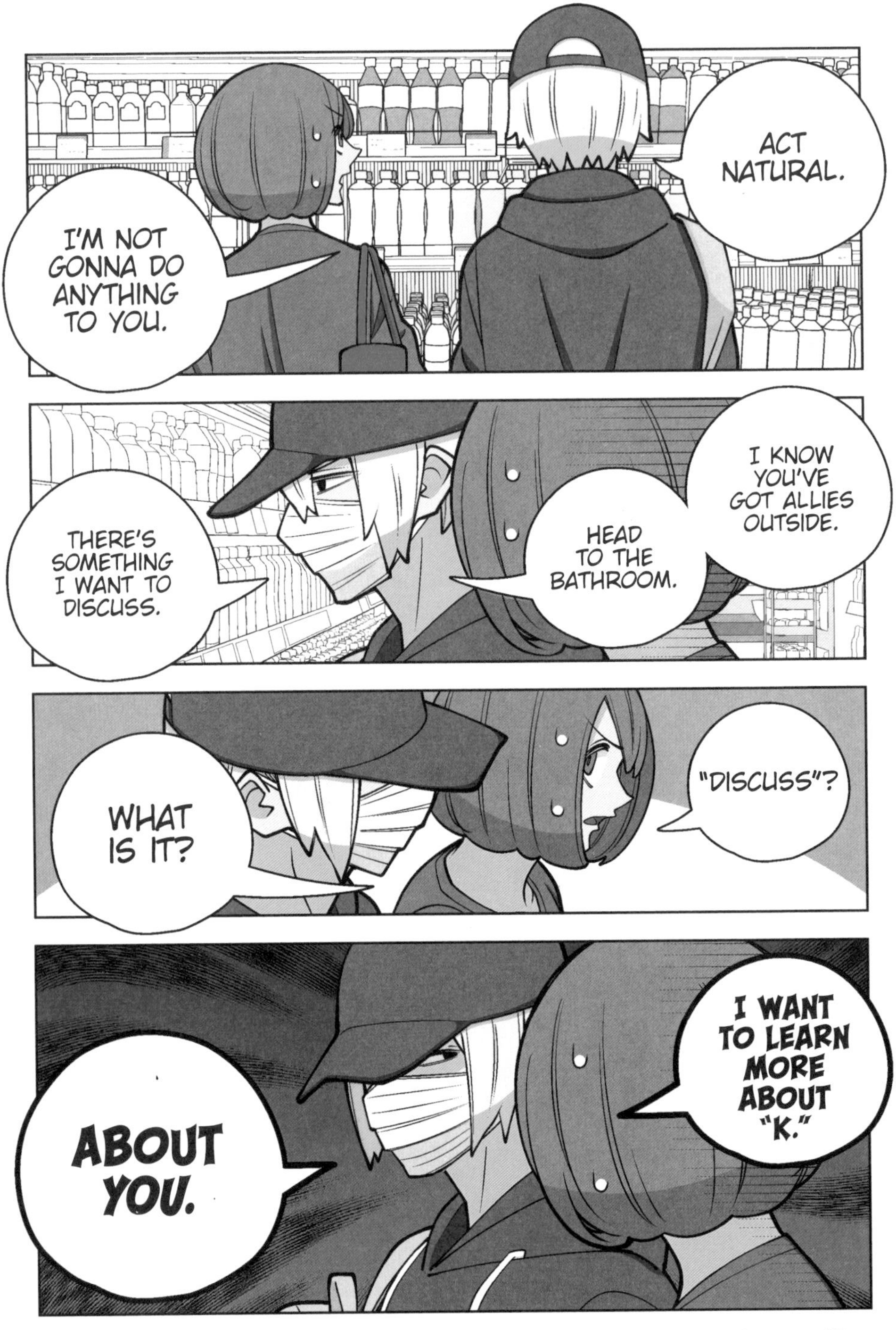
ACT NATURAL.
I'M NOT GONNA DO ANYTHING TO YOU.
I KNOW YOU'VE GOT ALLIES OUTSIDE.
HEAD TO THE BATHROOM.
THERE'S SOMETHING I WANT TO DISCUSS.
"DISCUSS"?
WHAT IS IT?
I WANT TO LEARN MORE ABOUT "K."
ABOUT YOU.

☆ — What a flirt.

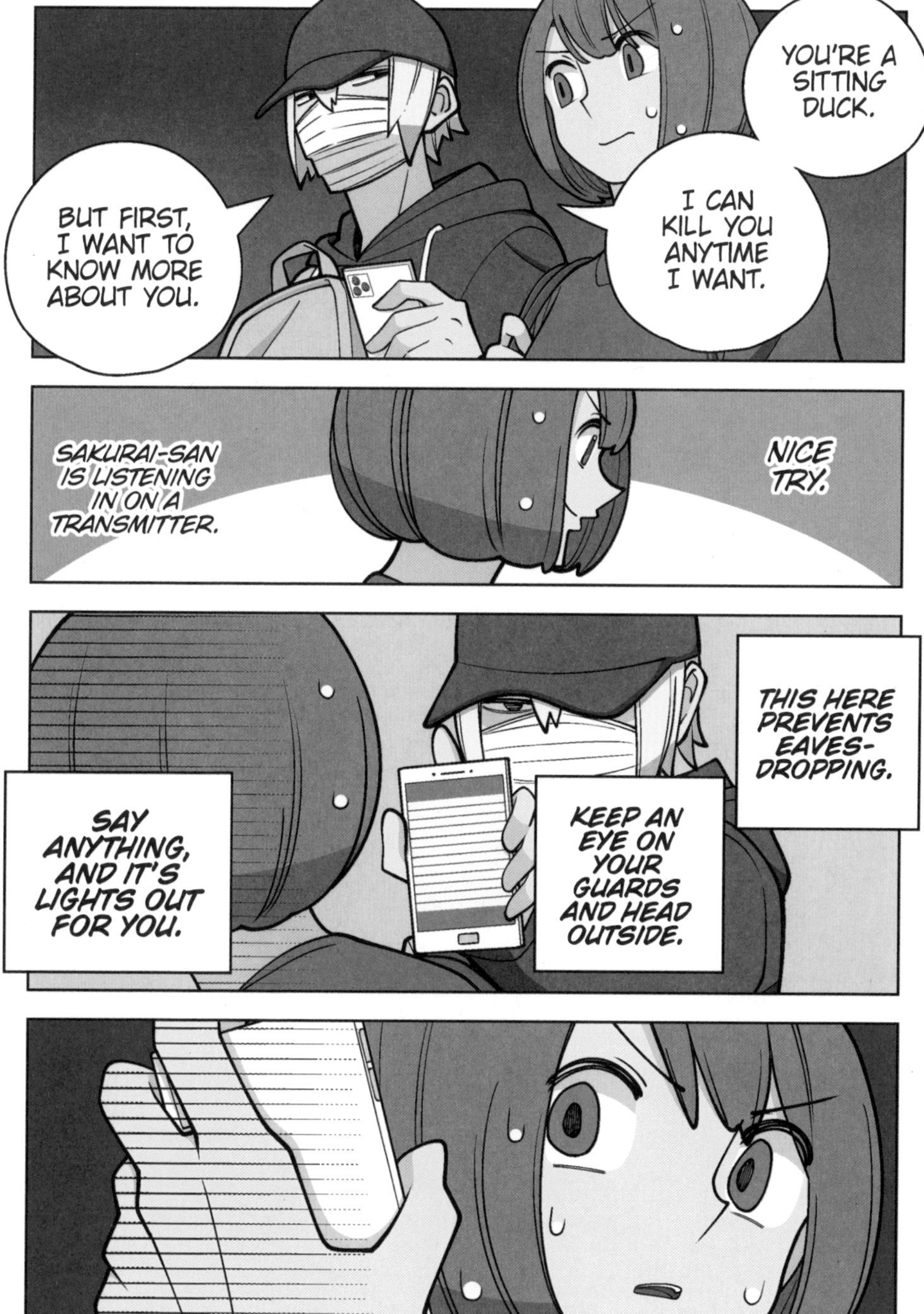
YOU'RE A SITTING DUCK.
I CAN KILL YOU ANYTIME I WANT.
BUT FIRST, I WANT TO KNOW MORE ABOUT YOU.
NICE TRY.
SAKURAI-SAN IS LISTENING IN ON A TRANSMITTER.
THIS HERE PREVENTS EAVES-DROPPING.
KEEP AN EYE ON YOUR GUARDS AND HEAD OUTSIDE.
SAY ANYTHING, AND IT'S LIGHTS OUT FOR YOU.

I'm in danger. ☆

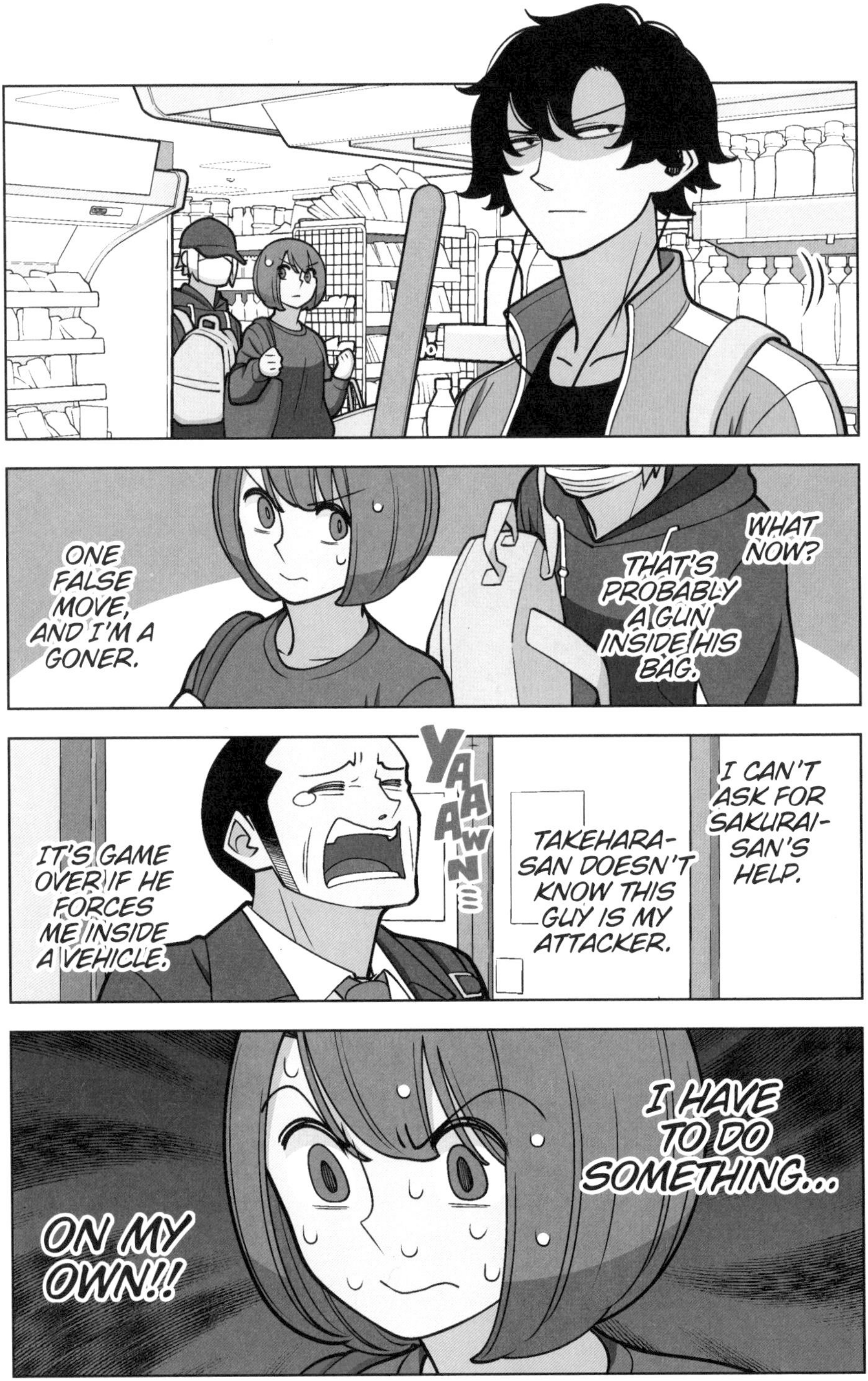
WHAT NOW?
THAT'S PROBABLY A GUN INSIDE HIS BAG.
ONE FALSE MOVE, AND I'M A GONER.
I CAN'T ASK FOR SAKURAI-SAN'S HELP.
YAAAAWN
TAKEHARA-SAN DOESN'T KNOW THIS GUY IS MY ATTACKER.
IT'S GAME OVER IF HE FORCES ME INSIDE A VEHICLE.
I HAVE TO DO SOMETHING...
ON MY OWN!!

☆ Can't stay a rookie forever.

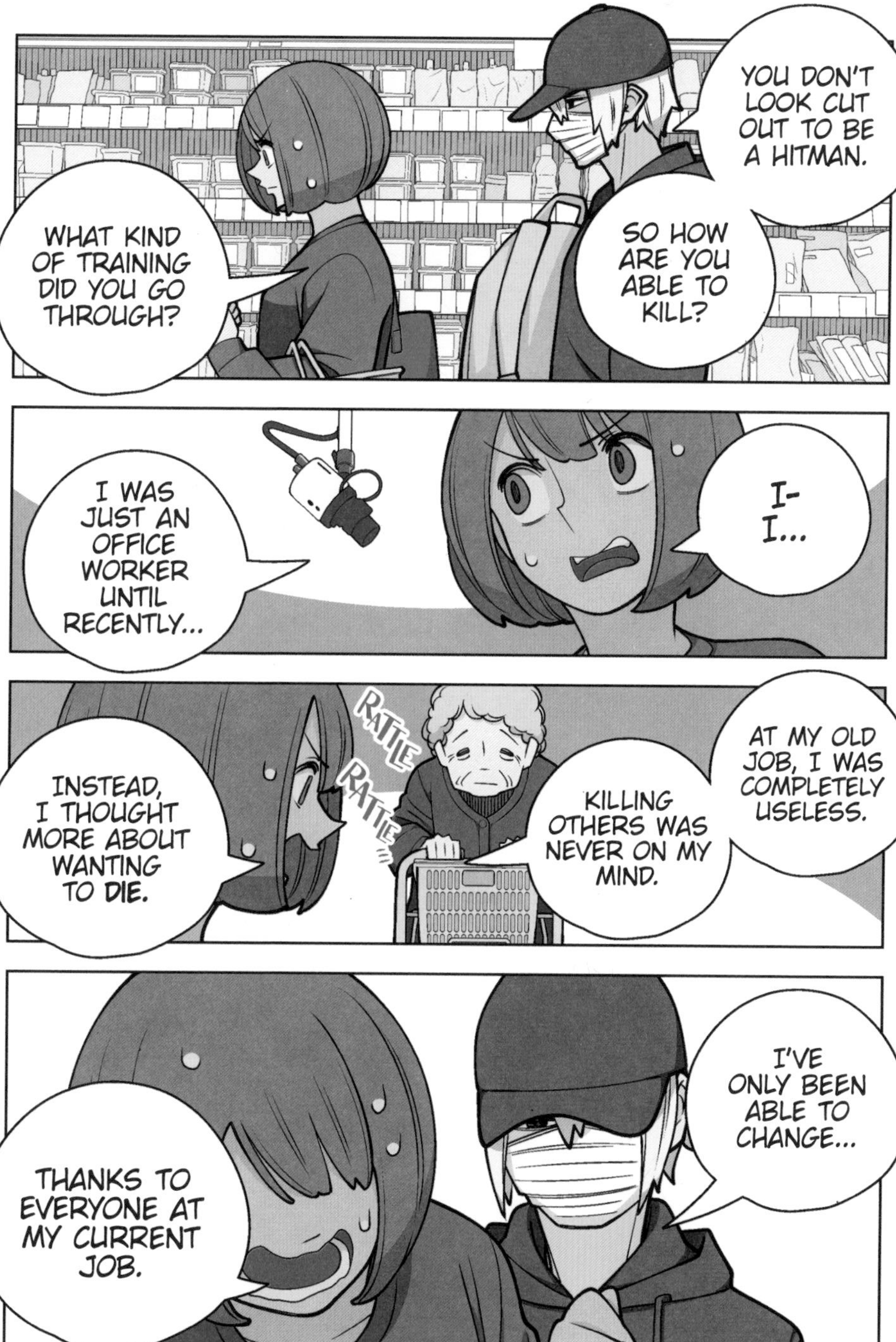
YOU DON'T LOOK CUT OUT TO BE A HITMAN.
SO HOW ARE YOU ABLE TO KILL?
WHAT KIND OF TRAINING DID YOU GO THROUGH?
I- I...
I WAS JUST AN OFFICE WORKER UNTIL RECENTLY...
AT MY OLD JOB, I WAS COMPLETELY USELESS.
KILLING OTHERS WAS NEVER ON MY MIND.
RATTLE
RATTLE
INSTEAD, I THOUGHT MORE ABOUT WANTING TO **DIE.**
I'VE ONLY BEEN ABLE TO CHANGE...
THANKS TO EVERYONE AT MY CURRENT JOB.

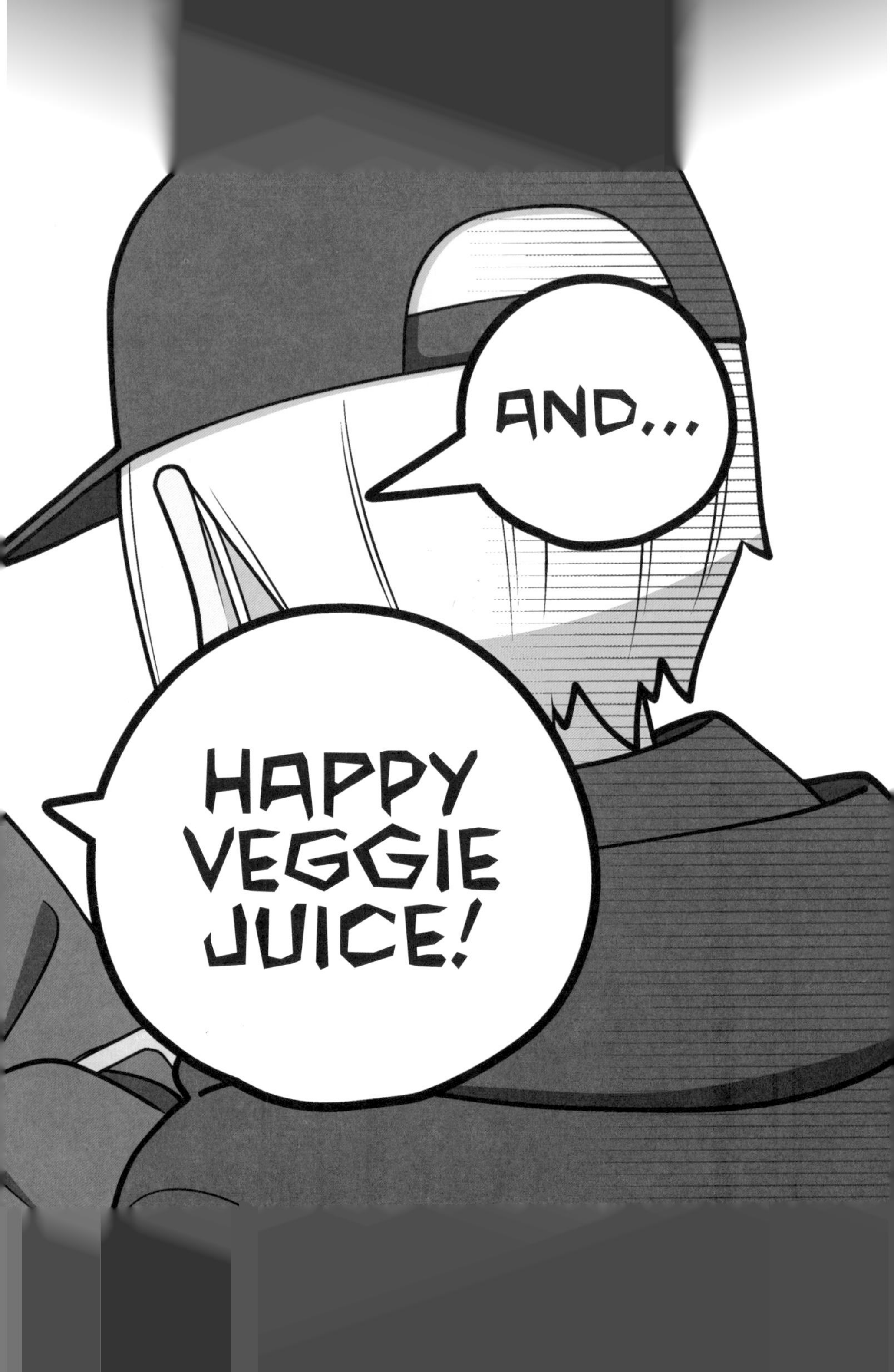
AND...
HAPPY VEGGIE JUICE!

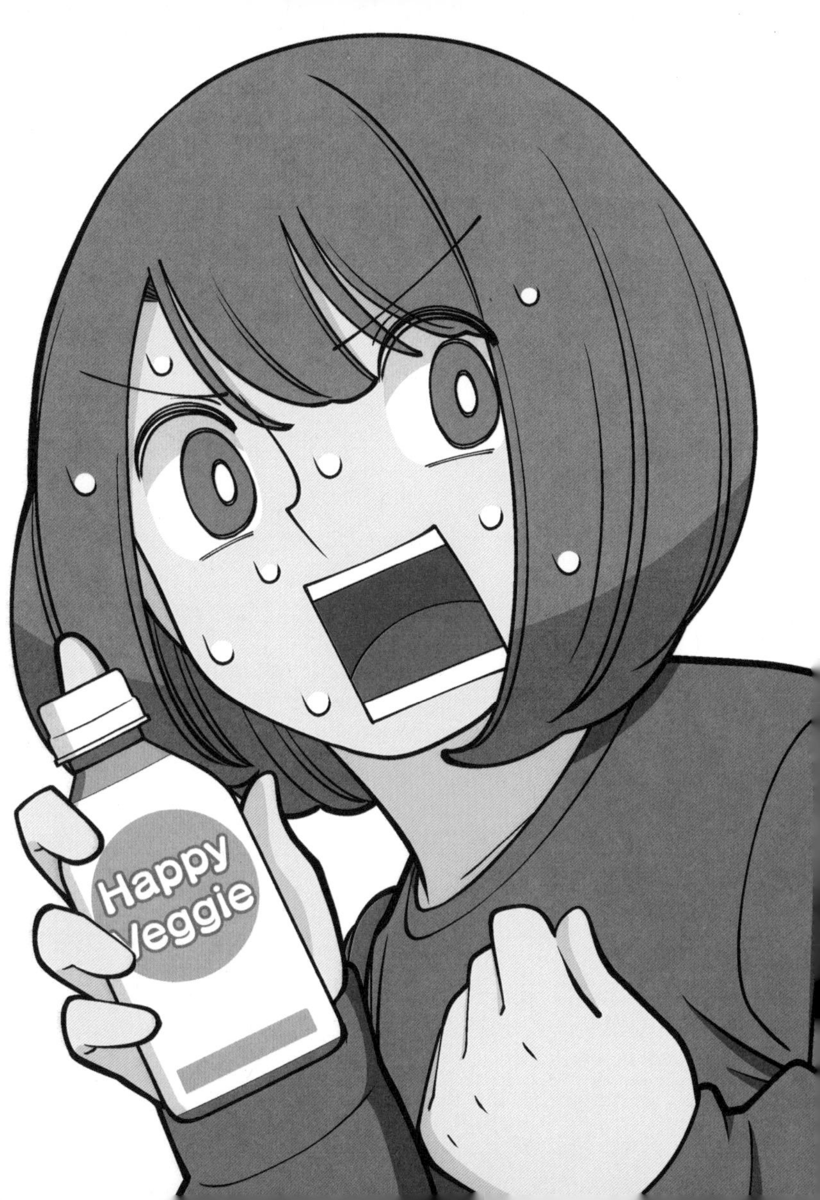
Happy Veggie

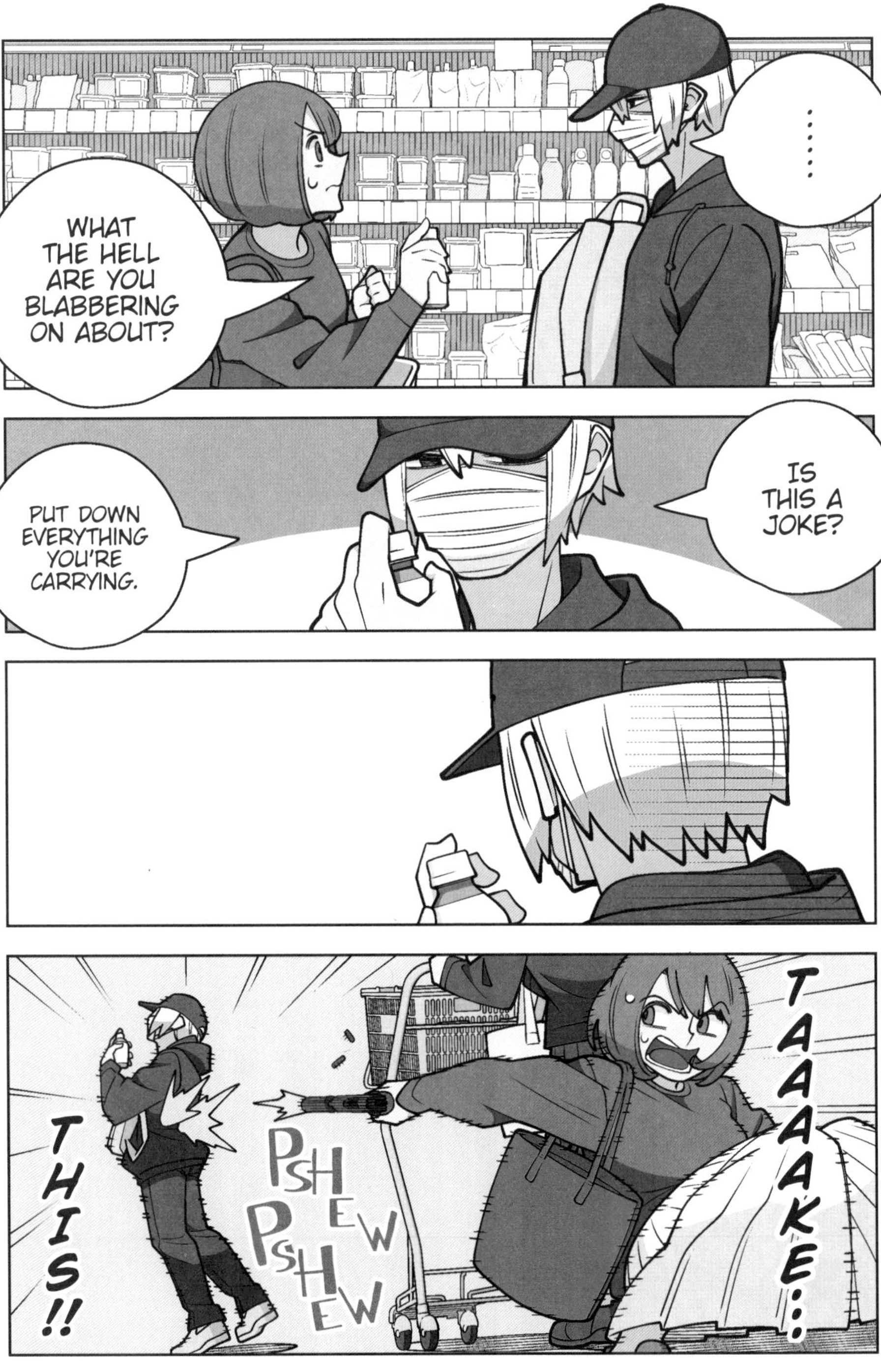
......
WHAT THE HELL ARE YOU BLABBERING ON ABOUT?
IS THIS A JOKE?
PUT DOWN EVERYTHING YOU'RE CARRYING.
TAAAAKE...
PSHEW
PSHEW
THIS!!

☆ Thank you, Veggie Juice.

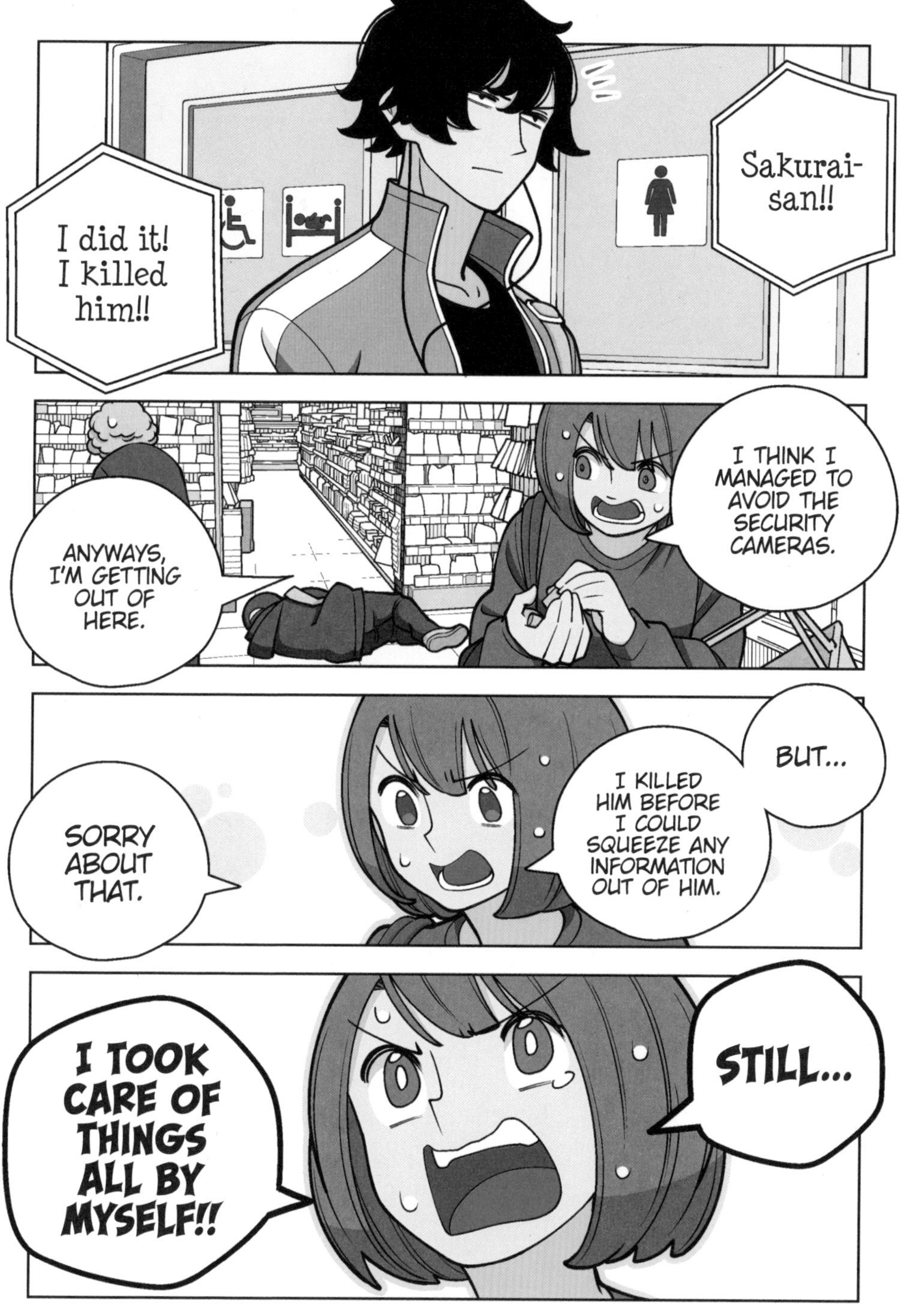
Sakurai-san!!
I did it! I killed him!!
I THINK I MANAGED TO AVOID THE SECURITY CAMERAS.
ANYWAYS, I'M GETTING OUT OF HERE.
BUT...
I KILLED HIM BEFORE I COULD SQUEEZE ANY INFORMATION OUT OF HIM.
SORRY ABOUT THAT.
STILL...
I TOOK CARE OF THINGS ALL BY MYSELF!!

A rookie no more! ☆

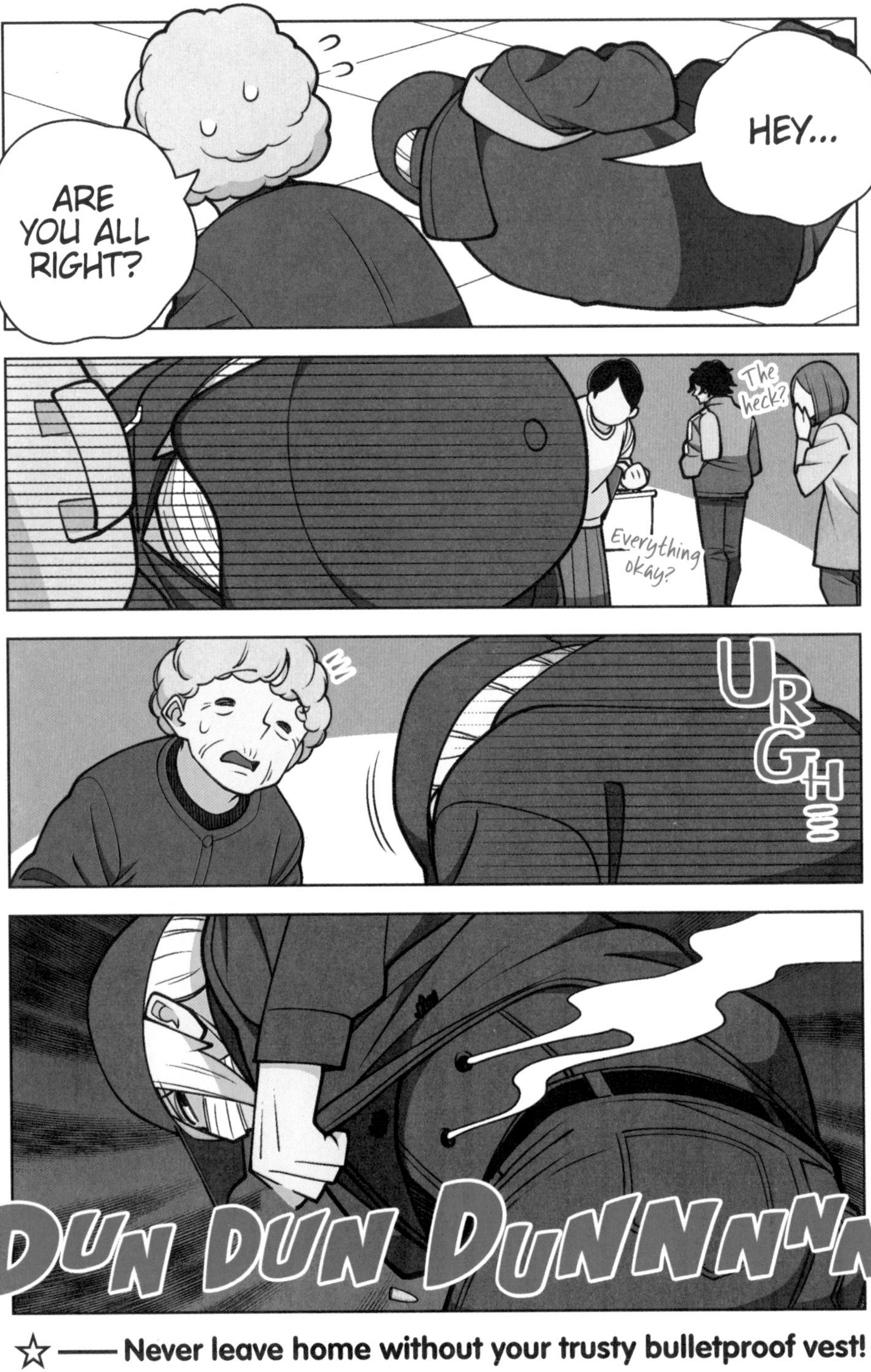
HEY...
ARE YOU ALL RIGHT?
The heck?
Everything okay?
URGH
DUN DUN DUNNNNN

☆——**Never leave home without your trusty bulletproof vest!**

Bonus

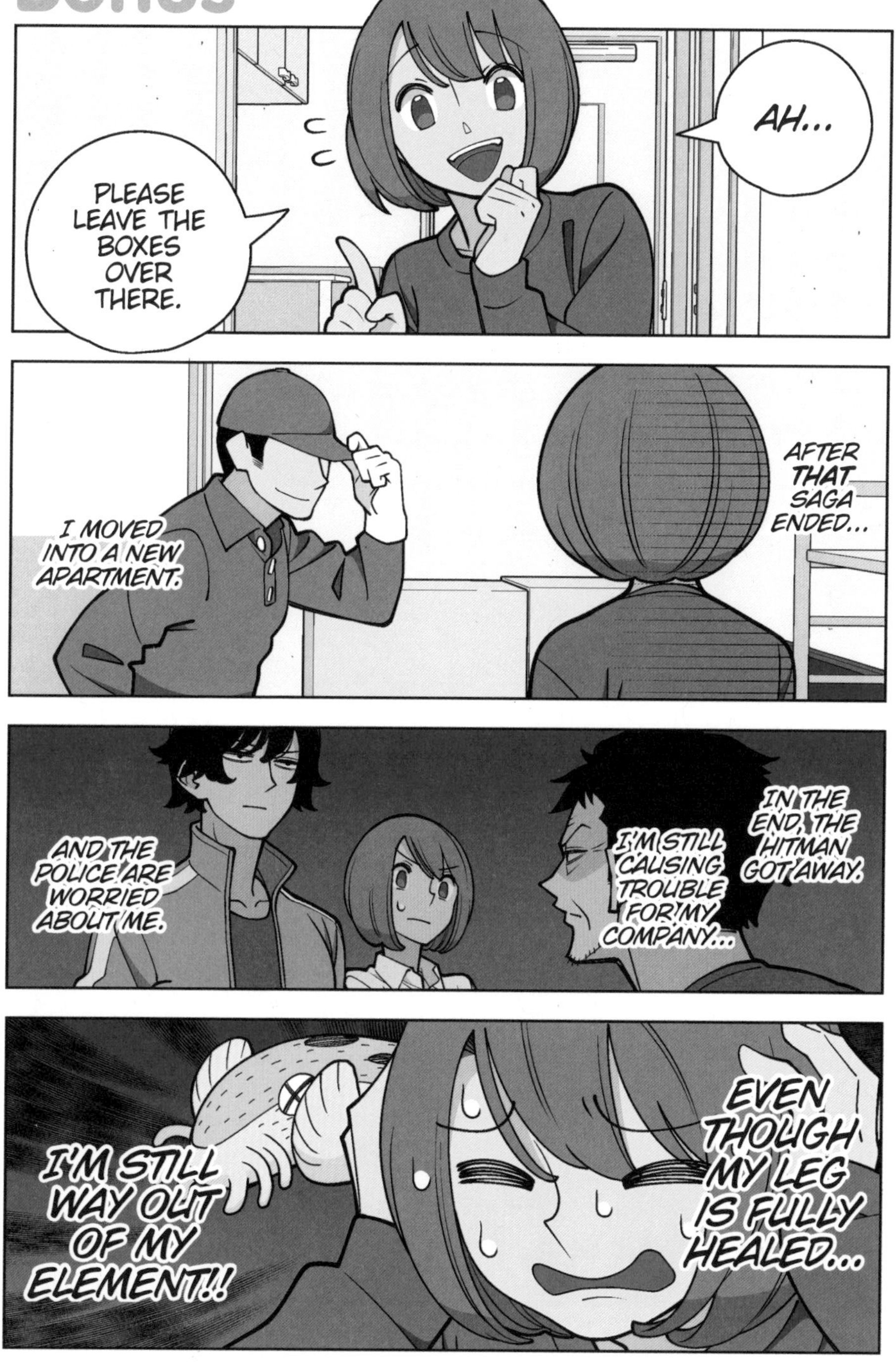
AH...
PLEASE LEAVE THE BOXES OVER THERE.
AFTER THAT SAGA ENDED...
I MOVED INTO A NEW APARTMENT.
IN THE END, THE HITMAN GOT AWAY.
I'M STILL CAUSING TROUBLE FOR MY COMPANY...
AND THE POLICE ARE WORRIED ABOUT ME.
EVEN THOUGH MY LEG IS FULLY HEALED...
I'M STILL WAY OUT OF MY ELEMENT!!

Like a fish out of water! ——— ☆

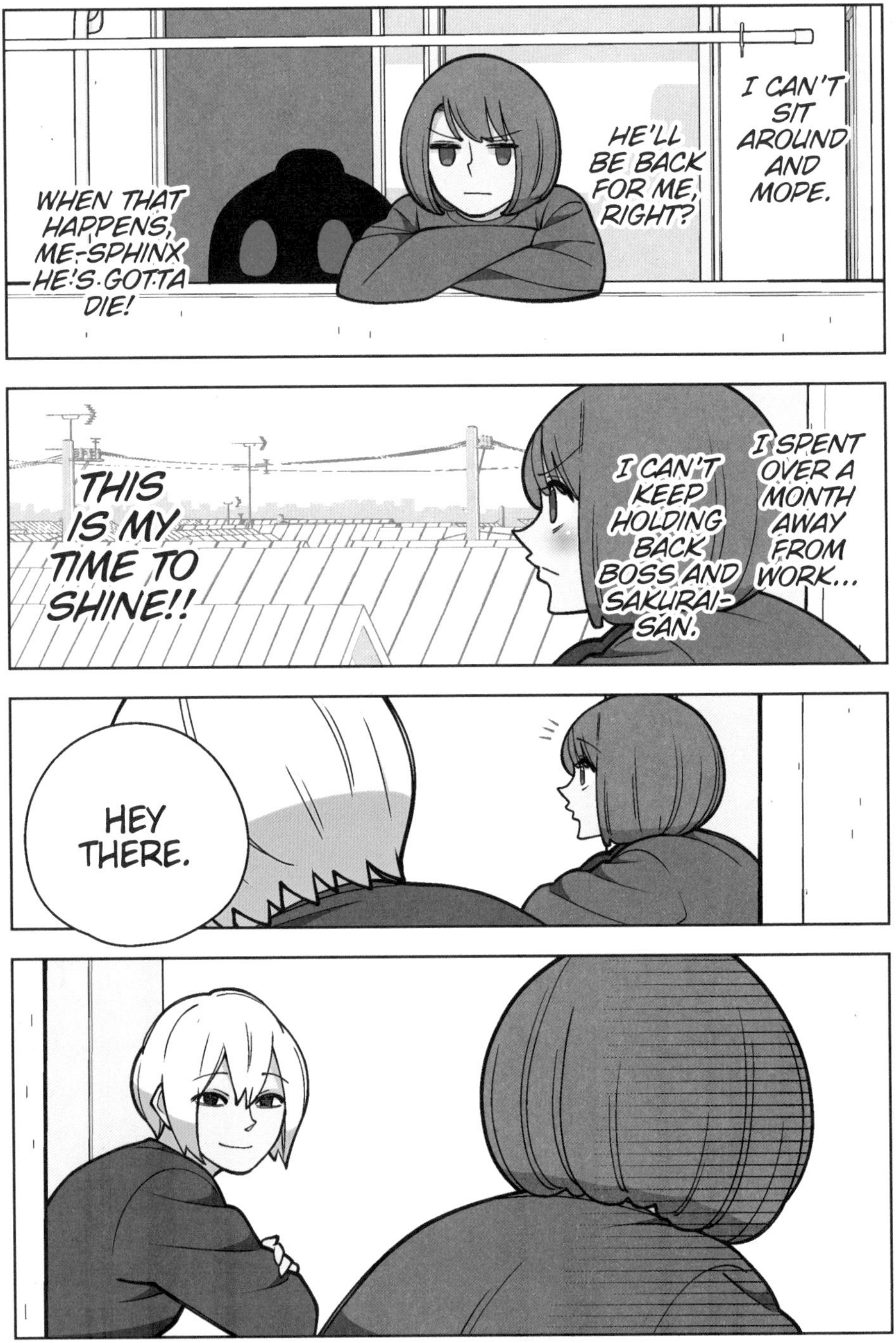
I CAN'T SIT AROUND AND MOPE.
HE'LL BE BACK FOR ME, RIGHT?
WHEN THAT HAPPENS, ME-SPHINX HE'S GOTTA DIE!
I SPENT OVER A MONTH AWAY FROM WORK...
I CAN'T KEEP HOLDING BACK BOSS AND SAKURAI-SAN.
THIS IS MY TIME TO SHINE!!
HEY THERE.

☆ — **Hi, neighbor.**

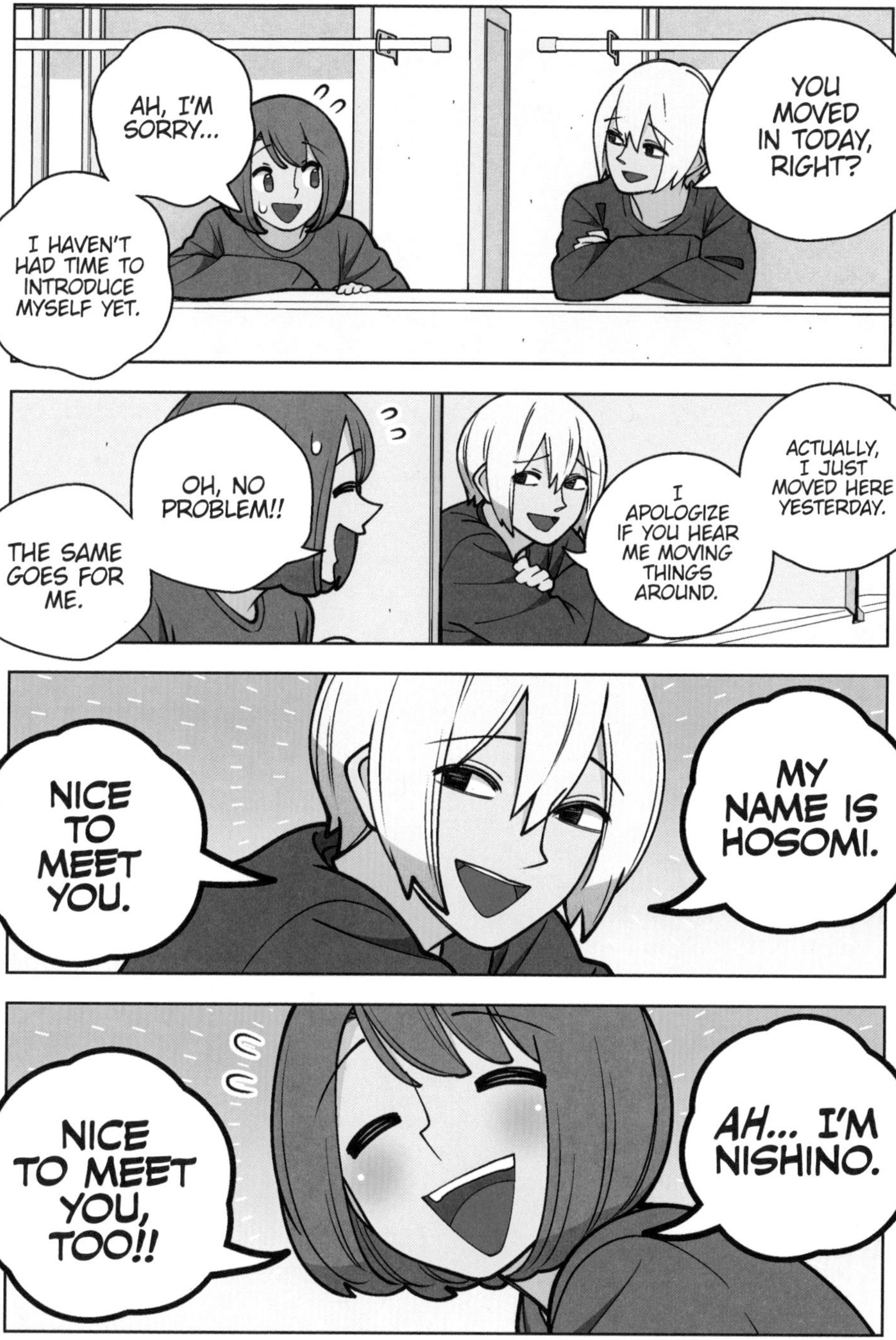
YOU MOVED IN TODAY, RIGHT?
AH, I'M SORRY...
I HAVEN'T HAD TIME TO INTRODUCE MYSELF YET.
ACTUALLY, I JUST MOVED HERE YESTERDAY.
I APOLOGIZE IF YOU HEAR ME MOVING THINGS AROUND.
OH, NO PROBLEM!!
THE SAME GOES FOR ME.
MY NAME IS HOSOMI.
NICE TO MEET YOU.
AH... I'M NISHINO.
NICE TO MEET YOU, TOO!!

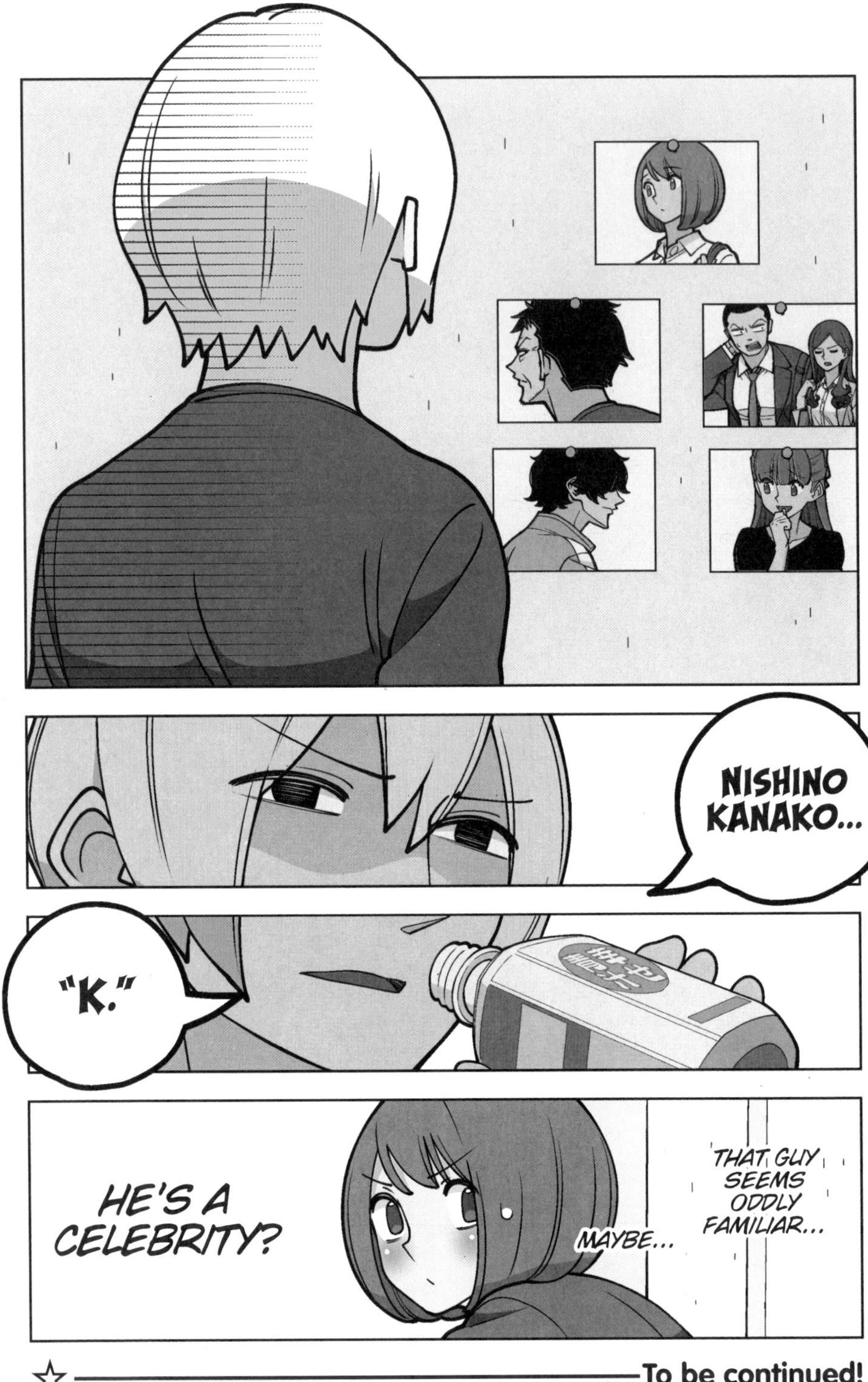
NISHINO KANAKO...
"K."
THAT GUY SEEMS ODDLY FAMILIAR...
MAYBE...
HE'S A CELEBRITY?

☆ —— To be continued!

Happy Kanako's Killer Life

NISHINO ...
BECOME A LEGEND.

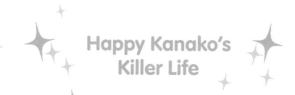

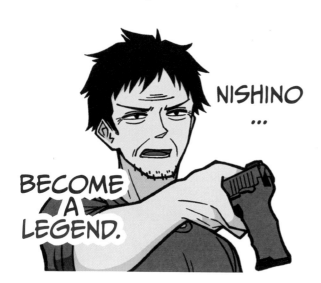

Thank you for reading!! Fighting every day means you're bound to experience some setbacks!!

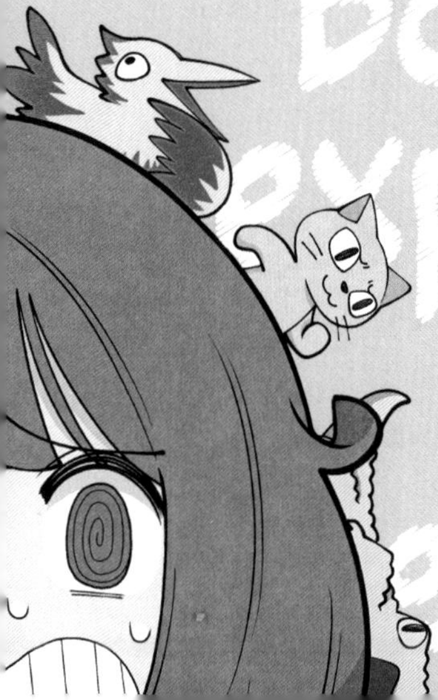

Kanako is giving it her all right along with you!! She'll be fighting next time, too so keep on living!!

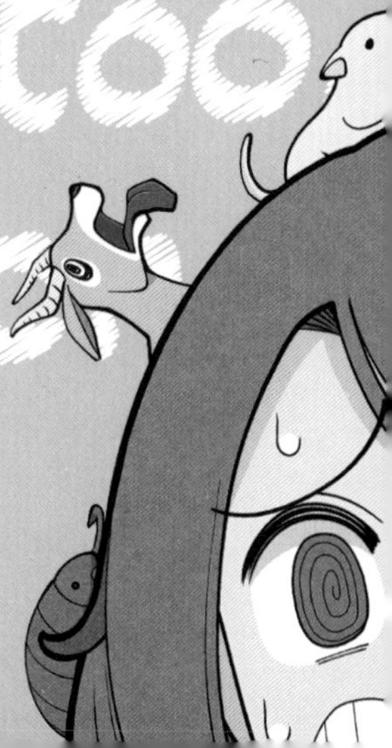

From

Toshiya Wakabayashi

SEVEN SEAS ENTERTAINMENT PRESENTS

Happy Kanako's
Killer﹒Life

story and art by TOSHIYA WAKABAYASHI — VOLUME 3

SHIAWASE KANAKO NO KOROSHIYA SEIKATSU VOL. 3
© Toshiya Wakabayashi 2020
All rights reserved.
Original Japanese edition published by Star Seas Company.
English publishing rights arranged with Star Seas Company
through KODANSHA LTD., Tokyo.

Seven Seas press and purchase enquiries can be sent to Marketing Manager Lianne
Sentar at press@gomanga.com. Information regarding the distribution and purchase of
digital editions is available from Digital Manager CK Russell at digital@gomanga.com.

Seven Seas and the Seven Seas logo are trademarks of
Seven Seas Entertainment. All rights reserved.

ISBN: 978-1-64827-377-3
Printed in Canada
First Printing: January 2022
10 9 8 7 6 5 4 3 2 1

TRANSLATION
Jenny Tran

LETTERING
???

???
J.Y. Sullivan

PROOFREADER/EDITOR
Kaleena Uhmori

???
???

PROOFREADER
Kurestin Armada

PRODUCTION MANAGER
Lissa Pattillo

MANAGING EDITOR
Julie Davis

ASSOCIATE PUBLISHER
Adam Arnold

PUBLISHER
Jason DeAngelis

READING DIRECTIONS

This book reads from *right to left*,
Japanese style. If this is your first time
reading manga, you start reading from
the top right panel on each page and
take it from there. If you get lost, just
follow the numbered diagram here.
It may seem backwards at first,
but you'll get the hang of it! Have fun!!

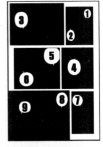